Mapping Dalits

Mapping Dalits

CONTEMPORARY REALITY AND FUTURE PROSPECTS IN PUNJAB

Paramjit S. Judge
Gurpreet Bal

RAWAT PUBLICATIONS
Jaipur • New Delhi • Bangalore • Mumbai • Hyderabad • Guwahati

ISBN 81-316-0268-0

Published by
Prem Rawat for **Rawat Publications**
Satyam Apts, Sector 3, Jawahar Nagar, Jaipur 302 004 (India)
Phone: 0141 265 1748 / 7006 Fax: 0141 265 1748
E-mail: info@rawatbooks.com
Website: www.rawatbooks.com

New Delhi Office
4858/24, Ansari Road, Daryaganj, New Delhi 110 002
Phone: 011 2326 3290

Also at Bangalore, Mumbai, Hyderabad and Guwahati

Typeset by Rawat Computers, Jaipur
Printed at Chaman Enterprises, New Delhi

To

Professor P.N. Pimpley

Contents

List of Tables

Chapter 2

APPENDIX of Chapter 2

Chapter 3

Preface

Social transformation in the age of globalisation has picked up a fast pace in India. Its signs are becoming more and more visible. The satellite media, emergence of the mall culture, cell phone use and rising expectations of the people in terms of material prosperity mark these changes. Relations are going to transform as well. Indian society, with the existence and prevalence of the caste system, has been facing the forces of globalisation in the spirit of competition in the world market. Are we going to change our caste inequalities in all walks of life? The present work is a grim reminder that we are way behind our agenda of achieving social equality despite the state interventions. More importantly, caste has offered the stiffest challenge to all attempts to end it or make it irrelevant in social life. At present, castes that have suffered all kinds of discrimination for centuries are demanding equal share in all aspects of the collective life of the society. They are asserting for their right to equal opportunity and good quality of life. How far these castes can go in achieving social equality? In this book, an attempt has been made, based on empirical data, to make a reasonable estimate about the present and future of these castes in Punjab.

Punjab having the largest proportion of the scheduled castes (SCs) offers a unique example, because a majority of its people belong to the egalitarian religion, namely, Sikhism. The fact that the Indian Constitution extends all kinds of protective discrimination to the SCs among the Sikhs, the existence of caste inequality is also accepted. As a matter of fact, caste system exists among almost all religious communities in the country, and more importantly, among the SCs themselves. This study not only maps the social mobility among the SCs of Punjab, but also examines its areas of continuity. The rising tide of intercaste contestation involving dalits is also a sign of emerging dalit consciousness and certain levels of organisation.

We are grateful to the University Grants Commission for sponsoring the project. We also acknowledge the help rendered by the university administration in facilitating the work. Gurpreet Singh and Manoj Kumar Birdi worked hard in collecting data efficiently and with commitment. We thank both of them. Bhupinder Thakur joined the project and remained with us all through. He made every difficulty look easy and we acknowledge his contribution to the success of the project.

Dr Rajivlochan went through the entire report and gave his critical comments in the light of which it has been revised. We are grateful to him.

The staff of the Department of Sociology, specially Sucha Singh, Kulraj Singh, Amarjit Kaur and Natha Singh, helped us in various ways. We thankfully acknowledge their assistance.

Last but not least, we are grateful to our respondents who spared their precious time and responded to our questions patiently.

This book is dedicated to our revered teacher, Prof P.N. Pimpley—a great and the major source of inspiration to a large number of students. In the Department of Sociology, Panjab University, Chandigarh, where he taught from 1960, at the time of its opening, to 1998 when he retired, he influenced and shaped the minds and perspectives of many generations of students. He has been the pioneer in the area of 'Dalit Studies'. He was the first to start a course on "Sociology of the Underprivileged" in 1970s at the M. Phil. level to expose the students to the study of the dalits and other marginalised communities in India. As his students, starting from M.A., then M. Phil. to Ph.D., we owe to him our initiation and sensitivity towards the issues concerning the underprivileged sections of the society.

Paramjit S. Judge
Gurpreet Bal

Introduction

The present study was conducted in order to examine, evaluate and interrogate the changing status of the dalits[1] in Punjab by taking into consideration four variables, namely, education and occupation, empowerment, entrepreneurship and emigration. All the four dimensions would provide a panoramic view of the trajectory of change among the dalits in Punjab. The term 'dalit' has gained currency in academic research and intellectual discourse by marginalising, if not eliminating, other denotative terms like scheduled castes, untouchables, ex-untouchables, Harijans, depressed castes, outcastes etc. Mendelsohn and Vicziany (2000) opt for the use of the term 'untouchables', which, according to them, is sociological and comprehensible in the western world, whereas the terms 'scheduled castes' and 'dalit' are legal and political respectively. However, all the western writers do not agree with this position. For example, Zelliot (1992) has used the expression 'from untouchable to dalit' in the title of one of her books, which suggests the contemporary relevance of the use of the word 'dalit'. She writes, "*Dalit* implies those who have been broken, ground down by those above them in a deliberate and active way. There is in the word itself an inherent denial of pollution, *karma,* and justified caste hierarchy" (ibid.: 267). Prasad (2006) is of the view that dalit signifies a set of castes against whom untouchability is practised. The present Punjab is regarded as the social site in which untouchability declined considerably under the influence of the Sikh religion though caste hierarchy and discrimination continue to exist. Therefore, the use of word 'dalit' is appropriate in comparison to 'untouchable'.

The emerging trend in the intercaste interaction in Punjab indicates that intercaste contestations are on the rise. It is being argued that the better off sections among the dalits are spearheading the struggle against caste inequality, discrimination and social exclusion. The 'Green Revolution'—a phenomenon of high agricultural productivity—has contributed towards the improvement in the economic conditions of the dalits. The international migration of the Punjabi dalits is still another important contributor in improving their conditions in certain areas of the state. The emigration of the dalits of Punjab is a specific feature that may be absent in other states. Recently, the process of empowerment as a state effort in the formal structure through constitutional amendments has acquired significance worthy of probe.

One of the prevalent discourses in the analysis of caste system in India is the existence of caste stratification among the non-Hindus. Weber (1970), dealing with the issue of caste among the non-Hindus, makes it explicit that in the case of non-Hindus the Brahmin has lost his significance. The centrality of the position of Brahmins has remained unchanged in the Hindu social system. In spite of this limited insight that Weber provided, no attempt has been made to explore it further. The prevalent discourse thus makes an attempt to create a world-view that there is something specific about the Indian subcontinent that can be situated in the Indian civilisation. Thus, we have studies of empirical nature that affirm and substantiate the presence of caste stratification among the Sikhs, Muslims and Christians. Such empirical observations draw strength from the historical fact that the Sikhs, and the Indian Muslims and Christians have their roots in Hinduism and their co-existence has been influenced by the Hindu ideology, way of life and world-view. Such a view has implications for the understanding of the dalits of Punjab. Privileging oneself by exercising exclusion is invariably a function of power. Classes in power tend to exhibit behaviour in which they create social distance from others. Such a behaviour that is analogous to caste and not sanctioned by religion can be observed in many cases. One obvious instance is that of the British in India, who, despite their not constrained by caste and religion, kept distance from the Indians. Kasturi (2002) has shown in her study of the Rajputs that there was close association between upward mobility and adoption of presumed higher caste diacritical marks including greater sanction for untouchability, female infanticide, stricter acceptance of purity-pollution norms etc. Similarly, Judge (2002b) also argues that despite the emergence of different caste hierarchy among the Sikhs from the ideal typical Hindu social order in which the Jats, essentially belonging to the Shudra varna, emerged at the top and began to enforce disabilities on the lower castes in the fashion similar to the caste system in general.

With 59.9 per cent of the total population of Punjab, the Sikhs constitute a majority in the state and the Sikh dalits are eligible for the benefits under the reservation policy (Puri, 2003). The politics of recognition has played the role in confusing the issue. Though Sikhism is an egalitarian religion, yet the caste stratification exists and is perpetuating through endogamy, exclusion and certain degree of restriction on social interaction. At the same time, the caste hierarchy among the Sikhs is different from that of the Hindus. Among the Sikhs the castes that occupy the top positions may become lower in the Hindu caste hierarchy. In this regard, the caste system among the Sikhs is largely based on power and privilege paradigm, whereas the Hindu caste system has strong ideological basis, which supports and legitimises the given system of inequality. As a result, the privileged position of the upper castes in the Sikh community has been facing constant challenges from the egalitarian ideology of Sikhism. The modern Indian state has decisively intervened in the evolutionary process of the Sikh community through the affirmative action programme. Contemporary writings in the 19th century tend to suggest that Sikhism was fast moving towards the merger with Hinduism (Bingley, 1985). The Singh Sabha movement and the British colonial policies combined to create a Sikh identity along Khalsa lines for which the emphasis on equality among castes within the community became a rallying point to demarcate it from Hinduism. No wonder that one of the major ideologues of the Singh Sabha movement, Giani Ditt Singh, was a dalit (Ramdasia).

To further illustrate the issue of the dalits with regard to the religious communities, we may take the example of 'temple entry'. It is a well-known fact that the dalits were prohibited from entering the Hindu temples (Zelliot, 1970; Virdi, 2000). Deliége (1999) points out that prohibition was not simply confined to the temple entry, but also applied to the streets that approached the temples. Dr B.R. Ambedkar organised the movement of the Mahars on this issue in the earlier stages of his struggle. This movement for temple entry met with strong resistance, opposition and violence from the upper caste Hindus in Maharashtra. Conversely, we do not find such struggle of the dalits for the entry into the Sikh Gurdwaras. There are separate Gurdwaras for all castes in most of the villages in Punjab and the same may be true in the cities as well where such things remain hidden. This empirical fact is generally quoted and explicated to argue that 'untouchability' exists among the Sikhs. It is important to remind that a dalit is not prevented from entering the Gurdwara belonging to the upper castes. Still another notable feature is that the priests in the Gurdwaras belong to the lower castes, particularly the backward classes, such as Chhimbas, Bhatras, etc. and one may also find a dalit priest in the Gurdwara belonging to the Jat Sikhs—the fact that has been elaborated in this study.

There are certain ways of investigating whether change has occurred in the status of dalits. One way is to identify the parameters of change in the caste system. In this context, the effective way to do so is to evaluate whether various features, such as endogamy, hereditary occupations, and restrictions on interaction and food have undergone a limited or complete change. Whatever may be the degree of change in these features of caste system, the shift from the ideal construction could be regarded as an instance of transformation. If we take into account all these features, then, we may find that the major change has occurred in the hereditary character of occupations, whereas the practice of caste endogamy has not undergone much change so far as the dalits are concerned.

Placed in the broader Indian context is the social structure of Punjab, which has certain unique features with regard to the dalits and the caste system. In fact, the issue is much more complex than one may anticipate. While discussing Punjab's social structure, there is a need to pinpoint these distinctive elements, particularly with regard to the dalits. It may be appropriate to start the discussion by identifying such elements.

First, the proportion of the dalits in the total population of Punjab was 28.31 per cent according to the 1991 census and it has gone up to 28.85 per cent in 2001. This proportion is the highest in the country if we compare it with other states. However, the percentage of dalits owning land is quite low, that is, 4.3 per cent and according to the Punjab Human Development Report (2004), more than half of them were agricultural labourers in 1991. Gill (2004) has provided the data on the wages of the agricultural labourers with base of 1960–61 converted to 1980–81 and he has shown that the real wages of the agricultural labourers have gone up between 1980 and 2000. Second, within Punjab, the population distribution of the dalits is not uniform. Of all the districts, Nawanshehar with 40.46 per cent of the total population has the highest percentage of the dalits, followed by Jalandhar, Faridkot and Hoshiarpur districts (see Table 1). Firozpur has the lowest percentage (22.82%) of the dalits, which is still higher than the all-India average.

Third, according to the official list, Punjab consists of 37 castes[2] of dalits, out of which two, namely, Chamar/Ad-dharmi and Balmiki/Mazabi, are the most numerous. In the list of scheduled castes (SCs) these castes are differently listed. If we combine all the different names of a caste, then these two constitute the overwhelming majority. In most of the cases the change in nomenclature has emerged due to their different religious affiliations. For example, Balmikis are Hindus, whereas Mazabis are Sikh though both were originally known as 'Churhas'. It is evident from Table 2 that for the purpose of enumeration these castes are separately identified and adding all these different names would give the above-mentioned two castes numerical supremacy.

Table 1

Districtwise Population of the Scheduled Castes in Punjab in 2001

District	*Total population of the SCs*	*Percentage of the SCs out of the total population of the state*
Gurdaspur	520,691	24.75
Amritsar	891,164	28.78
Kapurthala	225,787	29.92
Jalandhar	739,762	37.69
Nawanshehar	237,664	40.46
Hoshiarpur	507,544	34.28
Rupnagar	266,672	23.89
Ludhiana	757,962	24.99
Firozpur	398,409	22.82
Faridkot	199,257	36.17
Muktsar	293,539	37.75
Moga	284,939	31.84
Bathinda	354,652	29.97
Mansa	208,889	30.33
Sangrur	551,476	27.57
Patiala	425,280	23.05
Fatehgarh Sahib	165,036	30.67
Total	7,028,723	28.85

Source: Statistical Abstract of Punjab, 2005.

Table 2

Population of Major Scheduled Castes in Punjab, 1991 and 2001

Name of the Scheduled Castes	*Population in 1991*	*Population in 2001*
Ad-dharmi	9,15,098	10,45,126
Bauria, Bawaria	78,429	1,02,232
Bazigar	1,62,804	2,06,442
Charmakar (including Jatia Charmakar Rehgar, Raigar, Ramdasi, Ravidasi)	14,84,268	18,39,032
Balmiki, Churha, Bhangi	6,40,210	7,85,464
Dhanak	57,997	66,646
Dumna, Mahasha, Doom	1,58,357	1,81,810
Kabirpanthi, Julaha	65,028	73,705
Mazabi	17,65,798	22,20,945
Megh	1,05,157	1,24,210
Sansi, Bhedkut, Manesh	81,062	1,05,337

Sources: Human Development Report, 2004: Punjab, p. 146, Census of India, 2001.[3]

Fourth, various castes of the dalits are unevenly distributed in the state. In Jalandhar, Hoshiarpur, Gurdaspur, Rupnagar and Faridkot districts the Chamars are most numerous, whereas in Amritsar, Tarn Taran, Bathinda, Mansa and Firozpur districts the Mazabis are preponderant. One common aspect of these castes is that despite their concentration in certain pockets they are found in all the districts of the state. Other castes are small in size and each one of them is confined to a particular region of Punjab. For example, the Dumnas are largely confined to the Gurdaspur district.

Finally, the most significant dimension of the dalits is related with the religious composition of present Punjab. The Sikhs are predominating community both in terms of political domination and numbers, as they constitute 59.9 per cent of the population. Hindus come next being 36.9 per cent of the population of the state. Both the Christians and Muslims are considerably smaller in proportion than the Sikhs and Hindus. The Muslim and Christian dalits are not recorded as the scheduled castes. They are identified as backward classes. The Sikh dalits are officially recognised as the scheduled castes as a result of which they are at par with their Hindu counterparts since both are eligible for benefits under the reservation policy of the government. Ironically, Sikhism claims, professes and preaches social equality among human beings. It is expected that the caste equality be practised among the Sikhs. It seems that the politics and economics of reservation policy combined with centuries' old traditions, customs and practices have led to this paradoxical situation. It is all the more important in the light of the fact that in recent decades the Sikhs have fought and struggled for rewriting and revising of the Article 25 of the Constitution of India to recognise Sikhism as a distinct religion from Hinduism. No such attempts have been made in the direction of getting the dalits derecognised as the scheduled castes. On the other hand, the Rai Sikhs/Mahatams have been added to the list of the scheduled castes and Ramgarhias have been accorded the status of other backward castes (OBCs).

The above described features of the scheduled castes of Punjab give us an idea of plurality of the social structure across regions in the Indian subcontinent. In this study we have defined social mobility as the improvement in the status and conditions of the scheduled castes in terms of social inclusion through four parameters, namely, education and occupation, empowerment, emigration and entrepreneurship. Of these four dimensions, one, that is, emigration, is specific to the Punjab situation. It is a well-known fact that Punjab has been the place of origin of a large number of international migrants. An attempt was made to see how far the scheduled castes form a part of the Punjabi diaspora. To contextualise these four parameters, it is important to mention that each of them is dependent upon many factors. Sociological literature has identified some variables as independent, which influence the other variables. However, to use the Marxian expression, most of the independent variables are also "determined determinants". The pattern of interaction of these variables is so complex that it is not advisable to work out a linear progression of forces and their influences.

The discussion in this introductory chapter is divided into five parts. The first part deals with the important issue of alternative strategies of social mobility of the scheduled castes, whereas the second part takes stock of the emerging issue of social inclusion with the special focus on the scheduled castes. Objectives of the study are given in the third part and the fourth part deals with the methodology of the study. The plan of the study is succinctly explicated in the fifth part.

I
Alternative Means of Status Improvement

To understand the issue concerning the improvement in the conditions of the dalits, it is important to identify various alternative strategies and their success. Four major strategies that are discussed here are: reform movements, intervention of the Indian government, efforts of the dalits through sanskritisation and political mobilisation, and economic development.

Socio-Religious Reform Movements

During the medieval period India experienced a series of invasions from the north-western frontier. These invasions changed the outlook of the Indian masses largely under the impact of the egalitarian ideology of Islam, which was the religion of the invaders. The interaction between certain Hindu traditions of Bhakti and Islamic Sufism gave birth to what is now popularly called the Bhakti movement. Protagonists of the Bhakti movement like Kabir, Guru Nanak, and Nam Dev attacked the caste system and preached equality among all human beings. The most significant dimension of the Bhakti movement was the emergence of a class of religious sages belonging to erstwhile Shudra castes, including the untouchables. However, one common thread among them was that they all belonged to the artisan castes. Whereas the Sikh Gurus belonged to the upper caste of Khatri, the saints were from the lower castes. Kabir belonged to the Julaha caste, Ravi Das was an untouchable Chamar, and Nam Dev was Chhimba. There is a reasonable basis to argue that the arrival of Islam in India accelerated the international trade. The increase in the volume of the trade might have led to the rise in artisan production, which brought prosperity to the artisan castes. The rise in consciousness and quest for human equality could have been the consequence of the changing economic conditions of the artisans.

Interestingly, the second wave of religious reform movements emerged during the British rule in 18th and 19th century in India. The impact of the British rule was more profound than the medieval Islamic appeal of equality that had already degenerated into the caste system. The Satnami movement launched by Jagjivan Dass in the 18th century and popularised by Gasi Dass, was one such movement that flourished in the Chhattisgarh region of Madhya Pradesh. It was aimed at the abolition of both the caste system and the authority of Brahmins (Dube, 2001). Yet another movement, under the leadership of Narayana Guru, occurred among the Ezhavas of Kerala. Narayana Guru taught the doctrine of equality among all and he successfully led Ezhavas to enter temples (Sachchidananda, 1974).

In the late 19th century and the beginning of the 20th century, the trend in reform movements was towards combining the social reform with the agenda of freedom of the country. The Arya Samaj movement, launched by Swami Dayanand

Saraswati, was primarily the religious and social reform movement with a critique of the Brahminic domination within the framework of Hinduism by re-establishing the authority of the Vedas. The movement later oriented itself towards the social reform by attacking the caste system. It also introduced Shudhi (purification) movement, which was aimed at bringing back those who had converted to Islam or Christianity to the Hindu fold. Most of those who were reconverted to Hinduism belonged to the dalit castes and were renamed Mahashas or Aryas (Sharma, 2000). Leaders of the Indian national movement also undertook steps to end untouchability. The most notable among them was Gandhi who gave them the name of Harijans—the sons of God. While commenting on Gandhi's role in ameliorating the conditions of the dalits, Nagaraj (1993: 6) writes, "The caste system in India is not only a structure of cultural values but also a certain pattern of inequitable distribution of power and wealth of different kinds along the lines of caste hierarchy. One who appreciates the spiritual beauty of the revolt against the caste system should also accept the horror of materialist demands. Gandhiji could deeply respond to the spiritual beauty of the revolt, but he recoiled in utter embarrassment when confronted with its material form". However, among the nationalist leaders in the colonial period, Gandhi remains the towering figure who genuinely sought to bring changes in the conditions of the dalits.

It is generally understood that the reform movements failed to change the conditions of the dalits in India. Such an observation is partially correct, because we expect too much from these movements. The ideological paradigm of social reform movements in the country was linked with religion. The word 'reform' is invariably connected with religion in the existing literature. Since both the social structure and the social reform had their roots in religious tradition directly or indirectly, the one negating the other had the remotest possibility. Notably, the principle of 'Karma-Dharma' was widely regarded as the ideological principle of the caste system. The social and religious reform movements could not have changed the conditions of the dalits without refuting this principle. It should be reminded here that most of the nationalist leaders used *Gita* and sought to provide interpretation of this text by regarding it as the most sacred of the Hindu scriptures. Similar observation could be made about the earlier Bhakti movement, but there was one difference. The religious leaders in the Bhakti movement did not have familiarity with the egalitarian philosophy of the West, whereas most of the nationalist leaders had got education in England. It is strange that despite their knowledge they did not try much to end the caste system. The piecemeal approach to reform did not prove as effective as its leaders thought it to be. In spite of all these weaknesses of the reform strategy, these social reforms in the colonial period laid the foundation for the attack on the caste system from the dalit castes that were the worst sufferers in the system. For example, the Ad-dharm movement in 1920s could be traced back to the Arya Samaj's efforts to educate the dalits.

Efforts of the Post-Colonial State

After independence the Government of India undertook measures to abolish untouchability and check discrimination against and end atrocities on the scheduled castes. It sought to introduce the affirmative action programmes to improve their economic conditions. The following governmental measures could be identified in the post-colonial period:

Abolition of Untouchability

Articles 14, 15, 16 and 17 of the Indian Constitution mention right to equality, prohibition of discrimination on grounds of caste in matters of public employment and abolition of untouchability. Article 17 of the Constitution declares: "Untouchability is abolished, and its practice in any form is forbidden, the enforcement of any disability arising out of 'Untouchability' shall be an offence in accordance with law."

The Government of India has sought to end untouchability through various legislations with tremendous commitment. The Untouchability Offences Act, 1955 and the Scheduled Castes and the Scheduled Tribes (Prevention of Atrocities) Act, 1989 could be cited as illustrations of this commitment. The 1989 Act clearly enlists the nature of offences with the condition that the offender must be non-SC and non-ST and must be of aware of the status of the person against whom the offence is committed. It is quite comprehensive and perhaps the strongest ever enacted. Interestingly, Dalit Jan Kalayan Samiti (2003)—a voluntary organisation of the dalits—noted that no case had been filed till then. However, it may be kept in mind that the Indian state has moved from the end of untouchability to the endeavour towards ending caste-based atrocities.

Special Provisions for the Scheduled Castes and Scheduled Tribes

These include promotion of educational and economic interests of the scheduled castes and other weaker sections, and reservation of seats for them in the Lok Sabha and State Assemblies. Their claims to services and posts are provided under Articles 46, 330, 332, 334 and 335.

What is now called reservation policy should be understood from the perspective of liberal philosophy in which the individual is the unit of privileges and change. It is important to note that there is some sense in assuming that if some members of the oppressed communities are empowered through education and employment, there are great chances of breaking the age-old occupational barriers that were determined by the caste to which one belonged. The reservation of seats in the educational institutions has helped the dalits to get education despite all limitations. The recent demand of the OBCs to have reservation gives us an indication that whatever might have been the limitations of this policy certain benefits have reached the dalits.[4] It is also being argued that better off among the dalits—creamy layer—are reaping the benefits of reservation policy. The matter is not as simple as is popularly portrayed in the media and newspapers. The scheduled castes are given preferential treatment, because they suffer from social disabilities that are marked by atrocities, exclusion and discrimination and are based on their caste status. On the other hand, the OBCs have not been facing such social exclusions and disabilities. Therefore, the reservation policy has much wider implications and concerns in the case of the scheduled castes.

The rise of dalit intellectuals in the field of academia, literature and arts, and social activism could be related with the opening that the reservation policy provided to most of them. One may be critical of the entire phenomenon by saying that the benefits of reservation policy have reached only the rich dalits. Let us remember, something is better than nothing. The reservations in the public sector jobs have created many contestations. Till recently, the Class I jobs remained unfulfilled for want of qualified dalits. Now, the situation has changed though not completely (as we shall see in the second chapter). This changed situation has created more resentment among the upper castes.

There have been certain changes in the political reservations. It is well known that certain seats are reserved for the members of the SCs and STs in the Lok Sabha and the state assemblies. The political reservations for the scheduled castes are to be ratified after every ten years by the Lok Sabha. The idea behind this periodic ratification was that the moment the dalits were empowered this provision would be withdrawn. However, it has not happened so far. On the contrary, further attempts have been made to empower various excluded groups through constitutional amendments. The 73rd and 74th constitutional amendments provide for reservation for the scheduled castes in the local bodies in rural and urban areas respectively. At present, the issue of empowerment has acquired the centre stage.

Development Efforts

The government has initiated certain schemes that seek to uplift the scheduled castes economically. These schemes focus on those living below poverty line. Among the various schemes is the Special Component Plan (SCP) introduced in the Sixth Five-Year Plan under the 20-point economic programme. The SCP is aimed at the overall economic prosperity of the scheduled castes. Among the various programmes, which are to be made effective to achieve the targets are the Integrated Rural Development Programme (IRDP) and the National Rural Development Programme (NREP). As a matter of fact, the development programmes tend to cover all aspects of the economic life of the scheduled castes and have been in operation for many decades.

Similarly, the Ministry of Social Justice and Empowerment, Government of India, recently announced, "The key to empowering the scheduled castes/tribes is to provide top class education opportunities to meritorious students."[5] The government has been awarding post-matric scholarships to promote education among the dalits.

An objective evaluation of these programmes provides mixed results. A general observation has been that there is a creamy layer among the scheduled castes that has been monopolising over the benefits that should accrue to all the castes and classes among them.

Efforts of the Scheduled Castes

To understand the perspective of efforts made by the scheduled castes to ameliorate their socio-economic conditions marked by exclusion may be understood from two perspectives. First, they never accepted their position in the social system (Gupta, 2000). In other words, the ideology of the 'Karma-Dharma' did not completely envelope the consciousness of the oppressed sections of the Indian society despite its strengths in providing justification to the social hierarchy and occupational distribution. From this perspective one could map out the struggles of the dalits for improvement in their conditions. The second perspective is based on the understanding of the Indian society as not necessarily rigid in terms of the provision of various avenues for mobility. It has been argued that whereas the 'Varna' system was rigid, the caste was dynamic (Srinivas, 1966). From these two above-mentioned perspectives emanated two different kinds of strategies of the dalits to improve their conditions.

Sanskritisation

The concept of 'sanskritisation' gained tremendous popularity as a process of status improvement. Srinivas (1966: 6), who coined this term, defines it "as the process by which a low caste or tribe or other group takes over the ritual, beliefs, ideology and style of life of a high and in particular, a twice-born (*dwija*) caste". The way sanskritisation has been explained, it fits into the perspective of change without questioning or rejecting the ideological principles of the caste system. At the same time, the sanskritising caste/tribe is aware of what it aspires to do. Among the mainland Indian tribes, the adoption of high-caste rituals amount to Hinduisation. Among the Tadvi tribes in Bharuch district in Gujarat the practice of becoming Bhakata by adopting vegetarianism could as well be taken as the adoption of Hindu values.[6] However, in the case of the low castes, vegetarianism could be an attempt to remove the stigma of untouchability and thus improving the status. Srinivas' observation about sanskritisation as a process that could be seen in a historical context is an important dimension of understanding how castes have been changing their varna positions over a period of time. He gives the example of Kshatriya caste. He informs that in the Maurian period there was only Nanda caste, which had Kshatriya status, but at present the number of Kshatriya castes has increased manifold. Obviously, these castes have raised their status from the lower caste positions. In a way, sanskritisation presupposes improvement in the economic condition of the caste, which further improves its way of life. Assuming that a caste could imitate or adopt the ways of life of an upper caste without the necessary means at the minimum level seems unfounded. A caste, which is low in the social hierarchy where caste and occupation correspond with each other, may not go for sanskritisation as a means unless it has gained in economic conditions. From this perspective, sanskritisation becomes a consequence of certain changes in the society. According to Lynch (1969), sanskritisation is a cultural phenomenon rather than a structural one. However, the fact remains that sanskritisation has been the process through which certain castes sought to improve their status. Bailey's (1957) study amply establishes the fact that sanskritisation occurs (i) as a result of economic improvement in the conditions of a caste, and (ii) as a choice of that caste. Gupta (1991: 132) puts the issue aptly thus: "The concept of Sanskritisation very imperfectly understands the incongruence between deemed occupation and actual occupation. Any move on the part of the lower castes to appropriate life styles that were not traditionally theirs is interpreted as if these lower castes are ashamed of their identity." Ultimately, the entire process is reduced to some kind of elite emulation and nothing more.

Use of Political Means

Dr B.R. Ambedkar gave the slogan to the dalits thus: "Educate, Organise and Agitate". This slogan epitomises the collective struggle of the dalits for equality and a social space that could make them equal partners in all walks of life. There are, however, a few instances of the use of political means by the scheduled castes to raise their status. Notably, they adopted political mobilisation approach after alternative means had failed. The three cases that are mentioned prominently in this regard are: the Mahars of Maharashtra, the Jatavs of Agra and the Nadars of Tamil Nadu. We may describe each case in a little detail to see how political mobilisation approach could succeed in these three cases.

The Mahars of Maharashtra, under the leadership of Ambedkar, got organised and started a systematic struggle for the improvement in their status. In the beginning, the movement was led within the framework of Hindu values, such as efforts at entering temples. Obviously, attempt to enter Hindu temples was a tacit approval of the basic tenets of the Hindu religion. Ambedkar understood the contradiction and abandoned the efforts. Even before the temple entry movements, Ambedkar took to the political means and exploited all possible channels. The demand for separate electorate for the dalits led to the Gandhi-Ambedkar confrontation. Gandhi almost forced Ambedkar to withdraw the demand, which he finally did and the Poona Pact came into existence. It demonstrated the strength of the dalits in the sense that they could make things happen. In the post-independence period, Ambedkar did two things. First was the organisation of a political party called the Republican Party of India and secondly, he led the Mahars to conversion to Buddhism (Zelliot, 1970). Ambedkar's decision to abandon Hinduism and convert to Buddhism epitomises the crucial role of religion in forging identities.

The Jatavs of Agra are another dalit caste that politically mobilised to achieve a higher status and they were quite successful. Lynch (1969) points out that in the beginning its reference group of imitation was the Kshatriya caste in which it failed to reach anywhere. After that the Jatavs joined the Republican Party of India formed by Ambedkar and also converted to Buddhism by rejecting the caste values. They occupied an important place in the shoe-making business of Agra. They began to participate in local politics and held important offices in the local bodies. The entire phenomenon led to their empowerment and improvement in the status.

The Nadars of Tamil Nadu, who were traditionally the toddy-tappers, had experienced the worst sort of exploitation at the hands of Brahmins. Their women were not allowed to cover their breasts. They could not wear shoes and were not supposed to enter certain streets. After converting to Christianity and getting some education they started struggling against various disabilities imposed upon them by the Brahmins and upper castes. It was strongly resisted by the Brahmins. There were instances of violent clashes between the Nadars and the Brahmins during that period. Following a prolonged struggle they were able to improve their status. One of them was Kamraj who became the President of the Congress Party (Hardgrave, 1970).

All the above-discussed cases are a part of the historical experiences. To these cases could be added the Ad-dharm movement of Punjab in which the dalits were able to change their position and create a new religious identity of Ad-dharmi (Juergensmeyer, 1982). The Ad-dharm movement, though important as a part of historical process of the dalits assertion, did not have the kind of objectives that the other movements had. Unlike the Mahars and Jatavs who converted to Buddhism and the Nadars who converted to Christianity, the dalits of Punjab sought to seek an identity that formed the part of the larger Hindu tradition of Bhakti.

Some micro-studies at village level tend to suggest that an organised protest plays an important role in changing the self-image and others' perception of the scheduled castes (Seth, 1981). One positive element in this perspective is that the scheduled castes themselves organise to wage a struggle to improve their status. However, it presupposes certain conditions without which an organised struggle is not possible. One condition that is generally referred to in the existing literature is the consciousness that emerges as a result of ideological codification of subordination, discrimination and oppression for which there is a need for leadership that could perform this task. It has been noted that in most of the cases the leaders of the dalit movements belonged to the dalit castes. Mangoo Ram, who organised the Ad-dharm movement in Punjab, belonged to the Chamar caste. The caste background of the leader has been both positive and negative for the dalit movements. The leadership that emerged from within the dalit castes was aware of vicissitudes and sufferings of the dalits and they articulated the same well that resulted in the mobilisation of dalits. At the same time, most of the dalit leaders could only mobilise the dalits of their own castes. Other dalit castes became suspicious of them. Saberwal (1990) rightly points out that most of the Ad-dharmis were drawn from the Chamar caste.

The meaning of political mobilisation is shifting towards empowerment through electoral politics in recent years. Mayawati, the Chief Minister of Uttar Pradesh, along with Kanshi Ram, who was the supreme leader of the Bahujan Samaj Party (BSP) till his death, belong to this new emerging trend. Instead of mobilising the dalit masses to collectively assert their rights and claim equality, this new perspective entails mobilisation for votes. In other words, the dalit leaders treat the dalits as vote banks and then become political actors as well as players at both the state and national level politics. This perspective introduces new trend in the sense that it has all the ingredients and potential of providing better bargaining space to the dalit leaders. Moreover, after forming the government, the BSP could always initiate, revive or implement policies meant for the dalits. For instance, the allotment of land to the dalits has been one of the successful ventures of Mayawati in her earlier stint as the Chief Minister. However, in the politics of coalition government, Mayawati has contributed to reinforce Hindutva forces that earlier were labelled as *Manuwadi* by her. The implication of all this is quite clear. After a particular stage of political development capturing power becomes an end in itself rather than a means to an end of social inequality.

The new electoral approach of empowerment is rooted in the perspective of change from above. Social reform and the reservation policy are two other well-examined efforts, which also aim at improving the status of the dalits in India. The reservation policy has given rise to ambivalent situation, as the better off sections among the dalits have been able to make use of opportunities provided by it. At the same time, the division of society into upper castes, backward classes, other backward castes, scheduled castes and scheduled tribes has been created, reinforced and reaffirmed by the reservation policy. Within each category of people, there could be diversification, but we also witness 'reverse status orientation in public' among the members of hitherto existing upper castes. The Jats of Rajasthan and the Ramgarhias of Punjab are now officially the OBCs. This reverse status orientation in public is characterised by 'double consciousness' to use the term coined by Du Bois (Watson, 2002). However, the content of this double consciousness is qualitatively different from what Du Bois had in mind with regard to the American Blacks. In this case members of the caste are aware of their dominant position in the region and it is clear that this position is unchallenged and irreversible. Thus, the redesignation as OBCs would only give them benefits in the form of reservations in government jobs. The latter aspect of consciousness that gives reasons for exploiting the electoral, constitutional and legal structures is a new emerging phenomenon in Indian society and it has all chances of picking up the momentum. Once the reservation policy is isolated from the basis of the birth-ascribed status and social disability, it turns into a populist and rhetorical political action. It may just be reminded that the basic premise of the reservation policy was that if the socially degraded castes could get political representation, education and government jobs, then the birth ascribed status might be replaced by the achieved status. What has actually happened in India is that both kinds of status have begun to co-exist. The politically powerful groups are seeking to broaden the base of reservation policy, which, as it has started happening, may become the main impediment against the overall development of the dalits.

Development Process and its Trickle-Down Effect

Economic development is seen as the vehicle of social transformation, which trickles down to the poor classes. The economic improvement opens the avenues for the poor to improve their living conditions. Educational attainment and occupational change are realised only after the economic conditions improve. One of the illustrative processes that automatically lead to the status enhancement of the scheduled castes is westernisation. According to this view, when a group changes its way of life and secures material benefits or position in the political party, its status improves (Sachchidananda, 1974).

It is also argued that the process of industrialisation is closely associated with urbanisation. As a part of economic development, the process of urbanisation is equally important, as it is linked with the transformation of social space. When a society industrialises the traditional occupations, village community and traditional customary relations begin to decline in strength. An urban space separates the social relations from the occupational roles as a result of which functional relations emerge where caste tends to become irrelevant in interpersonal interaction in the market situation. Ambedkar asked the dalits to leave the villages and live in cities (Virdi, 2004) even if they had to do lower jobs than what they were doing in villages.

The economic change that affected the rural life most was the Green Revolution that began in the second half of 1960s. As a process of high agricultural productivity, it was due to the deliberate policy of the Indian government to be self-sufficient in foodgrains production after the Indo-Pak war of 1965. Punjab was chosen in the first phase where certain conditions, such as water for irrigation and the experience of the peasantry of the canal irrigation, etc. were already available. In 1970s there was heavy influx of the migrant labour, which depressed the rise of agricultural wages. The local labourers, who were mainly drawn from the scheduled castes, had to look for other avenues though they continued to work as agricultural labourers. Over a period of time, many of them moved out of the agricultural wage labour—the process that also began to erode the domination of the landowning classes (Judge, 2002). The dalits of Punjab began to assert for their rights and honourable living.

It may be added that economic development aided by other strategies could be quite effective. As such it has taken quite a time to reap the harvest of economic development. The trickle-down effect is slow and the gap between the rich and the poor has remained unchanged. Obviously, the perspective of evolutionary and automatic change has its limitations. It is thus clear from the above discussion that there is need for combined strategy to ameliorate the conditions of the dalits. Development process that must have a trickle-down effect, efforts of the government in assuring social equality and the organised efforts of the dalits to change their conditions are the necessary combined strategies to achieve the goal.

II
Social Inclusion[7]

Bouglé (1971) used the concepts of repulsion, hierarchy and hereditary to explain Indian social system. His notion of repulsion was later on interpreted as social exclusion that was practised in intercaste interactions. However, the term 'social exclusion' did not become very popular among the social scientists in the case of caste system and other dimensions of Indian social reality. Concepts like discrimination, deprivation, repression and exploitation were used to describe the condition of the lower castes. The concept of social inclusion became current in the West, particularly as a programme for social equality among various racial groups and between immigrant, ethnic/cultural communities and the host society. When Alexander (1980) made an attempt to understand social inclusion, the forces of globalisation had not been unleashed. He confined his analysis to the ethnic inclusion. He thought that the inclusion of any ethnic group depended on two factors, namely, "(i) the external, or environmental factor, which refers to the structure that surrounds the core group; (ii) the internal, or volitional factor which refers to all relationships between the primordial qualities of core group and outgroup". He identified economic, political, religious systems as external factors, whereas the internal factors, for him, were much more complex and depended on features like the complimentarity of the cultures of the two groups. One of the major failings of Alexander's perspective was that it was not possible to work out the process of inclusion where the differences between the two groups were immutable as a result of which it remained confined to the understanding between two different groups sharing more or less the common racial identity.

In recent years, much more serious attempt has been made to understand social inclusion from a broader perspective. For example, according to Duncan (2003), "A society that is socially inclusive is a society that grants access to everyone to the vehicles of the good life, as it is defined by that society". It is clear that a major shift has occurred in the conceptualisation of inclusion. The emphasis has shifted from outgroup's effort to the core group's orientation and practices to the society as whole. In the specific context of caste, (im)migrants and religious minorities, social inclusion is generally understood as equal participation of different groups and communities distinguished from each other on the basis of class, ethnicity, religion and/or culture and caste in social, cultural and economic life and opportunities offered by that society. Exclusion signifies discrimination and deprivation of those groups that are low in the hierarchy of relationships.

Social inclusion operates at both public and private levels. The process of inclusion is complex and implicates various dimensions of interaction between the immigrants and the host society. One of the most important elements is the labour market. It is to be ascertained whether the absorption of migrant labourers in the labour market is free from discrimination and deprivation. This brings into the focus the nature of labour market, that is, whether labour market is neutral and egalitarian characterised by due recognition to merit in matters of appointments and promotions with regard to the differences in other social dimensions like caste, ethnicity and religion. At the public level the social inclusion is the responsibility of the society that manifests through the rule-making function of the state. How does the society respond to the exclusion of caste, ethnic and religious groups in terms of their rights? This leads us to the analysis of public policy issues.

However, there is something more to the idea of social inclusion than the content of the discussion above tends to suggest. Social inclusion is rarely examined at the private level, because it is difficult to achieve as well as enforce it. The private space of inclusion is strongly linked to the idea of liberal space in which an individual is free to make personal choices so long as he/she does not violate the law. The issue of inclusion at the private level implicates the dispensation of the state with regard to the rights and liberties of the individuals. The Indian democracy is based on the notion of liberal state with a legal framework to ensure that the violation of the rights of the individual is punished. State is the only legitimate agency to exercise force. The liberal philosophy ensures that the state cannot force the individual to construct his world of interaction in a particular manner. To illustrate this point, the state has legislated against any discrimination on the basis of caste in the restaurants and hotels, but it cannot force the upper caste people to invite the dalits at home to dine. The state cannot force an individual to love people of all ethnic backgrounds. The important issue therefore is to go beyond the identified variables of social inclusion in general and try to situate inclusion/exclusion in the specific context of a particular excluded group.

III
Objectives of the Study

In the light of the above discussion, it is important to make an empirical assessment of the extent to which social change contributing to the conditions that facilitate improvement in the status of the scheduled castes in Punjab has occurred. Four variables that have been taken for examination, as pointed out in the beginning of the discussion, are education and occupation, empowerment, entrepreneurship and emigration. All the four variables are central to the understanding of their mobility. *Education,* as we all know, is the key to employment and awareness, which are important dimensions of the economic and cultural growth of the individuals as well as the road to empowerment. *Empowerment* has two sources, namely, the efforts of the government and the mobilisation of the dalits on their own. *Entrepreneurship* is considered to be a modern economic activity. One who has inculcated the characteristics of innovativeness, leadership, farsightedness, decision-making and risk-taking ability besides the organisational abilities may be called as an entrepreneur. *Entrepreneurship* involves the efforts of the government through the Entrepreneurship Development Programmes as well as their own personal initiatives. What is significant among the dalits is their participation in manufacturing, business and trading activities. Such entrepreneurial functions carry high prestige. Thus, the emerging entrepreneurship is an important aspect of the social mobility among the dalits. As mentioned at the outset, the dimension of emigration is a unique aspect of the scheduled castes of Punjab and it is expected that it must have played a significant role in changing their conditions. *Emigration* to the western countries as well as the Middle East is an important feature of the dalits belonging to the Doaba region consisting of Hoshiarpur, Jalandhar, Kapurthala and Nawanshehar districts.

Following objectives were set for the study:

- To know the overall profile of the scheduled castes with regard to various social, ecological, demographic and economic variables in both the urban and rural areas.
- To examine and analyse the hierarchical differentiation among the scheduled castes and its implications for the mobility.
- To examine the educational level and the occupational pattern of the scheduled castes in the rural and urban contexts.
- To investigate the level of empowerment of the scheduled castes at all levels to assess whether it is real or has remained confined to the formal expression.
- To identify and examine various enterprises in which the scheduled castes are involved and the resulting change in their status in the community.

- To assess and observe the changes those have taken place among the scheduled castes as a result of emigration to the Gulf countries as well as the western countries.

An attempt at mapping the changing society or its people remains incomplete without identifying areas that either partially change or remain unchanged. The present study is also an investigation into what has not changed. Or if it is changing, whether it is due to slow pace. The development of understanding that the required level of change has not been achieved is based on normative expectations and ideal construction of various strategies the most important being the state intervention after independence.

IV
Methodology

The present study is descriptive and comparative in nature. Though there have been several studies on the scheduled castes in Punjab as well as the country as a whole, yet these studies have limited applicability to the problem largely due to the passage of time and the issues to be examined in this study.

It was planned to make a comparative study of the rural and urban areas of the two districts of Punjab. These two districts were chosen by keeping in mind the level of development of the scheduled castes. Thus, the study was conducted in the rural and urban areas of Jalandhar and Amritsar districts. The distinctive features of the Jalandhar district are: (i) the percentage of the scheduled castes was the highest in the state before the Nawanshehar district was carved out of it; (ii) the dalits are aware, organised and politicised; (iii) as a part of the Doaba region it represents the emigrant and entrepreneur dalits; and (iv) both Jalandhar city and the district have remained the major centre of the activities of the dalits in various aspects of their cultural and political life. On the other hand, the Amritsar district has remained relatively ignored and as such, there is an absence of empirical studies on the scheduled castes of this district. The general impression based on various sources of colonial period is that the dalit population in Amritsar district is distinct from Jalandhar in terms of religion and castes.

For the purpose of the study it was decided to have a total sample of 1,600 households of the scheduled castes of which 800 households were studied in each district. In each district, 400 households each from rural and the urban areas were interviewed. Four localities of each city and five villages of each district were selected. First of all, one tehsil from each district was randomly chosen and then the villages were randomly selected. To draw the sample of 400 from five villages the method of 'proportionate random sampling' was used in view of the tremendous variations in the population of the scheduled castes among the selected villages. The villagewise population of the scheduled castes was obtained from the population census data of 2001. The total population of the scheduled castes in all villages was worked out. Then, the proportion of the scheduled castes from each village out of the total population was calculated. Finally, to determine how many households should be taken, the proportion of the scheduled castes of the each village was multiplied with the size of the sample. After going through this whole procedure we were able to know the exact number of households to be taken from each of the five villages in each district. The sample size selected from each village has been shown in Table 3.

Table 3

Sample Size

Village	*Total Population of the Scheduled Castes*	*Proportionate Sample*
Mahem	893	54
Bath	1,709	104
Mehatpur	2,747	167
Udhowal	538	33
Adraman	681	42
Galowali	2,820	119
Bhoma	1,250	53
Kotli Dhole Shah	996	42
Gehri	2,907	123
Nawan Pind	1,493	63
Total	—	800

Note: First five villages fall in the Jalandhar district and rest are in Amritsar district.

In the case of the cities, the selection of the sample was little different in the sense that there were variations in the number of the scheduled castes in each ward. After frequent visits to the wards that had substantial proportion of the scheduled castes, it was discovered that the wards could not be used as the basis of the selection of the sample, as it did not represent the social dimension. Instead of ward, locality, locally called *mohalla,* was more important. It was found that each of the localities (Judge and Bal, 2005) were inhabited by a particular scheduled castes. As a result, it was decided to study 100 households in each locality as the sample size from the four localities that were randomly selected among the wards with significant population of the scheduled castes. In Amritsar the localities that were selected included: Gowal Mandi, Haripura, Guru ki Wadali and Tapai. In Jalandhar the selected localities were Boota Mandi, Mithapur, Ali Mohalla and Bhargo Camp. There was one common feature of the localities that were selected in both the cities. Guru ki Wadali in Amritsar and Mithapur in Jalandhar were erstwhile villages that were enveloped by the expanding cities towards the end of the last decade of the last century.

For drawing the desired number of households from each category, simple random sampling method was used. For each district the similar method of selecting the sample was used in both the urban and rural areas. One adult member of the sample household was interviewed.

For the purpose of data collection interview method was used. Both the village schedule and interview schedule were administered. The data were then processed and finding that most of the information was highly skewed it was decided not to administer any statistical test.

V
Plan of the Study

The book covers all the issues raised above in six chapters. Following the standard rules of the empirical research in sociology, the first chapter covers various socio-economic and demographic characteristics of the respondents. The data on socio-economic and demographic variables, besides providing the clear-cut profile of the respondents, situates the dalits in comparative social context. It becomes clear that there are certain basic differences between rural and urban dalits. Various family characteristics provide insights into the changing world of the dalits that may or may not have any implications for their status improvement. Ownership of assets and nature of the house owned are some of the aspects of the economic conditions that have been taken into consideration for elaboration in order to have a reasonably accurate estimate of position of dalits. It is generally expected that in the present age of fast growing economies, such as ours, there is likelihood of economic heterogeneity among the dalits.

The second chapter deals with education and occupation. In certain respects education has become one of the most contested domains with regard to the dalits. Owing to the reservation policy in the educational institutions for the scheduled castes, it is perceived as if they have been able to utilise those provisions and in the process the non-scheduled castes have been deprived of their legitimate claim based on merit. In general perception there is a tendency to confuse between availability, accessibility and utilisation of certain facilities, privileges or provisions. How many scheduled castes do actually utilise the reservation policy? It is not a simple question, but an important issue of sociological concern. Inseparably linked with the education are the occupational levels of the dalits, as the modern occupations become accessible only after one has got requisite education to acquire skill and knowledge. There is also a provision of reservation of jobs for the scheduled castes. It has also been examined whether occupation of the dalit respondents is linked with education or not.

Powerlessness of dalits is not just linked with the formal political institutions, but it manifests more in their everyday life relations with the upper dominant castes at the informal level. The third chapter takes cognizance of both the formal and informal channels of empowerment of the dalits. By situating the issue of empowerment in the historical context of dalits' struggles for a better deal in all aspects of their lives, the discussion elaborates on two major themes with the help of data.

Firstly, it records major and micro-level political contestations between the dalits and upper dominant castes on diverse issues like conflict over wages, clashes during panchayat elections, contestations over religious places, and political mobilisation at the larger level. Secondly, the landmark constitutional amendments (73rd and 74th) in which the provisions for the scheduled castes have been made are examined with the help of data. In this chapter case studies have been given to elaborate the mechanism through which the dalits are striving for developing an ability to realise their will.

There is something the dalits of Punjab do not share with their counterparts in the rest of the country, namely, emigration to the western countries. Chapter four traces the history of the emigration of dalits to the foreign countries and examines how it has contributed to their social mobility however limited it might be. The pattern of emigration of the Punjabi dalits has been traced from the colonial period beginning in the early 20th century. The post-colonial period is marked by the rise of the dalit emigration particularly to England and Canada. However, major migration has occurred to the Middle East in 1970s and has continued till date. Since the migrants to Middle East ultimately return to their original homeland, their impact on the socio-economic process of their native localities could be more noticeable. Attempt has also been made to see castewise differences in the pattern of emigration of the dalits.

Economic dependence on the upper caste is generally considered a major hurdle not only before their social mobility but also empowerment. Movement towards new occupations as a result of education or otherwise is a sign of empowerment as economic independence provides autonomy to the dalits to take decisions about themselves. Running business/trade/industry is the most important economic activity. The main objective of the fifth chapter is to examine the extent and the level of entrepreneurship among the Punjabi dalits and see how it has helped them to attain better status and gain power. With the help of the case studies it has been shown how some of the dalits used their acumen and skills to start the business or establish the factory.

The last chapter examines the paradox involved in dalit mobility in terms of how the perpetuation of caste is not seen as the major obstacle against their status improvement. The best way for the dalits to end caste discrimination and ameliorate their conditions is to struggle for the end of caste system. If the dalits indulge in the social construction of their identity on the basis of caste, then, the purpose of ending caste system is defeated. However, it is important to examine whether certain aspects of social life change slowly in comparison to educational and occupational changes. Sociologists recognise the realm of values, traditions and religion that do not undergo change at a rapid pace. The issue of articulation of dalit identity in the public sphere in elections becomes an important issue that has been examined.

Note

1. In this book, the expressions 'scheduled castes' and 'dalits' have been used interchangeably. The use of the word 'dalit' is preferred owing to its current sociological relevance and meanings, whereas the name 'scheduled castes' is constitutional. In Punjab the word 'dalit' was first used in 1930s (Virdi, 2000).
2. Two more castes have been added to the list of the scheduled castes making it a total of 39 castes. These two castes are Mochi and Mahatam or Rai Sikh by the Constitution (SC) Order (Amendments) Act 2007 (Act No. 31 of 2007). The information regarding the total population of Mochis is not available, but the unofficial estimate of the population of Mahatams/Rai Sikhs is 8, 00,000 putting them at the fifth position in terms of numerical strength.
3. Source of data for 2001 is from the Act mentioned in note 2 above.
4. The adoption of the reservation policy for the OBCs by the Indian government sparked off debate on the issue of reservation that brought out the question of creamy layer among the scheduled castes.
5. "Scheme of Post Matric Scholarships to the Students Belonging to the Scheduled Castes for Studies in India". A circular sent to all universities by the Ministry of Social Justice and Empowerment, Government of India, 2007.

6. The observation is based on the work on the displaced tribals in Gujarat as a result of the construction of Sardar Sarovar over Narmada. One of the authors was involved in the monitoring and evaluation of the resettlement and rehabilitation of the displaced tribals in Gujarat.
7. Social inclusion/exclusion has recently made entry into the sociological imagination in India the reason for which is the University Grants Commission (UGC) has begun to encourage teaching and research in the area of social exclusion and inclusive policy. In accordance with this policy, the UGC has sanctioned grants to many universities to open centres across the country for the purpose.

1

Mapping the Dalits

Confining the discussion to the paradigm of academic research, it may be stated at the outset that this chapter has two distinct but inseparable objectives. These are: to provide the demographic and social profile of the dalits in the rural as well as urban settings, and to understand the level of heterogeneity among them. These two objectives of the chapter are linked with the issues of education and occupation, empowerment, entrepreneurship and emigration in various ways. The most important link is with regard to the caste heterogeneity and various avenues of social mobility. The second is the differences between the rural and urban dalits in terms of religion, caste and other family characteristics. Called as background variables, these would determine the significance of analysing all other variables.[1] Sociological imagination assumes that the nature of the socio-economic conditions under which one lives has direct relationship with what he/she does, experiences and how he/she performs in life. It becomes still more relevant to explore the continuity and the changes the underprivileged sections of the society have experienced with the impact of great modernising forces of urbanisation, industrialisation and education and, at present, the way globalisation is operating in our society.

Classical sociological literature distinguished between two kinds of status, namely, ascribed and achieved. Ascribed status is immutable and remains with the person throughout his/her life. Sex, race and caste are some of the instances of the ascribed status. On the other hand, whatever individual attains through his/her own efforts is called achieved status. The issue is important for the present study, because its main purpose is to examine social change among the dalits. To put it in the idiom/conceptual framework of status, the main objective of the study is to examine how the castes that occupy low position in the hierarchy are able to change their status through various modernising forces as well as their own efforts. It is by virtue of having certain ascribed variables that the probability of achievements is determined. In the caste-ridden Indian society we may expect only a certain level of socio-economic achievements among the scheduled castes.

Who are the dalits/scheduled castes? Ibbetson[2] (1974) traces their history and mentions that they are the aboriginals and lived as the vagrants, leading a nomadic life and then many of them settled in Punjab villages.[3] They carried on various menial and filthiest jobs such as scavenging. Some of them desirous of rising in life stopped scavenging and took to tanning and working in leather. They moved a step forward by changing the nature of the job; still, some of them stopped working in leather and took to weaving—a less degrading work to have clean life. There are also instances where they skipped the leatherwork and took to weaving. Thus, there is always an intermixing of caste and occupations and hence the hierarchy of caste groups has been created closely associated with the nature of their work. We hardly know whether such a construction of the anthropological past of the lower caste could be validated with help of sufficient evidence though Ibbetson is not alone in making plausible conjectures. There are many other scholars/British administrators during colonial rule, who have tried to make sense of the complexity that the Indian society offers to an outsider. Since Ibbetson was talking about the castes in Punjab his empirical observation could be taken for further analysis.

With the rise in social hierarchy, there are also instances of change in religion and in turn religion has its effect on occupation. Ibbetson (ibid.: 268) further writes, "The scavenger on becoming a Musalman will refuse to remove night soil and on becoming a Sikh will take to tanning and leather working. The tanner or leather worker on becoming Musalman will give up tanning, and on taking the Sikh *pahul* will turn his hand to the loom and so forth". It is clear that changing the religion has remained a means to their social mobility the notable element of which is that it was invariably accompanied by occupational changes. The occupational mobility has a direct relationship with the social mobility of the dalits. It is probable that as one moves up in the occupational ladder, he/she also moves up on the social ladder. The existing literature reveals many such instances where the low-caste people in all parts of India have been able to move up in the social hierarchy as a result of change in occupation. The pace of change has accelerated due to the industrialisation, which requires diversified occupational skills. The process has further been speeded up due to ample opportunities available in the market economy geared through the process of globalisation.

The discussion of the socio-economic background of the respondents has been divided into four parts. The first part takes stock of demographic variables, whereas social profile of the respondents has been presented in the second part. The third part deals with the family background of the respondents and the last covers the ownership pattern among the respondents. The chapter concludes with the discussion of findings of the socio-economic background of the respondents.

I
Demographic Profile

In this part we have taken up two variables for discussion, namely, age and sex.

Age

The age distribution of the respondents is very important to know as it would point towards the level of mobility the respondents have experienced. Age reveals the levels of fixation to the values and practices of the society. Miller and Form (1980) inform that conservatism often increases with age and acts as a psychological blockage to adapt to new habits, practices and occupational choices. Young persons may be more actively accepting the new ways and practices of life. New enterprises may be attracting young and energetic persons, while the older people may be found sticking to traditional occupations, practices and values.

Table 1.1
Age of the Respondents

Age Group (years)	*Urban*	*Rural*	*Total*
Up to 20	47 (5.88)	39 (4.88)	86 (5.38)
21–30	214 (26.75)	164 (20.50)	378 (23.62)
31–40	237 (29.62)	244 (30.50)	481 (30.06)
41–50	182 (22.75)	184 ((23.00)	366 (22.87)
51–60	61 (7.63)	99 (12.37)	160 (10.00)
61–70	41 (5.12)	60 (7.5)	101 (6.31)
71 and above	18 (2.25)	10 (1.25)	28 (1.75)
Total	800 (100)	800 (100)	1600 (100)

Figures in parentheses are columnwise percentages.

Table 1.1 reveals that a little more than three quarters of the respondents, that is, 59.06 per cent, are in the age groups of upto 20, 21–30 and 31–40 years. In a way the sample is predominantly represented by young people though there are more than 8 per cent of the respondents who are above sixty years of age. Their proportion falling in rural and urban areas is by and large same. Looking at a high proportion of young persons in our study, we may expect a significant level of occupational and social mobility as well as change-oriented attitude amongst the scheduled castes both in urban and rural areas. At the same time, it may be foreseen that if change is taking place among the dalits, it would emerge clearly due to the young people in the sample.

Sex

The demographic distribution of the scheduled castes in Punjab, according to 2001 census, for rural areas, is 52.80 per cent males and 47.20 per cent females. Almost similar is the pattern in urban areas where the proportion of males is 52.99 per cent and females is 47.01 per cent. In this study, out of the total respondents, nearly three-fourths (76.12%) are males and one-fourth (23.88%) are females. Interestingly, in urban areas, the proportion of males is 81.87 per cent as compared to 70.37 per cent in rural areas. Accordingly, the female respondents are represented more in rural areas, i.e., 29.63 per cent, in comparison to their urban counterparts, that is, 18.13 per cent in the sample.

II
Social Profile

In this section, the two most important variables, which have been discussed, are religion and caste. As a matter of fact as well as expectation, it is assumed that caste is found among the Hindus only. Since the Sikhism claims to be egalitarian, the issue of caste becomes a little out of place at least in theory. As we have pointed out in the introductory chapter, the Sikh dalits are eligible for all the benefits under the reservation policy of the Indian government due to which the existence of castes among the Sikhs cannot be ideally or theoretically brushed aside. Furthermore, other religions have been in existence in Punjab. It may be reminded that Punjab is one of the few states that have Hindu minority population.

Religion

Religion is an institutionalised way of practising one's beliefs and values in relation to some sacred and divine forces. It is a matter of one's faith in some eternal powers and practices. It is a curious mixture of ascription and achievement. One can change his/her religion in a democratic society, but at the same time either it rarely happens or if it happens there could be strong reaction to it. Marx is of the view that religion is like opium and is the heart of the heartless society, which basically meant that religion impedes social change. However, in *Capital,* Vol. I, Marx (1975) also dealt with the role of Protestantism in the emergence of capitalism in England though it was quite a different explanation from what Weber did later on. He pointed out that after

Calvinism became the official religion of Anglican Church all the Roman Catholic monasteries and lands were confiscated. Most of these confiscated properties were given to the emerging aristocracy, which ruthlessly pursued the goal of making money at the time when Enclosure movement began by evicting the peasants from their lands in order to transform the entire land into pasturage. Weber (1976) shows a strong relationship between the Protestant ethic and the spirit of capitalism. Taking both the views into consideration, it becomes significant to note that religion does play a role at all stages of one's life. Throughout the history of India and in the 19th century Punjab, we find that many socio-religious reform movements were carried on with an attempt to remodel the social structure on the basis of modified explanations of religious doctrines. They propagated the modern ideas of social equality and equal access to economic opportunities to all sections of the society. The introduction of modern education system had a powerful impact to inculcate scientific and modern outlook of life.

The role of Christian missionaries also remains significant in changing the values of the downtrodden mainly through conversion from Hindu fold to Christianity. Besides this, the Arya Samaj through its Shudhi movement brought many low-caste people back into the Hindu fold. Though the purpose of such an effort was communal, but the reconverted lower caste persons were given the title of Mahashas and Aryas to make it sure that after their coming back to the fold of Hinduism they would live a life without any stigma of lower status. Whereas the Nirankaris rejected the supremacy of Brahmin priests and proposed a casteless society, the Namdhari/Kuka reform movement upheld the religious orthodoxy by practising Puritanism and untouchability quite similar to the orthodox Vaishnav tradition. In certain respects it was the negation of what the Sikh Gurus had regarded as the most important element of their preaching, namely, equality of worship. The most important movement among the Sikhs that occurred after the British annexed Punjab was the Singh Sabha movement. However, these movements lacked sustained and concerted efforts to remove the untouchability though they were able to create a social consciousness among the scheduled castes to aspire for social privileges, economic advancement and political power on egalitarian basis (Brar, 1985).

According to the Census of India, 2001, the percentage distribution of religious communities in Punjab is as follows: Hindus (36.9%), Sikhs (59.90%), Christians (1.2%), Muslim (1.6%), Buddhists (0.2%) and Jain (0.2%).[4] Tables 1.2 and 1.3 provide castewise information of the religion of the respondents in urban and rural areas respectively. By comparing data in both the tables we get certain interesting results. First, the number of Hindu dalits is more than the Sikhs. This finding is important in the light of the fact that Punjab is a Sikh-majority state. The religious representation of the scheduled castes in this study is almost reverse of the Punjab pattern. Though the percentage of the Hindu respondents is low in villages, yet they remain in majority. It may be added here that among the rural dalits in Amritsar district the percentage of the Sikhs (81.25%) was more than the Hindus. It may be concluded that most of the urban dalits are Hindus and the Sikh dalits are unevenly distributed in rural areas. There is a need to comment on five respondents, who recorded their religion as Christian, because their religious status excludes them from the status of scheduled castes. Interestingly, despite the conversion to Christianity, the respondents have not lost their status as scheduled castes. It implies that officially they continued to retain their original religion. The presence of one Buddhist respondent shows that Ambedkar's movement has not made an impact at the level of religious change. It may be inferred from the census data as well as our sample that Buddhism has not been a part of the dalit assertion as it was the case with the Mahars of Maharashtra. It was observed that most of the Ad-dharmis/Chamars continued to follow Guru Ravi Das.

Long discussions were held with many dalit leaders and intellectuals on this issue. S.L. Virdi—a noted dalit leader and activist—gave two reasons for this lag between the popularity of Ambedkar and low level of conversion to Buddhism in Punjab. First, he pointed out that owing to the impact of Sikhism the practice of untouchability had considerably declined. Both the Singh Sabha movement and the Arya Samaj made efforts to engage dalits in the egalitarian discourse. The aftermath of these efforts provided better social space to the dalits of Punjab than their counterparts in Maharashtra or rest of India. Second, following Ambedkar certain dalit activists converted to Buddhism, but the dalit leaders in the Congress party made all out efforts to suppress it. In his book, Virdi (2000: 221) has noted that this effort at converting to Buddhism occurred on June 17, 1958 at village Chak Hakima in Jalandhar district in which 5,000 dalits embraced the new religion. Well-known Punjabi dalit

Table 1.2

Caste and Religion of the Respondents in Urban Areas

Religion/Caste	*Hindu*	*Sikh*	*Christian*	*Buddhist*	*Total*
Chamar/ Ad-dharmi	205 (31.59)	2 (1.38)	1 (20.00)	1 (100)	209 (26.12)
Megh/Kabir-panthi	242 (37.29)	5 (3.45)	–	–	247 (30.88)
Balmikis	188 (28.97)	2 (1.38)	3 (60.00)	–	193 (24.12)
Mazabi	–	133 (91.72)	1 (20.00)	–	134 (16.75)
Sansi	–	3 (2.07)	–	–	3 (0.38)
Dumna	14 (2.16)	–	–	–	14 (1.75)
Total	649 (100)	145 (100)	5 (100)	1 (100)	800 (100)

Figures in parentheses indicate columnwise percentages.

Table 1.3

Caste and Religion of the Respondents in Rural Areas

Religion/Caste	*Hindu*	*Sikh*	*Christian*	*Total*
Chamar/ Ad-dharmi	242 (53.54)	13 (3.89)	1 (7.14)	256 (32.00)
Balmiki	150 (33.19)	–	13 (92.86)	163 (20.38)
Mazabi	–	299 (89.52)	–	299 (37.37)
Sansi	3 (0.66)	13 (3.89)	–	16 (2.00)
Bazigar	–	9 (2.69)	–	9 (1.12)
Od	57 (12.61)	–	–	57 (7.13)
Total	452 (100)	334 (100)	14 (100)	800 (100)

Figures in parentheses indicate columnwise percentages

writer, Des Raj Kali expressed the similar views by arguing that social oppression of dalits was less than what it was in other states—the reason being the egalitarian appeal of the Sikh religion.

However, one aspect of the history of dalit struggles is ignored while explaining the reasons for not opting for conversion to Buddhism at mass level. In the colonial Punjab the most important struggle of the dalits was organised by the Ad-dharm Mandal, which strived towards constructing and creating the new religious identity of the dalits. Recognition to the Ad-dharm by the government in 1931 was the successful culmination of the movement. Within three decades of the acquiring of new religious identity it seems least probable that the same community would go for another religion. It is because of this reason that only those dalits who were active in the Republican Party of India embraced Buddhism. Within three decades of the establishment of new religious community, Guru Ravi Das occupied a position that became part of the collective social, cultural and religious life of the Ad-dharmis. Bhagwant Rasoolpuri (2008), a noted Punjabi dalit writer, has recently written a story, "Jarhan" (Roots) that revolves around the tension between Ad-dharm and Buddhism. The story is about the efforts of a diaspora Punjabi dalit to construct Budh Vihar in his village. His effort is perceived by the dalits of the village (including his parents) as a threat to Guru Ravi Das. A group of dalit boys physically assault him, but he succeeds in constructing the Budh Vihar. However, no dalit from the village visits the place. In other words, it is not only the egalitarian influence of the Sikh religion that decisively created conditions against religious conversion, but also the way the dalits understood their religious identity. After all, Islam was also egalitarian in its appeal.

Caste

The institution of caste is the pivot around which the Indian society revolves. The caste system has several unique features ranging from segmental division of society, restrictions on occupation, marriage and social interaction to civil rights. An individual's status and social prestige is determined by his position in the varna hierarchy. Brahmin is at the top and Shudra is at the bottom of the hierarchy. Still another group, which was not even included in the social hierarchy, was that of untouchables. Their touch or even reflection could pollute the upper-caste persons. They were kept at the margins though they were performing vital functions for the people in the centre. Under the impact of various modernising forces, some aspects of caste have undergone change while others are still persisting in its old fold.

In Punjab there are 37 scheduled castes,[5] and 92 per cent of the total scheduled castes are comprised of only ten castes, viz., Mazabis, Ramdasia, Ad-dharmi, Balmiki, Bazigar, Dumana, Megh, Sansi, Julaha and Dhanak. Therefore, it may be discerned that these are the major caste groups in Punjab and others are marginally represented. Representing the universe, the sample in the study also represents only eight different caste groups. They are: Ad-dharmi, Mazabi, Balmiki, Megh, Od, Sansi, Dumna and Bazigar. The Ad-dharmis' (29.06%) occupation is snaring of skins and hides, tanning, and leatherwork. They are also the most progressive community in Punjab among the scheduled castes. They excel in their hereditary skills of handling hides and skins. They predominantly are the Chamars particularly of the Doaba region of Punjab who chose to become Ad-dharmis under the influence of Ad-dharm (first/primeval faith) movement led by Mangoo Ram in 1920s. The level of formal education, immigration and mobility is much higher amongst them than other castes. In comparison to all the other dalit castes, they are numerically, economically and politically powerful.

The Mazabis (27.06%), the second most represented group, are found all over Punjab but with dominance in Amritsar and Firozpur. The Balmikis, who were baptised to Sikhism are known as Mazabis. In some other parts of Punjab, they are called Bhangi, Churhas and Doms and they are all traditionally scavenging castes, that is, they are sweepers, cleaning the household of landlords and removing night soil (Fuchs, 1981). That is why, they were ranked lowest in the caste hierarchy. These days they are engaged in agricultural activities largely as attached labourers to the landlords. Their women mainly work in the household of farmers. Most of them are found in villages though a few of them are also settled in cities by becoming industrial workers and also doing government jobs. Balmikis (22.25%) are the Bhangis in the cities. In villages they are commonly referred to Churhas as whose hereditary occupation was scavenging and they claim their descent from legendary Saint Balmiki. They are still found more in villages carrying on agricultural labour activities and their women engaged in agricultural households, making cow-dung cakes etc. Their primary occupation in urban areas is scavenging besides providing 'other services'.

The Meghs (15.44%) are Kabirpanthis. They are also known as Bhagat at some places. In Jalandhar they are concentrated in Bhargo Camp locality where they settled after the partition in 1947. They also settled in Amritsar in Haripura locality. They have mainly migrated from Sialkot, now in Pakistan. Their hereditary occupation is weaving, but many of them took to making surgical instruments at Sialkot and after settling in Jalandhar they are concentrated in sports goods industry and making surgical instruments. They rank themselves higher than the Chamars as they have changed to cleaner and modern occupation. Ods (3.56%) are mainly the Muslims who were rearing sheep. It is said that the breed of dog kept to protect the sheep was known as Od. Therefore, they are called Od and their number is relatively small. The Hindu Ods identify themselves as Khatris. Sansis (1.19%) are also known as Bhedkut and Manesh. They claim Rajput ancestry. They trace their origin from Rajasthan from where they were expelled by a Muslim ruler in the 13th century. They are essentially a wandering tribe and are predominant in rural areas. In Punjab they used to rear wild cats, jackals and dogs and were engaging them for hunting. They were mainly dependent upon hunting for their livelihood. Some of them also took to agricultural labour and low jobs. Dumnas (0.88%) are also known as Dum or Mahasha. The name 'Mahasha' was given to them by the Arya Samajis to upgrade their status after their re-conversion to Hinduism from Islam. Their traditional work was scavenging and bamboo work. Presently, most of them are agricultural labourers, factory and construction workers, and rickshaw-pullers. In the cities, they are also engaged in preparing bamboo goods. Bazigar (0.56%) was a nomadic community and now they are distributed in all the districts of Punjab, concentrating mainly in the rural areas. Bazigar is a Persian word which means "he who does bazi (acrobats)" or any sort of game or play (Ibbetson, 1974). Their primary occupation is to perform acrobatics and they are still lagging behind other scheduled castes in terms of literacy rate.

It is relevant to mention that in our study the Bazigars and the Ods are not found in urban areas and they are concentrated only in villages. Conversely, Megh and Dumna are the urban castes and none of them is found in the villages. The data would be more explicit from Tables 1.2 and 1.3 separately for urban and rural areas showing the cross-comparison of religion and caste.

It is clear from Table 1.2 that the Meghs and the Chamars/Ad-dharmis are more numerous than other castes in the cities. Combining Mazabis and Balmikis would make them the largest among the dalit castes. However, both Chamars and Churhas along with their other names changed according to religious affiliation are in majority in the state in the light of which these castes are expected to be preponderant. On the other hand, Meghs who constitute a small percentage of the dalits of Punjab are 30.88 per cent of the total urban respondents. It shows that the Meghs are essentially an urban caste. In the case of villages the Mazabis, the Balmikis and the Chamars/Ad-dharmi have the overwhelming presence. The obvious absence of Meghs indicates that they may be largely confined to the cities.[6]

Another fact with regard to these castes is the presence of hierarchy among them. We did not find any religion-based exclusion within the caste groups. For example, the Mazabis did not articulate their superiority over the Balmikis. The same was the case among the Meghs who were divided along religious lines. However, the Meghs perceived themselves as the higher caste than the Chamars, whereas the Chamars thought themselves to be superior to all other dalit castes.

III
Family Background

Family, as the primary institution of socialisation of individuals, is the door to understand the social life lived at the micro level.

Over a period of time, the radicals and conservatives in sociological tradition have debated the indispensability of family without any final answer. One is immediately reminded of Murdock's (1965) notion of the universality of family and Cooper's (1971) assertion of the death of the family. So far family's role seems indispensable for the individual as well as society. It continues to be the first window to peep into institutional practices of any society for sociologists. In this section three dimensions have been discussed with the help of the data, namely, family type, its size, and earning members of the family.

Family Type

It is relevant to find out the type of family in which the respondents are living. In India, the usual trend is to live in joint families though now it has shifted towards the nuclear families due to the pressure of the modern forces. However, single parent living with one of the sons/daughters has also become a common occurrence. Such a case where single parent/both parents live with the nuclear family is called extended family. Table 1.4, which provides data on the type of the respondents' family, reveals that a large majority (77.62%) of the respondents are living in nuclear families and only a few of them stay in extended families besides the joint families. If we compare it with regard to the rural and urban contexts, we do not find any remarkable difference. The trend for both rural and urban areas is by and large same.

Despite the absence of marked differences between rural and urban families, two aspects could be treated as trends in the case of the dalits though these are the features of the middle classes of Punjab. First, the cases of extended family are more in cities than villages. Still, the joint families exist in rural areas and in cities they have not disappeared. The existence of extended families is typical of middle class in India where both husband and wife are working and they require somebody to look after their children. Mostly, the parents of any of them provide this kind of help. The logic of joint family is not simply linked with the modern life. It is much more complex than it is generally thought. Whatever is the case, the data on the type of the family among the respondents clearly show that the dalits show a pattern similar to the contemporary trends towards nuclear family.

Table 1.4
Type of Family

Family type	*Urban*	*Rural*	*Total*
Nuclear	660 (82.50)	582 (72.75)	1242 (77.62)
Extended	20 (2.50)	2 (0.25)	22 (1.38)
Joint	120 (15.00)	216 (27.00)	336 (21.00)
Total	800 (100)	800 (100)	1600 (100)

Figures in parentheses indicate columnwise percentages.

Size of the Family

Table 1.5 provides data on the size of the family of the respondents. Three class intervals revealing the size of the family could be categorised as small (2–3), medium (4–6) and large (7 and above). The trend, which is by and large same for both urban and rural areas, is the medium size of the families that constitutes more than half of the sample. In view of the fact that there are extended and joint types of families among the dalits, the likelihood of large family size is there. In case of cities 65 per cent families and in villages 54 per cent families have medium size. There is a reasonable basis to argue that as compared to urban areas the number of respondents in the rural areas having large size families is on the higher side. If we compare the data on the size of family with those of type of family, then it becomes clear that the number of families having large size is more than the number of joint families. In contrast to 21 per cent joint families of the total, there are 34.06 per cent of the respondents whose family size is seven and above. Even, the sum of joint and extended families in rural areas in particular is less than the families with large size. Therefore, it is relevant to mention that in both rural and urban areas, the respondents live in large-sized nuclear families.

Table 1.5
Size of the Family

Number of members	*Urban*	*Rural*	*Total*
2–3	46 (5.75)	52 (6.50)	98 (6.13)
4–6	522 (65.25)	435 (54.38)	957 (59.81)
7 and above	232 (29.00)	313 (39.12)	545 (34.06)
Total	800 (100)	800 (100)	1600 (100)

Figures in parentheses indicate columnwise percentages.

Earning/Non-Earning Members

Let us begin by exploring the earning members of the family. Table 1.6 indicates the number of earners in the family of the respondents in both urban and rural areas. The highest proportion, that is, 34.75 per cent of the respondents, told that they had two earning members in the family; another 23.81 per cent had only one earning member. Taking a rural-urban comparative view of the data we find that the predominant trend in urban areas is one/two earning members. This empirical fact corresponds with the existence of nuclear family life in the cities where both husband and wife are engaged in income-generating activities. Whereas in rural areas 32 per cent have four or more earning members, the distribution of earning members in other categories is even. While in the urban areas 30.75 per cent of the respondents have one earning member, in the rural areas only 17 per cent have just one earning member. Such a relationship shows that either the respondents did hide the information on the work of the members in the cities, particularly of their women, or more number of members of a family are engaged in work outside the household in rural areas. In fact, it was found that a considerable number of respondents did not either record their occupation or their spouses' occupation.[7] While exploring this issue further, an attempt was made to find out the distribution of non-earners in the family of the respondents. Nearly 55 per cent of the respondents mentioned that they had four or more number of family members who were (Table 1.7) non-earners, 22 per cent had three and other 14 per cent had two non-earning members. There is a correspondence between the increase in number of non-earners in the family and the increase in the number of respondents having large number of non-earners. For example, 60.88 per cent of the urban respondents and 49.75 per cent of rural respondents had four or above members who are non-earners. Interestingly, villages have less number of non-earners in the family and if we take into account the data in Table 1.6, it becomes clear that rural respondents have more earning members in the family.

Table 1.6

Number of Earners in the Family

Number of Earners	*Urban*	*Rural*	*Total*
One	246 (30.75)	135 (16.88)	381 (23.81)
Two	301 (37.62)	255 (31.87)	556 (34.75)
Three	161 (20.13)	154 (19.25)	315 (19.69)
Four and above	92 (11.50)	256 (32.00)	348 (21.75)
Total	800 (100)	800 (100)	1600 (100)

Figures in parentheses indicate columnwise percentages.

Table 1.7

Number of Non-earners in the Family

Number of Non-earners	*Urban*	*Rural*	*Total*
One	42 (5.25)	52 (6.50)	94 (5.87)
Two	92 (11.50)	136 (17.00)	228 (14.25)
Three	171 (21.37)	187 (23.38)	358 (22.37)
Four and above	487 (60.88)	398 (49.75)	885 (55.31)
Not applicable	8 (1.00)	27 (3.37)	35 (2.19)
Total	800 (100)	800 (100)	1600 (100)

Figures in parentheses indicate columnwise percentages.

The data on earning and non-earning members in the family of the respondents provide a scope for varying interpretations.

First of all, it could be stated that rural respondents have more earning members in the family because of their poor socio-economic conditions, whereas a considerable percentage of the urban respondents has achieved middle class status as a result of which they have withdrawn their women from the labour market. It is also quite possible that the urban respondents are sending their children to school and colleges instead of pushing them to unskilled labour. Secondly, the high percentage of respondents with four and above non-earners in the family, as mentioned above, is a consequence of their unwillingness to give information.

IV
Ownership Pattern

This last section is aimed at examining the ownership pattern among the respondents. Variables that have been taken for examination are house, kitchen, electronic and household gadgets and vehicles. The level of ownership of the assets is of a great help in situating the respondents in the economic class hierarchy.

Type of House

Ownership of the house is the first major important economic asset that is required at the minimum level. However, in view of the fact that the urban centres receive lot of migrants who are in the process of settling themselves, it is expected that the number of respondents not owning the house in cities would be more than that of the villages where it is expected to be almost negligible. Let us further explore the type of house the scheduled caste people own and live in.

Tables 1.8 and 1.9 show the castewise distribution of respondents according to the type of house. In the case of cities there are 10 (1.25%) respondents who do not own any type of house, whereas all respondents own their houses in villages. The information reveals that a large majority of them, that is, 83 per cent own *pucca* houses, both in rural and urban localities, while another 16 per cent respondents own semi-*pucca* houses. Only one per cent of them live in *kutcha* houses though their number is more in rural areas. Looking at the castewise ownership of the type of the house, it is clear from Table 1.8 that in the urban areas, the quality of life in terms of living in *pucca* houses is better in case of the Ad-dharmis/Chamars (29.46%), the Meghs (31.22%) and the Balmikis (25.75%) than other caste groups. It is interesting to note that the Ad-dharmis are still better as nearly 97 per cent of them reside in *pucca* houses followed by the Meghs, i.e., 86 per cent. There are just 0.37 per cent persons belonging to Mazabi caste who own *kutcha* houses in the cities.

Table 1.8

Castewise Type of the House in Urban Areas

Type of House/Caste	*Pucca*	*Semi-Pucca*	*Kutcha*	*Not owned*	*Total*
Ad-dharmi/ Chamar	200 (29.46)	8 (7.41)	—	1 (10.00)	209 (26.12)
Megh/Kabir-panthi	212 (31.22)	35 (32.41)	—	—	247 (30.87)
Balmikis	175 (25.77)	13 (12.04)	—	5 (50.00)	193 (24.12)
Mazabi	78 (11.49)	50 (46.30)	3 (100)	3 (30.00)	134 (16.75)
Sansi	3 (0.44)	—	—	—	3 (0.37)
Dumna	11 (1.62)	2 (1.85)	—	1 (10.00)	14 (1.75)
Total	679 (84.88)	108 (13.50)	3 (0.37)	10 (1.25)	800 (100)

Figures in parentheses indicate columnwise percentages. (In the last row the percentages rowwise)

Whereas the data (Table 1.9) show that in case of rural residents a majority of the Chamars/Ad-dharmis has *pucca* houses followed by the Mazabis and the Balmikis. Out of all the caste groups, Mazabis have *kutcha* houses more than others, followed by Sansi, Balmiki and Od castes. The Bazigar is the only caste group, which has *pucca* residence. None of the Chamar/Ad-dharmi respondents is residing in *kutcha* house in the rural areas.

Table 1.9
Castewise Type of the House Owned in Rural Areas

Type of the house/Caste	*Pucca*	*Semi-Pucca*	*Kutcha*	*Total*
Chamar/Ad-dharmi	245 (38.16)	11 (7.69)	—	256 (32.00)
Balmiki	151 (23.52)	11 (7.69)	1 (6.67)	163 (20.38)
Mazabi	189 (29.44)	100 (69.93)	10 (66.67)	299 (37.38)
Sansi	5 (0.78)	8 (5.59)	3 (20.00)	16 (2.00)
Bazigar	9 (1.40)	—	—	9 (1.12)
Od	43 (6.70)	13 (9.09)	1 (6.67)	57 (7.12)
Total	642 (100)	143 (100)	15 (100)	800 (100)

Figures in parentheses indicate columnwise percentages.

Now it becomes important to know how spacious their houses are. Information was gathered on the number of rooms each house contains. Data (Table 1.10) reveal that they generally own moderate type of houses, as 68 per cent of them possess 2–3 room sets. Only 8 per cent of them have big houses of 5–6 and above rooms in the house. Similarly, there are only 7 per cent who own only one-room set. The trend is by and large same for both rural and urban areas. However, little more respondents live in bigger houses in urban areas and more number of respondents live in smaller houses in rural areas. Further while comparing the space with the number of family members occupying it, we find that in both urban and rural areas there is no direct relationship between the size of family and the number of rooms in the house. In fact, there is quite an equal distribution of respondents in all sizes of the houses. It means that the three-member families may be living in one, two, three, four, five and even six-room set. Therefore, no meaningful correlation could be found between the two variables. It may be discerned that there is a wide variation in their quality of life. We may put the scheduled castes on a scale of bad living conditions to excellent lifestyle. There are enough families particularly amongst the Chamars in the cities who live in big, palatial houses constructed in posh colonies.

Table 1.10
Number of Rooms in the House

Number	*Urban*	*Rural*	*Total*
1	56 (7.00)	53 (6.63)	109 (6.81)
2	255 (31.88)	304 (38.00)	559 (34.94)
3	256 (32.00)	279 (34.87)	535 (33.44)
4	153 (19.12)	109 (13.63)	262 (16.37)
5	56 (7.00)	37 (4.62)	93 (5.81)
6 and above	24 (3.00)	18 (2.25)	42 (2.63)
Total	800 (100)	800 (100)	1600 (100)

Figures in parentheses indicate columnwise percentage.

Ownership of Kitchen Gadgets

So far as the possession of kitchen goods is concerned, there are still 32 per cent of the respondents (Table 1.11) who do not make use of modern kitchen gadgets except for the fridge used by a quarter of the respondents. However, there is a great difference with regard to rural and urban areas in terms of possession of such goods. In rural areas a little more than half of the respondents do not own any such gadgets as refrigerator, food processor, cooking gas, microwave etc., whereas others do use refrigerator, gas and churning machine. In urban areas it is only 12 per cent who do not possess any such item, but even here a large majority, i.e., 46.50 per cent, uses only fridge in their houses. But, there are some respondents who even use microwave ovens for cooking. Surely, the quality of life of dalits in urban areas is better than those who live in the villages.

The ownership of kitchen gadgets simultaneously signifies the level of modernity and class mobility. The urban families may have moved up in the economic hierarchy, but the awareness that along with the economic mobility there is need to update the kitchen is an important dimension of modern life in which the urban respondents show obvious differences from their rural counterparts.

Table 1.11
Ownership of Kitchen Gadgets

Item	*Urban*	*Rural*	*Total*
Refrigerator/food processor/churning machine/microwave/gas	85 (10.63)	–	85 (5.31)
Refrigerator/food processor/microwave/gas	35 (4.37)	–	35 (2.19)
Refrigerator/food processor/churning machine/gas	40 (5.00)	–	40 (2.50)
Refrigerator, churning machine, gas	111 (13.87)	39 (4.88)	150 (9.37)
Refrigerator, gas	59 (7.38)	185 (23.12)	244 (15.25)
Refrigerator	372 (46.50)	18 (2.25)	390 (24.37)
Gas only	–	144 (18.00)	144 (9.00)
None of the above	98 (12.25)	414 (51.75)	512 (32.00)
Total	800 (100)	800 (100)	1600 (100)

Figure in parentheses indicate columnwise percentage.

Ownership of Electronic and Other Household Gadgets

Interestingly, the data in Table 1.12 show that there are only 1.5 per cent respondents who do not own any such item. Otherwise, all of them are making use of the modern electronic gadgets. The sources of entertainment and modern means of communications have been percolated to the lowest rungs of the Indian society. Nearly one-fourth of them do have TV, VCD, telephone, and cell phone. While making a rural and urban comparison, we find that only 0.75 per cent of the respondents have personal computers in rural areas, whereas in the urban areas their proportion increases to 8 per cent. The use of cell phones is much more in urban areas, whereas in rural areas it is more of telephone in use. The television and VCD are more popular amongst the rural people. These are their main sources of entertainment. There is only one respondent who does not have any other item but he has a mobile phone with him.

Table 1.12
Ownership of Electronic and Other Gadgets

Items	*Urban*	*Rural*	*Total*
TV, VCD, mobile, telephone/PC	65 (8.12)	6 (0.75)	71 (4.44)
TV, VCD, mobile, telephone	276 (34.50)	140 (17.50)	416 (26.00)
TV, VCD, telephone	68 (8.50)	172 (21.50)	240 (15.00)
TV, VCD, mobile	183 (22.88)	—	183 (11.44)
TV, VCD	104 (13.00)	182 (22.75)	286 (17.87)
TV1	98 (12.25)	279 (34.88)	377 (23.56)
Mobile	1 (0.12)	—	1 (0.06)
None	5 (0.63)	21 (2.62)	26 (1.62)
Total	800 (100)	800 (100)	1600 (100)

Figure in parentheses indicate columnwise percentage.

Ownership of Vehicles

In the modern times owning a vehicles has become a necessity as it makes the physical mobility of the people possible. Many times the place of work is far off thus requiring your own means of transportation. The data in Table 1.13 reveal that irrespective of rural-urban differences there are only 1 per cent respondents who do not own any vehicle of their own. A total 36 per cent have cycles and another 47 per cent of them have either scooter or motorcycle. However, the fast moving two-wheelers are replacing the cycles more in urban areas as compared to villages. There are 6 per cent respondents who own cars as well though the proportion of the urban respondents is much more than their rural counterparts in this case. Nevertheless, still 83 per cent of the respondents have either cycle or scooter/motorcycle as their main means of transportation.

Table 1.13
Ownership of Vehicles

Item	*Urban*	*Rural*	*Total*
Not owned	8 (1.00)	10 (1.25)	18 (1.13)
Cycle only	216 (27.00)	357 (44.63)	573 (35.81)
Scooter/motorcycle	377 (47.12)	374 (46.75)	751 (46.94)
Scooter and motorcycle	121 (15.13)	48 (6.00)	169 (10.56)
Scooter, motorcycle and car	78 (9.75)	11 (1.37)	89 (5.56)
Total	800 (100)	800 (100)	1600 (100)

Figure in parentheses indicate columnwise percentage.

To sum up the discussion on the socio-economic status and lifestyle maintained by the dalits in rural and urban areas of Punjab, we may state that with regard to various socio-economic variables there is a significant variation amongst the dalits in terms of their caste affiliations and differences exist with regard to their rural and urban background as well. The dalits in Jalandhar city could perform much better than those in Amritsar. The Chamar/Ad-dharmi caste has been found to be more progressive on a number of variables as compared to other caste groups. The respondents are largely the young males belonging to Hindu religion. Though there are 37 different caste groups among the scheduled castes in Punjab, yet we find that more than 90 per cent of them belong to only ten caste groups. This study represents all these caste groups except for the Dhanakas who are covered by the Ods as Chamar/Ad-dharmi and Megh/ Kabirpanthi have been clubbed into one category. Looking at these facts we may conclude that the sample is well drawn and may expect to draw some significant generalisations. Majority of them, living in nuclear families, have acquired modern means of communications and transportation. They have medium size of families living largely in *pucca* houses with many modern amenities of life. An overview of the emerging profile of the dalits points towards the plausibility of significant changes in their educational and occupational profile, process of entrepreneurship, emigration and empowerment. An important aspect that seems to have come up strongly is that there are discernible differences between the rural and urban dalits. The urban dalits have improved their quality of life in relation to all criteria, which have been discussed with the help of data. We can also observe that the Chamars/Ad-dharmis are the most mobile in comparison to other castes. There is also a class formation among the dalits in the sense that each caste is not economically homogenous though the only caste that seems to have come closer to the corporate mobility is the Chamar/Ad-dharmi caste.

Notes

1. Two important background variables have not been discussed in this chapter. These are education and occupation. The reason for doing so is that the next chapter exclusively focuses on education and occupation.
2. Ibbetson does not use both the concepts to trace the origin of these castes. His major expression is that of menial castes.
3. Max Weber had the similar views. Benedix (1962: 149) wrote that Weber thought, "In the course of Indian history the established caste order came into contact with ethnically distinct tribes that occupied territories of their own". Such tribes were assimilated in the Hindu social order.
4. The data are based on the Census of India, 2001. *The First Report on Religion Data.*
5. These proportions are likely to change as a result of the inclusion of two castes in the list of the scheduled castes. See note 2 of Introduction.
6. The query was informally made with regard to the urban character of the castes. It was discovered that the Meghs also live in villages in Kapurthala district. They trace their origin to the Jammu district where their distribution is both rural and urban.
7. See Chapter 2 for a detailed discussion on the issue.

2

Education and Occupation

The present chapter is aimed at providing a panoramic view of the educational profile of the respondents and the subsequent occupational changes that have occurred among them. Most of the societies in the contemporary world are marked by the occupational diversification and, to use the theoretical expression of Davis and Moore (1967), there is certain logic of acquiring a particular occupation. Most of the occupations in modern times require certain degree of skill, which could be obtained through education. At the same time, modern education is the means to attain high social status that is generally derived from occupation. The process of globalisation has radically altered the nature of labour market. The arrival of knowledge societies has become a major possibility in which the rules and law of controlling knowledge have become a bone of contention at the global scale. The issues regarding copyright, patent rights, etc., are turning into the decisive factors through the WTO. We are thus witnessing the times where research and production of knowledge have turned into the most important elements of capital accumulation. To reach such a stage, the societies are expected to have mass education and well-developed institutions of higher education and research. The traditional Indian society in which the principle of exclusion has remained the defining criterion provided limited access of education to the people. The dalits were an excluded category from the right to acquire education.

The British colonialism marked the phase of the beginning of the modern education. However, both traditions and caste system played decisive role in the identification of those who could have got modern education. Yagati (2003: 59) rightly observes, "Modern education during the early phase was the exclusive concern of the dominant castes and reinforced their traditional identity". However, it is worthwhile to understand that in agrarian societies based on the feudal mode of production, the peasants hardly gave due recognition to education. The working class castes were still behind the peasantry. Predictably, the access to education was limited to urban upper caste people only. Even then, the expansion of labour market and emergence of certain occupations that could only be got if the individuals had requisite qualifications altered the significance of education. In the first half of 20th century there was a definite expansion of modern education. Dr B.R. Ambedkar could get education during this period though the attempt to educate the members of the depressed castes began early through the efforts of the Christian missionaries. The role of the Arya Samaj in Punjab is commendable in this regard. In the post-independence period, the Government of India undertook various measures to assure that the dalits and the tribals acquire education.

The education was destined to play a radical role by contributing to the separation between caste and occupation. In the context of lower castes, Wankhede (1999) and Yagati (2003) consider education having twin aims, namely, enabling the people to change occupation and empowering people with the consciousness that helps them to mobilise for better status. A study conducted in 1980s on the self-images of scheduled caste girl students in Chandigarh colleges (Pathak, 1985) points towards the positive relation between educational level and the elated self-image. They were confidently mentioning their names, religion, sex and hierarchical position in the family besides having the status of a student. The paradox involving acquiring of modern education was pointed out by Pimpley (1980: 110) when he commented, "Since the spread of education is found to be related to the socio-economic status of the parents, there seems to be need to tackle the problem of the parent's status. However, since the socio-economic status depends in large measure in societies like ours on education, nothing short of a radical change in the social structure can break this vicious circle and help to improve the status of these groups". Acquiring education is also a class phenomenon that could be observed even in the societies that do not have birth-ascribed status system. For example, in the case of the USA, "... fully 80 per cent of 1965 high school seniors who graduated did not attend college in 1967 if their family income was under $3,000, as compared to only 13 per cent of those with family incomes of $15,000 and over" (Anderson, 1974: 140).[1] Thus, the radical role, which the education was destined to play by bringing separation between caste and occupation were stalled by the limitations imposed by the socio-economic status of the family. It may be reminded that the reservation policy for the scheduled castes was aimed at overriding the economic impediments, which still seemed to be operating.

The issue raised by Pimpley (1980) belongs to the period of the mixed planned economy and socialist commitment of the Indian state. The present times are best known as marked by liberalisation, privatisation and globalisation of economy. The state has started withdrawing from its social responsibilities leaving everything to the market forces for corrective measures. However, market subsumes economic inequality in which the ownership of commodities determines individuals' ability to negotiate their position. In other words, free market consolidates and reinforces economic inequalities. It has been observed that despite the secular character (exclusively economic) of the market, there are social forces that influence the labour market forces. Recent studies indicate that social exclusion occurs in the western societies due to the individuals' status as blacks, ethnics, or immigrants. To what extent the state could enforce the extinction of social forces in labour market that exclude social groups is difficult to gauge, but it becomes clear that market is not neutral to the social inequalities. The Indian society, where caste-based inequality is entrenched in the world-view and cultural milieu through long-drawn processes, is faced with the difficulty of assuming that market could be a corrective measure. In other words, the state intervention is needed for social inclusion.

The second important dimension that must be taken into account is that whether the education attained is sufficient to help in getting better jobs. Mere literacy will not help in getting better employment. Better employment is related to the attainment of higher educational levels and/or the acquisition of specific skills. Issue is not confined to the level of education so far as the scheduled castes are concerned. Two other deficiencies were pointed out by D'souza (1980) with regard to the educational characteristics of the scheduled castes of Punjab. First, in comparison to the non-scheduled castes, they were far behind in terms of education and, secondly, there were castewise variations among the scheduled castes so far as their education was concerned. For example, the Ad-dharmis had scored better than other scheduled castes. Added to the variation among them were the regionwise differences in the literacy rate. The scheduled castes belonging to the Hoshiarpur district had high literacy rate than those of any other districts. All these issues are related to many social, historical and cultural conditions of the region that is studied. As such, Punjab has been exposed to many experiences due to its proximity with the northwestern frontier through which the populations of traders, saints and invaders entered India. Islam and Sikhism brought notions of equality that pushed the Brahminic ideology to the margins. Access to scriptures and knowledge through the written language became better than the rest of the country. Even then everything remained and the caste never died.

Theoretically, education constitutes the axis around which the social mobility occurs in the modern world. It is important to see how in the case of the dalits education has helped them to rise in status hierarchy. The discussion on education of the respondents has been divided into three parts. The first part deals with the educational characteristics of the scheduled castes of Punjab as well as the respondents. The second part explores how education is related to different castes among the dalits, whereas the third examines whether education and occupation have logical and meaningful convergence.

I
Educational Characteristics

This section is mainly aimed to know the level of education of the respondents in the rural-urban comparative context. Before the presentation of the data, it is worthwhile to provide data on the education of the scheduled castes in Punjab. Districtwise literacy rate for the years 1991 and 2001 has been shown in Table 2.1. It is clear from the data that in addition to the rise in literacy rate by 14 per cent, the pattern of literacy varies according to the district. Some of the districts have lower literacy rate than the average rate among the scheduled castes in Punjab. Muktsar has the lowest literacy rate of 38.11 per cent, whereas Hoshiarpur tops the list with 77.66 per cent literacy rate.[2]

It is clear from the data that the overall scenario of literacy rate of the scheduled castes is far from satisfactory. Still, the proportion of the literate scheduled castes is slightly more than half of their total population. The data pertaining to the Amritsar district in comparison to those of the Jalandhar district clearly reveal that there are still tremendous variations in the literacy rate among the scheduled castes according to the region. The reason for emphasising the data on the Hoshiarpur district is to show that no such change has occurred that could disturb the pattern of literacy in the state. Right from the beginning the scheduled castes of the Hoshiarpur district enjoyed the status of being the most literate in the state and it has continued to be so.

After having discussed the literacy rate at the state and district levels, it is important to present the data on the educational characteristics of the respondents. It may be stated that the literacy rate among the urban respondents is likely to be higher than their rural counterparts. The second aspect that has been taken into cognisance is that of the level of education. Table 2.2 presents data on the educational level of the respondents in the cities and the villages.

Table 2.1

Districtwise Literacy Rate of the Scheduled Castes in Punjab in 1991 and 2001

District	*Literacy rate 1991*	*Literacy rate 2001*
Gurdaspur	47.60	64.03
Amritsar	33.71	46.76
Kapurthala	47.82	63.96
Jalandhar	56.61	70. 48
Nawanshehar*	—	73.53
Hoshiarpur	63.82	77.66
Rupnagar	57.38	70.17
Ludhiana	50.48	65.07
Firozpur	32.49	40.12
Faridkot	24.27	42.17
Muktsar*	—	38.11
Moga*	—	42.22
Bathinda	20.68	41.45
Mansa*	—	42.22
Sangrur	27.15	44.45
Patiala	38.53	53.47
Fatehgarh Sahib*	—	63.63
Total	41.09	56.22

Sources: (i) Statistical Abstract of Punjab, 2005.Government of Punjab.
(ii) Human Development Report 2004, Government of Punjab.

*All these districts were carved out of the existing districts between 1991 and 2001.

Table 2.2

Education of the Respondents

Education	*Urban*	*Rural*	*Total*
Illiterate	113 (14.12)	300 (37.5)	413 (25.81)
Literate	28 (3.5)	6 (0.75)	34 (2.13)
Primary	130 (16.25)	180 (22.5)	310 (19.37)
Middle	136 (17)	135 (16.88)	271 (16.94)
Matriculation	206 (25.75)	134 (16.75)	340 (21.25)
+2	80 (10)	25 (3.12)	105 (6.56)
College/Graduate	71 (8.88)	14 (1,75)	85 (5.31)
Post-graduate	11 (1.38)	1 (0.12)	12 (0.75)
Diploma/Professional Degree	25 (3.12)	5 (0.63)	30 (1.88)
Total	800 (100)	800 (100)	1600 (100)

Figures in parentheses are columnwise percentages.

It is evident from Table 2.2 that the scheduled castes living in the cities are more educated than those living in the villages. Notably, Amritsar has the population of more than one million, whereas Jalandhar is just below the one million mark.[3] It also implies that the bigger cities are attracting the educated scheduled castes. The second important fact that emerges from the data is that the level of higher education is considerably low. For example, less than 5 per cent in urban areas and 1 per cent in rural areas have got education at post-graduation level as well as in professional courses. While talking about the education level of the scheduled castes in higher education, Gill (2002: 13) informs, "In spite of the policy of reservation for Scheduled Castes, the SC students constituted 9.70 per cent of the total students in 1991 and 9.71 per cent in 1998. The system is unable to raise the proportion of SC students in higher education and end discrimination against them". The findings of the present study are in tune with the earlier research. One of the implications of low proportion of the dalits at the higher level of education is that they would mostly remain confined to the low level of occupations. However, for the purpose of the study, it is important to know whether the educational level has improved across generations.

Table 2.3 provides information about the education of respondents' fathers. It is clear from the data that there is tremendous change in the educational level across generations. In the case of the fathers of the respondents almost three-fourths were illiterate. Whereas the urban areas presented a reasonably good picture, the literacy rate in the rural areas has been very low. There was no post-graduate amongst them. One common thing between the respondents and their fathers is that a majority have got education at the matriculation level. In the case of the mother's education, the data in Table 2.4 give us an expected picture in the sense that most of them are illiterate. Only 13.44 per cent of the total are either literate or educated above matriculation, but none of them was a graduate.

Table 2.3
Education of Respondents' Fathers

Education	*Urban*	*Rural*	*Total*
Illiterate	477 (59.63)	694 (86.75)	1171 (73.19)
Literate	18 (2.25)	2 (0.25)	20 (1.25)
Primary	76 (9.5)	40 (5.00)	116 (7.25)
Middle	70 (8.75)	22 (2.75)	92 (5.75)
Matriculation	126 (15.75)	36 (4.50)	162 (10.12)
+2	30 (3.75)	5 (0.63)	35 (2.19)
College/Graduate	3 (0.37)	1 (0.12)	4 (0.25)
Total	800 (100)	800 (100)	1600 (100)

Figures in parentheses are columnwise percentages.

Table 2.4
Education of Respondents' Mothers

Education	*Urban*	*Rural*	*Total*
Illiterate	653 (81.63)	732 (91.50)	1385 (86.56)
Literate	15 (1.88)	10 (1.25)	25 (1.56)
Primary	44 (5.50)	36 (4.50)	80 (5.00)
Middle	28 (3.50)	3 (0.37)	31 (1.94)
Matriculation	43 (5.37)	14 (1.75)	57 (3.56)
Matriculation and above	17 (2.12)	5 (0.63)	22 (1.38)
Total	800	800 (100)	1600 (100)

Figures in parentheses are columnwise percentages.

If we look into the educational level of the grandparents of the respondents, it becomes quite clear that only less than 1 per cent of the respondents, as the Table 2.5 indicates, have grandfathers who were literates, while rest of them were illiterate. And, in none of the cases the grandmother had got education.

Table 2.5

Education of Respondents' Grandfathers

Education	*Urban*	*Rural*	*Total*
Illiterate	786 (98.25)	799 (99.88)	1585 (99.06)
Literate	4 (0.50)	1 (0.12)	5 (0.31)
Primary	6 (0.75)	—	6 (0.38)
Middle	1 (0.12)	—	1 (0.06)
Matriculation and above	3 (0.38)	—	3 (0.19)
Total	800 (100)	800 (100)	1600 (100)

Figures in parentheses are columnwise percentages.

The implications of these findings are quite clear. If we go into the past and compare three generations in terms of the educational level, we find that tremendous change has taken place. Still another important aspect that should be noted across three generations is the emerging rural-urban gap across time. There could be many plausible reasons for this. First of all, it could be stated that most of the respondents have rural background and the migration to the cities took place as a consequence of their or their father's education. Secondly, it is important to keep in mind that the process of urbanisation began with some pace only after independence. The growth of the cities remained slow and the culture of the cities did not remain conducive to the acquiring of education at the earlier stages. Thirdly, the consciousness that education would provide them better economic opportunities could have developed quite late. However, it has already been noticed that in comparison to these big cities, the other urban areas of these two districts do not show such a high literacy rate. It therefore implies that either migration made the difference or the better chances of getting education in big cities could be the reason. The increasing rural-urban gap is the expected trend in the development process at the macro level. The trend is not confined to Punjab or India. As early as 19th century, Marx (1975) pointed out the rural-urban contestations in *German Ideology*. It seems obvious that capitalism emerged by negating the feudal mode of production.

A sociologically important issue is whether literacy is a culture or an accident. In other words, it is generally expected that a literate or educated person would make it sure that his children acquire education. It generally happens due to many factors. One obvious advantage is better employment opportunities. However, it has become important to be able to read and write. A person has begun to encounter numerous situations—more numerous than fifty years back—where education helps him in negotiating the external, formal and communicative world successfully. From the payment of electricity bill to the opening of the bank account, from reading the sign boards to fill railway reservation form education comes into play. Obviously, the better employment opportunity is one of the advantages though it is the most important of all.

Tables 2.6 and 2.7 show respondents' and their fathers' education in urban and rural areas respectively. It is clear from the data that there is a great degree of diversity in the educational level of the father and the son. In both urban and rural areas more than 50 per cent of the illiterate fathers have sought to provide education to their sons. At the same time, however, the educated father seems to have made it sure that his son/daughter is educated. Despite all this change that could be discerned from father to son, it may be pointed out that still most of the dalits are educated up to matriculation. The role of education in raising the consciousness could be well taken into consideration, but the level of education among the dalits does not give much indication of possible and probable occupational change. However, there is one methodological problem that comes into the picture. Before stating the problem, it is important to mention that this problem could occur to any micro-level empirical study if its findings are not interlinked with the overall development process. What happens is that the empirical study focuses on its area of study and its population. Methodologically, it is the best way to conduct the research, but the study would take into account only those families that are residing at the time of data collection. In the present study ten villages and eight urban localities of two cities have been studied. It was observed at the time of data collection that many individuals had left the village or urban locality after getting better jobs. In the process, it is quite

Table 2.6

Education of Respondents and their Fathers (Urban)

Father's Education/Respondent's Education	*Illiterate*	*Literate*	*Primary*	*Middle*	*Matriculation*	*Graduation/ Post-graduation*	*Total*
Illiterate	111 (23.27)	1 (5.56)	–	1 (1.43)	–	–	113 (14.12)
Literate	22 (4.61)	2 (11.11)	3 (3.95)	1 (1.43)	–	–	28 (3.5)
Primary	104 (21.8)	5 (27.78)	11 (14.47)	3 (4.29)	7 (5.56)	–	130 (16.25)
Middle	106 (22.22)	4 (22.22)	15 (19.74)	8 (11.43)	3 (2.38)	–	136 (17)
Matriculation	106 (22.22)	2 (11.11)	31 (40.79)	30 (42.86)	35 (27.78)	2 (6.06)	206 (25.75)
+2	11 (2.31)	2 (11.11)	11 (14.47)	17 (24.29)	30 (23.81)	9 (27.27)	80 (10)
College/Graduate	12 (2.52)	–	2 (2.63)	5 (7.14)	41 (32.54)	11 (33.33)	71 (8.88)
Post-graduate	1 (0.21)	1 (5.56)	–	1 (1.43)	3 (2.38)	5 (15.15)	11 (1.38)
Diploma/Professional Degree	4 (0.84)	1 (5.56)	3 (3.95)	4 (5.71)	7 (5.56)	6 (18.18)	25 (3.12)
Total	477 (100)	18 (100)	76 (100)	70 (100)	126 (100)	33 (100)	800 (100)

Figures in parentheses are columnwise percentages.

Table 2.7

Education of Respondents and their Fathers (Rural)

Father's Education/Respondent's Education	*Illiterate*	*Literate*	*Primary*	*Middle*	*Matriculation*	*Above Matric*	*Total*
Illiterate	300 (43.23)	–	–	–	–		300 (37.50)
Literate	5 (0.72)	1 (50.00)	–	–	–		6 (0.75)
Primary	178 (25.65)	–	1 (2.5)	–	1 (2.78)	–	180 (22.50)
Middle	120 (17.29)	–	7 (17.50)	4 (18.18)	4 (11.11)	–	135 (16.88)
Matriculation	80 (11.53)	–	24 (60.00)	15 (68.18)	15 (41.67)	–	134 (16.75)
+2	10 (1.44)	–	5 (12.50)	3 (13.64)	7 (19.44)	–	25 (3.12)
College	1 (0.14)	–	2 (5.00)	–	7 (19.44)	4 (66.67)	14 (1.75)
Diploma/Professional Degree	–	1 (50.00)	1 (2.50)	–	2 (5.56)	2 (33.33)	6 (0.75)
Total	694	2	40	22	36	6	800 (100)

Figures in parentheses are columnwise percentages.

possible that the actual estimate of dalits with higher education was affected by class-based migration. This is despite the fact that urban localities are expected to be caste-neutral though that has not been the case.[4]

We may now take up the educational levels of the brothers and sisters of the respondents, which would help us in knowing whether the education of respondents was a part of the overall family situation or simply an accidental feature—positive or negative. The information given in Table 2.8 clearly provides us the understanding that the education of the respondents' siblings more or less corresponds with that of the respondents. The similar trends in rural-urban difference are discernable here. In a way the data on educational level of the brothers and sisters provide us an insight into the nature of change among the dalits of Punjab.

Table 2.8

Educational Level of Siblings

Educational Level	*Urban*	*Rural*	*Total*
All illiterate	134 (16.75)	230 (28.75)	364 (22.75)
Some illiterate, some literate	113 (14.12)	53 (6.63)	166 (10.38)
Some illiterate, some educated	66 (8.25)	246 (30.75)	312 (19.50)
All literate	73 (9.13)	10 (1.25)	83 (5.19)
Some literate, some educated	125 (15.63)	70 (8.75)	195 (12.19)
All educated	288 (36.00)	190 (23.75)	478 (29.87)
Not Applicable	1 (0.12)	1 (0.12)	2 (0.12)
Total	800 (100)	800 (100)	1600 (100)

Figures in parentheses are columnwise percentages.

So far we have largely discussed the family of orientation of the respondents. It is equally important to know about the family of procreation of the respondents. A caveat may be added before discussing the data on the educational level of the family of the respondents. In certain cases the family may be the family of orientation, as some of the respondents may be living with their parents. Table 2.9 provides data on the educational level of the members of the family of the respondents. It is interesting to note that the villages show more percentage of the families whose all members are educated than the urban areas. The difference in the families in terms of the percentages of the illiterate families is not much. If we take into consideration the data presented in Tables 2.10 and 2.11, which show the educational levels of the most educated son and daughter respectively, it becomes clear that still not many families have sons and daughters who have got education above matriculation. In the urban areas there is a stronger trend in going for higher education, but even that is not satisfactory. Whereas literacy has gone up, the job-related educational attainment is absent in the fourth generation.

Table 2.9

Educational Level of Family Members

Education	*Urban*	*Rural*	*Total*
All Educated	338 (42.25)	415 (51.88)	753 (47.06)
Some Educated	445 (55.63)	365 (45.62)	810 (50.63)
All Illiterate	17 (2.12)	20 (2.25)	37 (2.31)
Total	800 (100)	800 (100)	1600 (100)

Figures in parentheses are columnwise percentages.

Table 2.10

Educational Level of the Most Educated Son

Education	*Urban*	*Rural*	*Total*
Primary	97 (12.12)	90 (11.25)	187 (11.69)
Middle	99 (12.38)	237 (29.63)	336 (21.00)
Matriculation	325 (40.62)	405 (50.63)	730 (45.63)
College/Graduate	89 (11.13)	25 (3.12)	114 (7.12)
Post-graduate/Professional Degree	43 (5.38)	13 (1.62)	56 (3.50)
Not applicable	147 (18.37)	30 (3.75)	177 (11.06)
Total	800 (100)	800 (100)	1600 (100)

Figures in parentheses are columnwise percentages.

Table 2.11
Educational Level of the Most Educated Daughter

Education	*Urban*	*Rural*	*Total*
Primary	93 (11.63)	189 (23.63)	282 (17.62)
Middle	99 (12.37)	229 (28.63)	328 (20.50)
Matriculation	246 (30.75)	277 (34.62)	523 (32.69)
College/Graduate	77 (9.63)	29 (3.62)	106 (6.63)
Post-graduate/Professional	43 (5.37)	12 (1.50)	55 (3.44)
Not Applicable	242 (30.25)	64 (8.00)	306 (19.12)
Total	800 (100)	800 (100)	1600 (100)

Figures in parentheses are columnwise percentages.

It is thus clear from the discussion on the educational profile of the scheduled castes that there is a tremendous increase in the literacy rate among them. From grandfather to grandson/granddaughter the literacy rate has gone up. It is still higher in the case of the sons and daughters of the respondents. In a way, if we map the literacy rate across generations, it shows linear progression. Expectedly, the urban dalits are more literate than rural dalits. There is a likelihood of the greater number of urban people getting education than those of the villages owing to better educational facilities in the cities. However, the data provided by Ghuman et al. (2006) give us some startling information. According to them, in 1981–82, there were 8.86 per cent scheduled castes among the total students in graduate, post-graduate and professional institutions and universities in Punjab, which increased to 11.55 per cent in 1991–92 from where it declined to 10.23 per cent in 2001–02 and 10.25 per cent in 2003–04. They also inform that of the total enrolled students in the universities of Punjab only 4.96 per cent belonged to the rural areas in 2005–06. The scheduled castes constituted 14.60 per cent of the rural students.

Somewhere it also seems that class factor combined with the sense of traditional defeatism might have played the role in influencing the levels of education. It has already been pointed out that most of the dalits belong to the poor neighbourhoods.

Sometimes when the people find themselves helpless they tend to philosophise their position by rationalising their illiteracy. In fact, the linkage between education and better economic conditions looks quite remote. In the case of the rural areas of Punjab this tendency seems stronger. It also implies that the perception of education as a means to social mobility is losing its appeal. It may be noted that there is only one district (i.e., Hoshiarpur) in Punjab where the value of education in social enhancement was widely recognised by the scheduled castes. The percentage of the educated and literate dalits is the highest in this district. The overall trend shown by Ghuman et al. (2006) seems to suggest that education, as a human resource development measure as well as a means to improve people's conditions, is not serving its objective. There is also a possibility that after privatisation of education it is becoming more and more difficult for the poor dalits to get education.

II
Education and Caste

The relationship between caste and education in general has been highlighted even in the ideology of caste system in which the hereditary nature of occupation is emphasised. Ghurye and many other indologists consider that the restricted choice of occupation correspondence is the defining criteria of caste. There is also a view that the binary opposition of upper (*dwijas*, twice-born) and lower (once-born) castes is based on the division between manual and non-manual labour (Wankhede, 1999; Judge, 2002). Beteille's (1966) study of caste, class and power in a Tanjore village emphasises the emerging divergence and convergence between caste and hereditary occupation. Placed in the traditional context of hereditary character of occupations the education was believed to be the monopoly of the Brahmin caste, whereas the other upper castes could acquire education but their rights were limited. The famous controversy between Vashisht and Vishwamitra in the Hindu mythology revolves around the limits imposed on the degree to which the latter's education could be recognised. As Malagatti (2007) points out, Vishwamitra could not be given the status of *Brahmarshi* owing to his Kshatryia background. In other words, the access to education was limited to certain castes in the traditional sense of the term, and then, as the Vishwamitra's story reveals, there were prescriptions with regard to the kind of knowledge accessible to particular castes. The dalits were denied the right to education in the traditional Indian society.

The expansion of modern education began during the colonial period and it had specific purpose. The education was linked with the white-collar jobs at the low level in general. The post-independence period saw tremendous expansion of educational institutions in the country. Under the Constitution of independent India the access to education was made to every child. However, there is difference between accessibility and utilisation. The response to the accessibility varied from caste to caste among the dalits. All the dalit castes had never been at the same socio-economic level at any point of time. The story of Punjab has been no different.

D'souza (1980) and Pimpley (1980) have shown in their studies that there are castewise variations in the literacy rate of the scheduled castes in Punjab. For example, in 1961 and 1971, the literacy rate was the highest among the Ad-dharmis, whereas in the case of other major scheduled castes, namely, Balmiki and Mazabi, it was the lowest. There were other castes, such as Bazigar and Dhanak, which had literacy rate even lower than the Balmiki and the Mazabi, but their population was small. The situation has not undergone change even in 1991 (Government of Punjab, 2004). In the light of these facts, an attempt was made to examine the educational levels of the respondents in terms of their caste background.

Tables 2.12 and 2.13 show the castewise distribution of the respondents in terms of their educational levels in urban and rural areas respectively. It is clear from the data that in the case of both the urban and rural contexts the Ad-dharmis/Chamars have the highest literacy rates, whereas the Mazabis have the lowest in the urban areas. So far as the rural areas are concerned, the Ad-dharmis/Chamars remain at the top in literacy; the Ods, the Sansis and the Mazabis belong to the lowest categories. A fact that could be treated as sociologically important is the discrepancy in the literacy rates between the Balmikis and Mazabis. It may be reminded that the difference between the two castes is that of religion. They have been separately classified due to their different religious adherences as the Balmikis are Hindus and the Mazabis are Sikhs. It is generally believed that Sikh religion is egalitarian in ideology and practice. Secondly, there is a widely held belief that the Sikhs are more progressive in terms of certain development criteria, particularly in the case of the lower castes. The reason attributed to this belief is that the Sikh religion provided tremendous space to the deprived and oppressed sections of the society in terms of the right to worship at the religious places. The principle of social equality of the Sikh religion is expected to provide the much needed dynamism to its lower castes. Ironically, the religion that is based on the ideology of equality has community, which is divided along caste lines. The Government of India has duly recognised the scheduled castes among the Sikhs by making them eligible for the reservation policy. Thus, the prevalent belief of Sikh dynamism is shattered by the data presented in the two tables.

However, it is important to note that a majority of the Sikhs, consisting of Jats, and other peasant castes, lived in villages for centuries and for them education did not have any relevance. On the other hand, the upper-caste Hindus, consisting of Brahmins, Khatris and Aroras, were always literates, if not educated. Irrespective of religion, the condition of the dalits has remained as it was. At the same time, the aggregate data presented here do not give us the picture of each district so far as the rural areas are concerned. The Jalandhar district has no Mazabi respondent, whereas the Amritsar district has tiny number of Ad-dharmis/Chamars. The result is that owing to the regional variations in literacy and caste, we have data that show the dominant trend of literacy. Whether it is due to region or caste is difficult to state though the plausible explanation could be that both the factors have influenced the outcome. If we examine these tables in the light of the data given in Table 2.1, then, it becomes clear that literacy rate of the scheduled castes in the Amritsar district is lower than that of the Punjab state as a whole. It seems obvious that the region has affected the comparisons. At

Table 2.12

Respondents' Education and Caste in Urban Areas

Caste/Education	*Chamar/ Ad-dharmi*	*Megh/ Kabirpanthi*	*Balmiki*	*Mazabis*	*Sansis*	*Dumnas*	*Total*
Illiterate	14 (6.7)	29 (11.74)	16 (8.29)	50 (37.31)	1 (33.33)	3 (21.43)	113 (14.12)
Literate	5 (2.39)	10 (4.05)	8 (4.14)	4 (2.99)	—	1 (7.14)	28 (3.5)
Primary	23 (11.00)	33 (13.36)	34 (17.62)	40 (29.85)	—	—	130 (16.25)
Middle	36 (17.22)	36 (14.57)	46 (23.83)	17 (12.68)	—	1 (7.14)	136 (17.00)
Matriculation	64 (30.62)	64 (25.91)	60 (31.09)	16 (11.94)	1 (33.33)	1 (7.14)	206 (25.75)
+2	27 (12.92)	23 (9.31)	21 (10.88)	4 (2.99)	—	5 (35.72)	80 (10.00)
College/Graduate	29 (13.88)	32 912.96)	6 (3.11)	1 (0.75)	1 (33.34)	2 (14.29)	71 (8.88)
Post-graduate	7 (3.35)	2 (0.81)	1 (0.52)	—	—	1 (7.14)	11 (1.38)
Diploma/Professional Degree	4 (1.91)	18 (7.29)	1 (0.52)	2 (1.49)	—	—	25 (3.12)
Total	209 (100)	247 (100)	193 (100)	134 (100)	3 (100)	14 (100)	800 (100)

Figures in parentheses are columnwise percentages.

Table 2.13

Respondents' Education and Caste in Rural Areas

Caste/Education	*Chamar*	*Balmiki*	*Mazabi*	*Sansi*	*Bazigar*	*Od*	*Total*
Illiterate	43 (16.80)	39 (23.93)	162 (54.18)	11 (68.75)	3 (33.33)	42 (73.68)	300 (37.50)
Literate	2 (0.78)	1 (0.61)	3 (1.00)	—	—	—	6 (0.75)
Primary	60 (23.44)	55 (33.74)	54 (18.06)	—	4 (44.45)	7 (12.28)	180 (22.50)
Middle	49 (19.14)	36 (22.09)	43 (14.38)	2 (12.50)	1 (11.11)	4 (7.02)	135 (16.88)
Matriculation	72 (28.12)	27 (16.56)	29 (9.70)	2 (12.50)	1 (11.11)	3 (5.26)	134 (16.75)
+2	14 (5.47)	2 (1.23)	8 (2.68)	—	—	1 (1.75)	25 (3.12)
College	16 (6.25)	3 (1.84)	—	1 (6.25)	—	—	20 (2.5)
Total	256 (100)	163 (100)	299 (100)	16 (100)	9 (100)	57 (100)	800 (100)

Figures in parentheses are columnwise percentages.

the same time, the Meghs who are living in both Amritsar and Jalandhar cities have a high rate of literacy. Therefore, the question is why the Mazabis, who exclusively belong to the Amritsar city, have the lowest literacy rate of all the castes. One of the explanations could be that these Mazabis belong to the margins of the city. They originally belonged to the villages, but owing to the expansion of the city their villages were engulfed by the city. The classical example is that of Guru ki Wadali, which now falls under the municipal limit of Amritsar. Most of the dalits living here belong to the Mazabi caste. The Balmikis drifted away from their traditional relationship with the landowners as attached labourers and moved mainly to the cities. On the contrary, the Mazabis remained attached to the agriculture under the traditional 'sepidari' system. It may be argued that the reasons for their low literacy rate might be located in the land relations of the Mazabis.

It is important to see whether the similar literacy patterns have continued to prevail in the next generation. The broad conjecture is that the Ad-dharmi/Chamars are likely to keep their top position in terms of the education of the family. Tables 2.14 and 2.15 show the educational levels of the families according to the caste of the respondents.

Table 2.14

Castewise Education of the Family in Urban Areas

Education/Caste	*All educated*	*Some educated*	*All illiterate*	*Total*
Ad-dharmi/Chamar	128 (37.87)	78 (17.53)	3 (17.65)	209 (26.12)
Megh/Kabirpanthi	126 (37.28)	121 (27.19)	—	247 (30.88)
Balmiki	61 (18.05)	129 (28.99)	3 (17.65)	193 (24.12)
Mazabi	18 (5.32)	106 (23.82)	10 (58.82)	134 (16.75)
Sansi	1 (0.30)	2 (0.45)	—	3 (0.38)
Dumna	4 (1.18)	9 (2.02)	1 (5.88)	14 (1.75)
Total	338 (100)	445 (100)	17 (100)	800 (100)

Figures in parentheses are columnwise percentages.

Table 2.15

Castewise Education of Family Members in Rural Areas

Education/Caste	*All educated*	*Some educated*	*All illiterate*	*Total*
Chamar/Ad-dharmi	209 (50.61)	46 (12.53)	1 (5.00)	256 (32.00)
Balmiki	113 (27.36)	49 (13.35)	1 (5.00)	163 (20.38)
Mazabi	71 (17.19)	218 (59.40)	10 (50.00)	299 (37.38)
Sansi	8 (1.94)	8 (2.18)	—	16 (2.00)
Bazigar	7 (1.69)	2 (0.54)	—	9 (1.12)
Od	5 (1.21)	44 (11.99)	8 (40.00)	57 (7.12)
Total	413 (100)	367 (100)	20 (100)	800 (100)

Figures in parentheses are columnwise percentages.

The data present interesting findings. The Meghs who largely live in cities in the sample have done better in the sense that there is no family among them, which has all illiterate members. However, percentages of the all educated members remain the highest among the Ad-dharmis/Chamars in both urban and rural areas. Among the Mazabis the percentage of illiterates whatever it may be remains the highest.

In terms of castewise education patterns the data suggest that despite the overall improvement in the educational levels of the castes, there is no radical social change in the conditions of the castes. The castes that were ahead of others remain at the top. In a way, the Ad-dharmis/Chamars have continued to occupy the top position.

III
Education and Occupation

The relationship between education and occupation has always been very strong ever since modern education introduced in India in the colonial period. It is a widely held view that education and occupation have positive relationship. Different occupations require different kinds of education. Industrial development, occupational diversification and rise in educational level of the societies have gone up simultaneously. Modern societies are also educated societies, whereas one of the indicators of traditional societies is low level of literacy. In the case of India the emergence of positive relationship between education and occupation is an important indication of country's development. One should imagine a society in which there has been restricted choice of occupations. A person born in a particular caste could choose between limited options. Some castes are generally identified with occupation. For example, the Jats are supposed to be owner cultivators, the meaning of the word 'tarkhan' is carpenter and the same is the occupation of the person who belongs to the Tarkhan caste. As pointed out earlier, education is a means to shift away from the traditional caste occupation. Therefore, the occupational change signifies two important dimensions of society: first, the level of education and, second, the level of development of the society.

In this section, an attempt has been made to examine whether the occupation of the respondents could be related to their educational level. Or, the occupational change has occurred largely due to the development process of the society as a whole. It may be informed that all the occupations have been categorised in the descending order on the basis of the occupational prestige. The categories of occupational prestige in the present study have been taken from D'souza (1985). Some of the occupations not listed in the D'souza's study have been added to different prestige categories by identifying the similarities with other occupations. D'souza (1985) conducted the study in the villages of Punjab due to which it was thought proper to take his classification. So far as the urban occupations are concerned, the same prestige categories have been adjusted to the urban social milieu. In view of the fact that there were certain rural-urban differences in the occupations of the respondents, separate data have been presented for analysis. Before we analyse them, it is essential to mention an important aspect. It was found that a considerable number of the respondents stated that they were not doing any income-generating work. A closer examination of these respondents revealed that there were three kinds of respondents who informed that they were not having any occupation. The first category belonged to the old persons who were doing nothing at that time. The second category included women, who claimed that they were housewives and were doing the domestic work. The third category consisted of young men, who had got education but did not get the employment. As a matter of fact, those women respondents who informed that they were doing only domestic work were in fact involved in gainful employment in urban areas. They were largely doing domestic labour in the city in two or three houses. Their working time was confined to the period between breakfast and lunch. In view of the fact that they did not reveal the nature of their occupation, one may argue that they thought it to be of lower status. This perception acquires significance due to their caste-class status. As dalits, who are situated at the lowest rungs of the caste hierarchy, they have begun to aspire for better and honourable life. The status of domestic servant does not fit into such perception, aspiration and expectation leading them to hide their occupational identity. The third category consisting of young men who are unable to get 'good' jobs are also doing casual work. They hesitated to reveal their economic activity. In the backdrop of these empirical facts observed during the data collection, we may now move on to interpret the data on occupation of the respondents in both urban and rural areas.

Appendix Tables A and B show the occupation of the respondents in urban and rural areas respectively. The data in the Table A provide certain interesting insights. First of all, the percentage of the respondents in the first four prestige categories of occupations is quite low (17.13%) and the respondents belonging to the Jalandhar city involved in these occupations are in an overwhelmingly majority. Secondly, most of the respondents are doing low prestige work, which is evident from the data on the number of respondents in occupational prestige category VII. In the case of the lowest prestige category the number of the respondents belonging to Amritsar is higher than that of Jalandhar. A study of Haryana scheduled caste population reveals that the first-ranking scheduled castes like Chamars are found in artisan work while the second-ranking Bhangis or Balmikis are found in the service sector. This shows that scheduled castes generally follow low-prestige occupations in the urban areas (Kaistha, 1985). Therefore, one may expect that the scheduled castes would have taken to diverse kinds of occupations though majority of them would be engaged in the low-prestige occupations. The data in Table B indicate no different trend except for more concentration of respondents in the middle prestige-categories V and VI. There are few respondents in the high prestige categories—much less than those of the urban respondents—and most of them belong to the Jalandhar district. The percentage of the agricultural labourers among the respondents is 23.88, whereas only 4.25 per cent are attached labourers. It is evident from data that despite the concentration of respondents in the low prestige occupations, a major shift has occurred in the economic activities of the rural dalits. So far as the diversification of occupations is concerned, there is close proximity between urban and rural areas. The dalits are going to the cities for work as well as many occupations have emerged for the rural dalits in villages. Two things seem to have happened. First, owing to the overall development of Punjab, the nature of the service sector in both villages and cities has become homogenous. A considerable number of services are required in rural areas that have emerged due to the change in the consumption pattern in the villages. Secondly, the people have started going to the cities for work, which signifies that the transport system has improved making the movement of the labour possible.

A comment on the percentage of the agricultural labourers among the rural respondents is required. According to the 2001 census, the percentage of the agricultural labourers in Punjab is 16.4, whereas it is 17.2 and 11 in Amritsar and Jalandhar districts, respectively. In the case of the respondents their percentages are 36.25 and 11.50 in Amritsar and Jalandhar districts respectively. Obviously, the percentage of the scheduled castes as agricultural labourers is still higher among the workers. However, the change is tremendous. The occupational diversification has led to the decline in the proportion of the dalit agricultural labourers.

If we compare the data on the occupation of the respondents with that of their fathers, the change is obvious (see Appendix Table D). Slightly more than half of the respondents' fathers were engaged as either agricultural labourers or attached labourers. The mothers' occupation (Appendix Table F) clearly shows that almost three-fifth of them were engaged as agricultural labourers. An attempt was made to work out the percentage of agricultural labourers among the wives of the male respondents. It was found that the percentage of the wives of the male respondents, who were doing agricultural labour in rural areas, was 33.15. It may be further added that the percentage of the agricultural labourers is more in the Amritsar district than the Jalandhar district.

In the case of urban respondents the comparison with the father's occupation reveals certain interesting findings. It is clear that in comparison to the respondents, the percentage of the fathers involved in the high-prestige occupation is high. It seems that it is largely due to the fact that those respondents who have reported no occupation could be belonging to such families where father is alive but the respondent has not yet started his own work. Except for this finding it is evident from the data that the father's occupation belongs to the lower prestige category than the respondents in a considerable percentage of cases. For example, only 5.74 per cent of the respondents are casual/agricultural labourers, whereas in the case of the fathers it is 17.74 per cent. In the case of mothers two major occupations in the urban areas are those of sweepers and maidservants. It may be added on the basis of field observations that the number of sweepers and maidservant among the mothers could be still high, as the respondents tended to hide it.

In the end, we may make an attempt to see whether there is any relationship between education and occupation. It is expected that the better educational levels would also lead to the high-prestige occupations. It is also expected that the percentage of the respondents belonging to the urban areas occupying higher prestige occupation would be higher than the rural areas. In the light of this conjecture, we may examine the data given in Tables 2.16 and 2.17.

Table 2.16 indicates the occupations of the respondents according to their educational levels in the cities. It is clear from the data that there is not much effect of the education on occupation. For example, in the case of the matriculate respondents, there is no clear-cut pattern of occupation. However, the post-graduate and professional degree holders had occupations that belong to the higher prestige categories, but their number is so small that it cannot be stated that education has really made an impact on the occupational levels. All the illiterate respondents are involved in the low-prestige occupations. In the case of the data on the rural areas as shown in Table 2.17, the lack of education and the low-prestige occupation go together though the exception is of four respondents who are illiterate, but are involved in the high-prestige occupations. Among those respondents who are involved in the top three prestige categories of occupation, only four are illiterate and they constitute less than one-fourth of all such respondents.

To conclude the discussion, discernable changes in the field of education have taken place among the dalits across generations. Over a period of time in which three generations could be examined, the educational level of the respondents has gone up from less than 1 per cent to almost 98 per cent. This change implies that education has become the major important factor in the life of the dalits. Despite the rise in the literacy rate the level of higher education is quite low. It implies that the respondents cannot get better jobs because of their low educational levels. It is also evident from the data provided by the Government of Punjab (2006) on the proportions of the scheduled castes among the employees according to the class/group category of the jobs. Out of the total 3,68,022 employees 72,665 (22.81%) belong to the scheduled castes. Groupwise percentages are as follows: in Group A, there are 16.36 per cent scheduled castes, whereas in Group B, they are 20.14 per cent. In Group C, they constitute 20.22 per cent and they are overrepresented, that is, they are more than the proportions of their reserved posts in Group D with 33.92 per cent.[5] This finding is contrary to the general perceptions of the upper castes that the scheduled castes are getting all jobs as a result of the reservation policy. The way the reservation policy is regarded as beneficiary to the dalits is not the case. Why have the dalits failed to fill the government posts reserved for them at the higher level? It becomes clear when we look into data with regard to the level of higher education among them. They have failed to get adequate education in larger numbers—the failure seems to be a consequence of the poor

Table 2.16

Respondents' Education and Occupation in Urban Areas

Occupational Categories/Education	*I*	*II*	*III*	*IV*	*V*	*VI*	*VII*	*VIII*	*Total*
Illiterate	—	1 (2.17)	—	—	16 (9.36)	15 (12.10)	59 (25.54)	22 (16.06)	113
Literate	1 (4.00)	—	—	2 (3.45)	8 (4.68)	4 (3.22)	8 (3.46)	5 (3.65)	28
Primary	2 (8.00)	5 (10.87)	—	4 (6.9)	25 (14.62)	24 (19.35)	54 (23.38)	16 (11.68)	130
Middle	5 (20.00)	5 (10.87)	—	5 (8.62)	34 (19.88)	31 (25.00)	46 (19.91)	10 (7.30)	136
Matriculation	11 (44.00)	13 (28.26)	3 (37.50)	12 (20.69)	51 (29.82)	31 (25.00)	54 (23.38)	31 (22.63)	206
+2	1 (4.00)	4 (8.70)	3 (37.50)	11 (18.96)	15 (8.77)	12 (9.68)	9 (3.9)	25 (18.25)	80
College/Graduate	4 (16.00)	16 (34.78)	1 (12.50)	7 (12.07)	21 (12.28)	6 (4.84)	1(0.43))	15 (10.95)	71
Post-graduate	1 (4.00)	1 (2.17)	1 (12.50)	—	—	1 (0.81)	—	7 (5.11)	11
Diploma/Professional Degree	—	1 (2.17)	—	17 (29.31)	1 (0.58)	—	—	6 (4.38)	25
Total	25	46 (100)	8 (100)	58 (100)	171 (100)	124 (100)	231 (100)	137 (100)	800

Figures in parentheses are columnwise percentages.

Table 2.17

Respondents' Education by Occupation in Rural Areas

Occupational Categories/Respondents'	*I*	*II*	*III*	*IV*	*V*	*VI*	*VII*	*VIII*	*Total*
Illiterate	2 (12.5)	2 (22.22)	–	1 (5.00)	13 (8.84)	47 (35.34)	216 (54.55)	19 (24.36)	300
Literate	–	–	–	1 (5.00)	1 (0.68)	2 (1.50)	2 (0.50)	–	6
Primary	–	–	–	5 (25.00)	33 (22.45)	33 (24.81)	95 (23.99)	14 (17.95)	180
Middle	3 (18.75)	1 (11.11)	–	3 (15.00)	46 (31.29)	23 (17.29)	45 (11.36)	14 (17.95)	135
Matric	8 (50.00)	2 (22.22)	–	5 (25.00)	47 (31.97)	25 (18.80)	30 (7.58)	17 (21.8)	134
+2	2 (12,50)	1 (11.11)	–	1 (5.00)	5 (3.40)	3 (2.26)	7 (1.77)	6 (7.69)	25
College	1 (6.25)	3 (33.33)	1 (100)	4 (20.00)	2 (1.36)	–	1 (0.25)	8 (10.25)	20
Total	16 (100)	9 (100)	1 (100)	20 (100)	147 (100)	133 (100)	396 (100)	78 (100)	800

Figures in parentheses are columnwise percentages.

economic conditions of the majority of them as well as the impact of privatisation in which higher education has become so costly that they cannot afford it. In the beginning of the chapter, Pimpley's (1980) study was referred wherein he concluded that better economic condition is a prerequisite for the attainment of higher education. It is clear from our findings that the same factor still holds valid. In the light of the above empirical fact, it becomes clear that most of the debate on reservation policy is misplaced in the sense that instead of examining the mechanisms through which the dalits are excluded from getting higher education, the focus has remained confined to the issue of merit versus reservation.

The absence of the dalits in higher education and high-prestige occupations could also be understood as discrimination. Dhesi (1998: 1043–440) concludes, "There is sufficient evidence to suggest that discrimination, defined as absence of equal opportunities, exists before the market as well as in the market against certain social categories in India. Inequality in access to sources of human capital acquisition reinforces inequality in the labour market and vice versa. Apparently, caste-religious discrimination and class discrimination overlap. However, in the case of socially deprived lower castes and minorities, especially Muslims, caste-religious discrimination seems to accentuate class discrimination. The impact of secular ideologies and institutions of modernity notwithstanding, the inegalitarian sacral tradition of caste still has strong hold over the minds and lives of Indians."

The scholars have frequently highlighted the hierarchical differentiation among the dalits. To make an adequate analysis of the conditions of the dalits, it is important that their educational levels are examined according to their caste. It has been found that the Ad-dharmis have done very well in education in comparison to all other dalit castes. The Mazabis have been left behind. It is equally important to note that there is occupational mobility among the dalits across generations. Much of the occupational changes are the consequence of the development of the region—or to put it simply—the Green Revolution. The education does not seem to be as effective as it is generally expected.

Notes

1. Though the data on the USA are old, but the class basis of acquiring education is highlighted well to suggest that if we wish to make observations with regard to Indian dalits, the issue of class cannot be put aside despite the reservation policy.
2. Literacy rates among the scheduled castes in Punjab in 1971, 1981 and 1991 were 16.12 per cent, 23.85 per cent and 41.09 per cent respectively. All these years the Hoshiarpur district topped the list in Punjab with 29.16 per cent in 1971, 41.57 per cent in 1981 and 63.82 per cent in 1991.
3. According to the Census of India, 2001, the total population of Amritsar is 10,00,536 and Jalandhar is 7,12,631. Ludhiana tops the list of cities with the highest population of 13,98,467.
4. Judge and Bal (2005) have shown how the dalits of particular castes are concentrated in single localities in both Amritsar and Jalandhar making the name of the locality and the caste coterminous.
5. Economic and Statistical Abstract of Punjab, Government of Punjab, 2006 (c.f. Kallarmajri, 2008: 84).

APPENDIX

Table A

Occupation of the Respondents in Urban Areas

Occupation	*Amritsar*	*Jalandhar*	*Total*
Category I			
Industrialist/Manufacturer	2 (0.50)	22 (5.50)	24 (3.00)
Foreign Returned	–	1 (0.25)	1 (0.12)
Category II			
Wholesaler/Property Dealer	–	16 (4.00)	16 (2.00)
Large Businessman	1 (0.25)	13 (3.25)	14 (1.75)
Running a School	–	1 (0.25)	1 (0.12)
Commission Agent (animals)	–	7 (1.75)	7 (0.88)
Junior Government Officer (Working/Retired)	5 (1.25)	3 (0.75)	8 (1.00)
Category III			
Registered Medical Practitioner (RMP)	–	1 (0.25)	1 (0.12)
Pharmacist	3 (0.75)	3 (0.75)	6 (0.75)
Nurse	–	1 (0.25)	1 (0.12)

Cont'd...

Cont'd...

Category IV			
Medium shopkeeper	6 (1.50)	21 (5.25)	27 (3.38)
Depot Holder	2 (0.5)	1 (0.25)	3 (0.38)
Cable Operator	1 (0.25)	—	1 (0.12)
School Teacher	6 (1.50)	12 (3.00)	18 (2.25)
Supervisor	3 (0.75)	6 (1.50)	9 (1.12)
Category V			
Mechanic/Electrician/Technician	11 (2.75)	14 (3.5)	25 (3.12)
Carpenter	3 (0.75)	6 (1.50)	9 (1.12)
Plumber	—	1 (0.25)	1 (0.12)
Tailor	2 (0.5)	7 (1.75)	9 (1.12)
Painter	1 (0.25)	11 (2.75)	12 (1.50)
Weaver	7 (1.75)	1 (0.25)	8 (1.00)
Bandmaster	3 (0.75)	—	3 (0.38)
Singer/Orchestra	1 (0.25)	—	1 (0.12)
Embroidery Worker	7 (1.75)	—	7 (0.88)
Petty shopkeeper	14 (3.50)	12 (3.00)	26 (3.25)
Clerical worker	16 (4.00)	16 (4.00)	32 (4.00)
Driver/Conductor	8 (2.00)	16 (4.00)	24 (3.00)
Shoemaker	2 (0.50)	1 (0.25)	3 (0.38)
Barber	2 (0.50)	—	2 (0.12)
Mason	4 (1.00)	5 (1.25)	9 (1.12)
Category VI			
Skilled Worker	1 (0.25)	39 (9.75)	40 (5.00)
Salesman	4 (1.00)	9 (2.25)	13 (1.62)
Police Constable	2 (0.50)	9 (2.25)	11 (1.38)
Factory Worker	8 (2.00)	9 (2.25)	17 (2.12)
Powerloom Labourer	28 (7.00)	—	28 (3.50)
Coolie/Paledar	15 (3.75)	—	15 (1.88)
Category VII			
Watchman/Peon	14 (3.50)	1 (0.25)	15 (1.88)
Ward Boy	2 (0.50)	—	2 (0.25)
Vender/Stall owner	4 (1.00)	12 (3.00)	16 (2.00)
Whitewashing	2 (0.50)	2 (0.50)	4 (0.50)
Sweeper	38 (9.50)	38 (9.50)	76 (9.50)
Domestic/Shop Servant	34 (8.50)	18 (4.50)	52 (6.50)

Cont'd...

Cont'd...

Daily Wage Worker	17 (4.25)	6 (1.50)	23 (2.88)
Agricultural Labourer	19 (4.75)	4 (1.00)	23 (2.88)
Rickshaw Puller	16 (4.00)	4 (1.00)	20 (2.50)
Category VIII			
No work	86 (21.50)	51 (12.75)	137 (17.12)
Total	400 (100)	400 (100)	800 (100)

Note: Figures in parentheses denote columnwise percentages.

Table B

Occupation of the Respondents in Rural Areas

Occupation	*Amritsar District*	*Jalandhar District*	*Total*
Category I			
Foreign Returned	–	16 (4.00)	16 (2.00)
Category II			
Government Official	1 (0.25)	5 (1.25)	6 (0.75)
Large Farmer	–	1 (0.25)	1 (0.12)
Running Tannery	–	2 (0.50)	2 (0.25)
Category III			
RMP	–	1 (0.25)	1 (0.12)
Category IV			
Medium shopkeeper	1 (0.25)	6 (1.50)	7 (0.88)
Medium Farmer	–	7 (1.75)	7 (0.88)
School Teacher	–	2 (0.50)	2 (0.25)
Dairy Farmer/Commission agent animals	4 (1.00)	–	4 (0.50)
Category V			
Mechanic/electrician	1(0.25)	10 (2.50)	11 (1.38)
Mason	7 (1.75)	31 (7.75)	38 (4.75)
Clerk	4 (1.00)	7 (1.75)	11 (1.38)
Carpenter	–	16 (4.00)	16 (2.00)
Driver	3 (0.75)	7 (1.75)	10 (1.25)
Petty Shopkeeper	2 (0.50)	9 (2.25)	11 (1.38)
Tailor	5 (1.25)	7 (1.75)	12 (1.50)

Cont'd...

Cont'd...

Painter	—	7 (1.75)	7 (0.88)
Plumber	1 (0.25)	3 (0.75)	4 (0.50)
Singer/Orchestra	—	2 (0.50)	2 (0.25)
Shoemaker	6 (1.50)	2 (0.50)	8 (1.00)
Blacksmith	—	2 (0.50)	2 (0.25)
Embroidery Worker	3 (0.75)	2 (0.50)	5 (0.62)
Photographer	—	3 (0.75)	3 (0.38)
Small Farmer	2 (0.50)	2 (0.50)	4 (0.50)
Handloom/weaving	2 (0.50)	1 (0.25)	3 (0.38)
Category VI			
Skilled Worker	—	34 (8.50)	34 (4.25)
Police/armyman	14 (3.50)	7 (1.75)	21 (2.62)
Paledar	18 (4.50)	3 (0.75)	21 (2.62)
Factory worker	2 (0.50)	1 (0.25)	3 (0.38)
Cycle repair	—	2 (0.50)	2 (0.25)
Brick kiln Worker	47 (11.75)	5 (1.25)	52 (6.50)
Category VII			
Cobbler	—	2 (0.5)	2 (0.25)
Barber	1 (0.25)	3 (0.75)	4 (0.50)
Horse cart driver	2 (0.50)	5 (1.25)	7 (0.88)
Watchman/Peon	2 (0.50)	9 (2.25)	11 (1.38)
Vendor	2 (0.50)	2 (0.50)	4 (0.50)
White washman	—	6 (1.50)	6 (0.75)
Rickshaw puller	15 (3.75)	1 (0.25)	16 (2.00)
Shop servant	4 (1.00)	4 (1.00)	8 (1.00)
Sweeper	2 (0.50)	4 (1.00)	6 (0.75)
Maidservant	18 (4.5)	20 (5.00)	38 (4.75)
Casual worker	50 (12.50)	19 (4.75)	69 (8.62)
Agricultural Labourer	145 (36.25)	46 (11.50)	191 (23.88)
Attached Labourer	19 (4.75)	15 (3.75)	34 (4.25)
Category VIII			
No Work/Household work	17 (4.25)	61 (15.25)	78 (9.75)
Total	400 (100)	400 (100)	800 (100)

Figures in parentheses denote columnwise percentages.

Table C

Occupation of the Fathers of the Respondents in Urban Areas

Occupation	Amritsar District	Jalandhar District	Total
Category I			
Industrialist/Manufacturer	1 (0.25)	14 (3.50)	15 (1.88)
Immigrant	—	4 (1.00)	4 (0.50)
Businessman	1 (0.25)	32 (8.00)	33 (4.12)
Category II			
Junior Government Official	13 (3.25)	15 (3.75)	28 (3.50)
Property Dealer	4 (1.00)	3 (0.75)	7 (0.88)
Commission Agent (animals)	1 (0.25)	9 (2.25)	10 (1.25)
Medium Farmer	—	1 (0.25)	1 (0.12)
Category III			
Flourmill	1 (0.25)	—	1 (0.12)
Category IV			
Medium shopkeeper	3 (0.75)	11 (2.75)	14 (1.75)
School Teacher	2 (0.50)	8 (2.00)	10 (1.25)
Milkman	—	1 (0.25)	1 (0.12)
Category V			
Mechanic/Electrician	3 (0.75)	1 (0.25)	4 (0.50)
Mason/Carpenter	7 (1.75)	6 (1.50)	13 (1.62)
Tailor	4 (1.00)	5 (1.25)	9 (1.12)
Weaver	75 (18.75)	14 (3.50)	89 (11.12)
Bandmaster	4 (1.00)	—	4 (0.50)
Petty shopkeeper	3 (0.75)	5 (1.25)	8 (1.00)
Clerical	8 (2.00)	32 (8.00)	40 (5.00)
Driver	1 (0.25)	2 (0.50)	3 (0.38)
Shoemaker	4 (1.00)	8 (2.00)	12 (1.50)
Barber	1 (0.25)	1 (0.25)	2 (0.25)
Category VI			
Skilled Worker	9 (2.25)	83 (20.75)	92 (11.50)
Salesman	1 (0.25)	—	1 (0.12)

Cont'd...

Cont'd...

Army/Police	13 (3.25)	9 (2.25)	22 (2.75)
Factory Worker	17 (4.25)	7 (1.75)	24 (3.00)
Coolie/Paledar	11 (2.75)	1 (0.25)	12 (1.50)
Brick kiln worker	1 (0.25)	–	1 (0.12)
Category VII			
Vendor	1 (0.25)	1 (0.25)	2 (0.25)
Sweeper	77 (19.25)	91 (22.75)	168 (21.00)
Shop Servant	5 (1.25)	1 (0.25)	6 (0.75)
Rickshaw Puller	5 (1.25)	–	5 (0.62)
Casual Labourer	62 (15.50)	23 (5.75)	85 (10.62)
Attached Labourer	3 (0.75)	–	3 (0.38)
Agricultural Labourer	45 (11.25)	12 (3.00)	57 (7.12)
No response	14 (3.50)	–	14 (1.75)
Total	400 (100)	400 (100)	800 (100)

Figures in parentheses denote columnwise percentages.

Table D

Occupation of the Fathers of the Respondents in Rural Areas

Occupation	*Amritsar District*	*Jalandhar District*	*Total*
Category I			
Foreign Returned	–	2 (0.50)	2 (0.25)
Category II			
Large Farmer	–	1 (0.25)	1 (0.12)
Category III			
RMP	–	1 (0.25)	1 (0.12)
Category IV			
Medium Farmer	–	9 (2.25)	9 (1.12)
Dairy Farmer/Commission Agent (animals)	6 (1.50)	0	6 (0.75)
Category V			
Mason	1 (0.25)	18 (4.50)	19 (2.38)
Clerk/Government employee	3 (0.75)	14 (3.50)	17 (2.12)

Cont'd...

Cont'd...

Carpenter	1 (0.25)	10 (2.50)	11 (1.38)
Driver	—	3 (0.75)	3 (0.38)
Singer/Orchestra	—	—	—
Shoemaker	5 (1.25)	12 (3.00)	17 (2.12)
Small Farmer	—	2 (0.50)	2 (0.25)
Handloom/weaving	1 (0.25)	10 (2.50)	11 (1.38)
Category VI			
Skilled Worker	2 (0.50)	—	2 (0.25)
Police/army man	6 (1.50)	5 (1.25)	11 (1.38)
Paledar	14 (3.50)	3 (0.75)	17 (2.12)
Factory worker	—	3 (0.75)	3 (0.38)
Halwai	—	1 (0.25)	1 (0.12)
Basket making	3 (0.75)	1 (0.25)	4 (0.50)
Tannery worker	—	87 (21.75)	87 (10.88)
Brick kiln worker	37 (9.25)	4 (1.00)	41 (5.12)
Sports goods worker	3 (0.75)	2 (0.50)	5 (0.62)
Tonga driver	1 (0.25)	1 (0.25)	2 (0.25)
Category VII			
Cobbler	3 (0.75)	3 (0.75)	6 (0.75)
Vendor	4 (1.00)	4 (1.00)	8 (1.00)
Casual worker	60 (15.00)	38 (9.50)	98 (12.25)
Agricultural Labourer	205 (51.25)	132 (33.00)	337 (42.13)
Attached Labourer	35 (8.75)	32 (8.00)	67 (8.38)
Sweeper	10 (2.50)	2 (0.50)	12 (1.50)
Total	400	400	800

Figures in parentheses denote columnwise percentages.

Table E

Occupation of Respondents' Mothers in Urban Areas

Occupation	*Amritsar District*	*Jalandhar District*	*Total*
Category III			
Health Worker	1 (0.25)	3 (0.75)	4 (0.50)

Cont'd...

Cont'd...

Category IV			
School Teacher	4 (1.00)	9 (2.25)	13 (1.63)
Category V			
Clerical	2 (0.50)	2 (0.50)	4 (0.50)
Weaver	14 (3.50)	4 (1.00)	18 (2.25)
Category VI			
Skilled worker	8 (2.00)	6 (1.50)	14 (1.75)
Factory worker	1 (0.25)	1 (0.25)	2 (0.25)
Category VII			
Maidservant	43 (10.75)	21 (5.25)	64 (8.00)
Sweeper	20 (5.00)	35 (8.75)	55 (6.87)
Category VIII			
No Work	307 (76.75)	319 (79.75)	626 (78.25)
Total	400 (100)	400 (100)	800 (100)

Figures in parentheses denote columnwise percentages

Table F

Occupation of Respondents' Mothers in Rural Areas

Occupation	*Amritsar District*	*Jalandhar District*	*Total*
Category IV			
Beauty Parlour	1 (0.25)	—	1 (0.12)
School Teacher	—	1 (0.25)	1 (0.12)
Category VI			
Brick kiln worker	40 (10.00)	4 (1.00)	44 (5.50)
Category VII			
Sweeper	10 (2.50)	1 (0.25)	11 (1.38)
Maidservant	33 (8.25)	41 (10.25)	74 (9.25)
Agricultural Labourer	297 (74.25)	160 (40.00)	457 (57.13)
Category VIII			
No Work/ Household work	19 (4.75)	193 (48.25)	212 (26.50)
Total	400 (100)	400 (100)	800 (100)

Figures in parentheses denote columnwise percentages.

3

Empowerment

This chapter deals with the diverse notions of empowerment, and the different methods adopted to attain substantive empowerment by situating the dalits in the centre of discussion. The empowerment of dalits, as a socio-political phenomenon, is a combination of efforts from below as well as above. While dealing with the issue of status improvement in terms of various dimensions in the introductory chapter, it was pointed out that the political mobilisation of the dalits has been an important factor in their goal attainment. The political mobilisation remained limited in numbers and to castes in the pre-independence period, but it proved more effective than other means like social reforms in India. The post-independence period is marked by the combination of both the governmental efforts and the dalits' own mobilisation. Both the strategies have kept on evolving over a period of time. At present, the notion of empowerment is linked with the grass-roots level changes that have been brought about through the constitutional amendments. In fact, it is not much about how to formally empower the excluded castes, but the question is how that empowerment is sustained and what kind of empowerment that is. Does empowering dalits imply that they will be able to live with dignity? Is empowerment through the efforts of the government making them 'Government Brahmin'? Malagatti (2007), in his autobiography, points out that for the upper castes the dalit students are government Brahmins, as they get scholarships and have reservation in government jobs. The paradox between empowerment from below and from above has recently emerged—that too with the powerful arrival of the dalit intellectuals on one hand and the Bahujan Samaj Party (BSP) on the other. The paradox has nothing to do with the castes other than the dalits. At empirical level, there seems to be no such paradox being faced by the dalits, as both the strategies are operating simultaneously without any apparent contradiction.

Empowerment, as a concept, is related with the notion of power, which according to Weber (1970: 180) is "the chance of a man or a number of men to realise their own will in a communal action even against the resistance of others who are participating in the action". The acquisition of power is a phenomenon that is based on various conditions marked by contexts and issues and notions of legitimacy and authority give formal status to the exercise of power. In this regard, the process of empowerment in India, as we shall shortly see, is not much about power but about acquisition of authority. If formal authority structure leads to the empowerment of the caste groups, which had been suffering from various kinds of disabilities, then it is important to examine how the formal authority translates into the empowerment at the corporate level. Empowering the scheduled castes through state intervention could only be understood, in the light of Weber's definition, if the dalits are able to carry out their will even against the opposition of the upper castes. To carry out one's will, one has to have necessary resources. Therefore, the role of state intervention is aimed at providing that resource. The reservation of seats in the formal political democratic process is enabling some dalits to get elected and occupy positions of authority. In this regard, the state intervention has provided the resource and it requires to be examined whether this resource has been translated into empowerment. Theoretically, it is possible to state that with the given resources the empowerment is likely to occur. At empirical level, there are so many 'ifs' and 'buts' that without a proper examination of the situation it becomes difficult to make a categorical statement.

In the light of the above observation, let us begin by understanding different meanings and shades of empowerment. Mohanty (2001: 27) points out that the NGOs and governmental agencies have used the term 'empowerment' in various ways. For example, the NGO-led grass-roots level movements are identified by them as empowerment, and "the governmental agencies have also adopted this term to establish programmes such as the National Literacy Mission, women's development and the panchayati raj schemes aimed at 'empowering' people, especially women, poor peasants etc. In fact several models of 'empowerment have been popularised' ". Mohanty makes an insightful remark that "thus instead of allowing the oppressed to expand their realm of political struggle, this notion of empowerment actually limits it". Mohanty is highly critical of the way the governmental agencies have articulated and operationalised the concept of empowerment, because such a notion is formal rather than substantive. As a corollary to Mohanty's argument is Roy's (2001: 67–68) comment that empowerment may not be treated as "a thing or an object which can either be gifted or picked up by simply stretching one's hand".

It is quite clear from the above discussion that 'empowerment' could be understood as something that is substantive, informal, and achieved. It is linked with the collective action of the social groups that are located at the margins of the relations of power. In Indian society, with its unequal distribution of resources along with regulatory functions of the state to ensure that distribution, the only road to empowerment goes through the social movement strategy. However, the state intervention to ensure some degree of capacity building among the marginal groups could create conditions for the quest for empowerment. In such a situation, the word 'empowerment' becomes positive as it is related with the political assertion of the hitherto marginalised sections of the society based on caste, gender and race. However, the most important issue is how to enable these groups to employ strategies of empowerment. Beteille (1999: 597), after evaluating different channels of empowerment, suggests that

"... in the end, the Indian way of securing empowerment for the unempowered seems to be by the safe way of providing, as extensively as possible, quotas on the basis of community, caste and gender".

Beteille's total rejection of the social movement strategy particularly in the case of the caste is a significant departure from the prevalent view that dalit mobilisation holds the key. For him, anybody preaching caste war must be out of his/her mind. Inadvertently, Beteille has alluded to political mobilisation as the way to empowerment, which, for him, amounts to caste war. Narayanan (2003) looks into the effectiveness of the participation approach to empowerment. Obviously, the question on the nature and level of participation arises. He is of the view that the state-led participation is not effective unless certain conditions are not met. Incidentally, he comes to the conclusion that 'a degree of empowerment' is required for the participation of the excluded sections in the development process. It is clear that the relation between participation and empowerment is discursive. However, the important issue is to understand whether empowerment from above with the empowerment from below could be combined. Instead of treating both the strategies as exclusive, it is important to develop an inclusive strategy. What circumstances do lead to the combination of various strategies? Is it desirable to have empowerment by creating caste wars? The second question is normative. As a matter of fact, the question of power and empowerment is also normative. It is important to note that even the quota system, which, according to Beteille, is the best way, has also led to caste wars.

It is evident from the above discussion that the conceptualisation of 'empowerment' implicates certain aspects of the strategy for change in the existing relations of power. It is also quite obvious that the concept of empowerment is applied in limited sense, that is, it does not involve the classical notion of power in which the powerful have the ability to carry out their will even against the resistance of others. In the specific context of Indian dalits, empowerment is basically an ability in which they develop collective capability not to allow the upper castes to realise their will. Empowerment, despite its political and normative overtones, is a positive concept in the sense that it is linked with the lowest of the low in terms of enabling them to come at par with the upper castes. Historically, the example of middle castes, such as Yadavs and Kurmis in UP and Bihar, is a vindication of the model of Camus' slave. Camus (1992) argued that a slave becoming master would be as atrocious on his slave as his master was. The abolition of the *zamindari* system in India benefited the occupancy tenants and most of them were Yadavs and Kurmis in these two states. The Yadav and Kurmi castes have shown no distinction from the Camus' slave turning master. These castes were empowered economically that sustained their political aspirations that finally put them at the citadel of power in both the states. The empowerment of dalits is different from these castes. Whereas the scheduled castes (SCs) have got the reservation policy, the other backward classes (OBCs) are demanding it. The distinction is quite obvious and there is no need to further explore the matter along these lines.

The identification of various modes of empowerment requires the examination of the empirical situation. Two modes seem to be the most discussed and widespread. These are social movement and political reservation. Both these modes are linked with the strategies of status improvement discussed in the introductory chapter. Let us first discuss the social movement approach to empowerment that has captured the minds of voluntary action groups and, in certain respects, this approach has given dividends at the microlevel. However, the social movement approach assumes that the incumbents of the movement are from within the social group that has adopted this approach. An external agency as an initiator of action has always been taken for granted, particularly in the Marxist tradition.[1] Therefore, the action groups or voluntary organisations that adopt the social movement strategy involve the concerned social groups in the issue. In other words, they provide the necessary input of articulation of the issues and other guidance, but the people themselves do the real job. If we remove the element of external agency and see how certain social groups mobilise themselves, then, we find that there are certain conditions that enable the group to do so. In the specific context of Nadars and Vanniyars, Rudolph and Rudolph (1967: 70) have identified certain factors in the mobilisation, which are as follows: (i) the number and size of other caste groups; (ii) regional differences and their effect on the caste profile of particular states; (iii) differences in the level of and characteristics of relevant political systems; (iv) the relative significance of dominant and subject castes and related propensities towards vertical and horizontal mobilisation; (v) changes over time in social and political environment in which particular castes operate; (vi) the degree of self-consciousness and cohesion that characterise particular castes; and (vii) the countervailing power of other castes, interest groups, and integrative forces, particularly political parties.

Judge (1997a) identified four features that could be the reasons for political action of a caste, namely, population of a caste, its level of economic independence, level of consciousness that has been formed due to either education or tradition of protest and historical specificity of goal orientation of a caste. It is quite clear that both subjective and objective conditions are required for the mobilisation to take place. In the case of objective conditions, size of a caste and economic independence are important conditions. Let us first begin with the second, that is, objective conditions. Economic independence implies three things. First, it enables a caste to sustain struggle for a long time. Second and more important, an economically independent, in the present case, dalit caste experiences relative deprivation. It has been argued by Gurr (1971) that relative deprivation is the major factor behind political mobilisation. It is not the acute deprivation that provides the objective basis for collective action as is generally thought, but the perception that the conditions could be better after an experience of some prosperity. Thirdly, economic improvement becomes the context in which a caste could think of removing the lag between their economic conditions and social status. The size of the caste or the community is a quantitative feature, which turns into quality after mobilisation. A small number of people make little impact even when they are organised unless they resort to violent means. In a democratic-liberal set-up the larger the size of a caste, more are its chances of using democratic-legal methods of struggle and better are its chances of success.

At the subjective level, consciousness and tradition of protest constitute important conditions that actualise the potential of mobilisation that is available due to prevalence of objective conditions. Positivist position heavily depends upon the influence of objective conditions without essentially taking into cognisance why at a particular point of time a caste resorts to mobilisation. It hardly takes stock of subjective factors, which in the traditional sociological imagination are linked with the issue of actor and his/her choices in the given situation. The autonomy and voluntary character of the actor's cognition has been recognised in Marxist tradition in an oblique way, whereas the phenomenological perspective takes into account the goals, intentions, purposes and motivations of the actor. Consciousness, as Marx (1975) pointed out, is determined by the social existence of men. The kind of consciousness that strives towards changing the conditions of a caste is to be attained. In Marxist tradition, consciousness is not relative. It could also be acquired in a way that the present conditions are transcended. How is consciousness attained? There are two sources of it. First, it is generally seen that if there is a tradition of waging protest in a particular manner, it remains as a part of the consciousness. In the case of those castes that had been resorting to protest, the chances of their protesting again are high in comparison to others. The second aspect is education. Education is the major source of acquiring new ideas. The central contribution of the subjective conditions is that these play the role of articulation of the alternative modes of orientation to ameliorate the conditions of caste oppression. The mediation between the objective and the subjective conditions plays the decisive role in the political mobilisation and also in the paradigmatic shift in the use of political means.

The political reservation as a strategy of empowerment could be contextualised in terms of the liberal democratic way of creating equality among castes. It may be noted that we have not used the term 'casteless society'. The reason is too simple to be lost to any person. If the primary policy of the government is to give preferential treatment to certain castes, then, the identification of such castes is the pre-condition. Obviously, such a policy cannot claim to be eradicating caste and making an effort to usher in a society free from caste system. It may be understood that such an endeavour is not misplaced, because it assumes that there would be caste differences. This assumption is quite close to certain other differences around which social inequality emerged. Two of such differences are gender and race. The difference between the two is that whereas the caste differences are social and embedded culturally in the everyday consciousness of people, the gender and racial differences are biological and thus immutable. The obvious distinction between caste differences and other immutable differences have been obliterated by the caste-based affirmative policy of the Indian government. The World Conference against Racism and Related Intolerance (WCAR), held at Durban in South Africa in 2001, marks a significant shift in the nature of discourse on caste. Various contributions of the Indian intellectuals and sociologists with regard to caste and race (Thorat and Umakant, 2004) have opened a new phase in our understanding of the Indian society. Instead of joining the issue whether caste is race or not, it is important to examine why at this moment the dalits (whether all or sections of them is immaterial) of India wish the caste to be equated with race.

Two conclusions can be drawn from the entire controversy that emerged in 2001. First, the dalits of India have, at this moment, developed the ability to take the issue of caste-based discrimination to the international forums. Ironically, it also shows that to an extent the government policies have contributed towards the amelioration of the conditions of the dalits in India and there has been a rise of dalit intellectuals who can articulate the issues concerning dalits as such. Dalit voices are no longer muted. The pitch of these voices is going to rise further in future. How do we understand the position of dalits of Punjab in this emerging scenario? The present chapter is an attempt in this direction. The proceeding discussion would first take stock of social movement/political mobilisation strategy and then examine the governmental efforts.

I
Use of Political Means

The mobilisation of the dalits of Punjab began on the question a distinct religious identity. Interestingly, Ambedkar's struggle guided him to the rejection of Hinduism when he led his followers to conversion to Buddhism; the struggle of the dalits began and ended on the issue of religious identity. The Punjabi dalits (Juergensmeyer, 1982; Ram 2004a and 2004b), who fought for a distinct religious identity, were able to achieve their goal and were recorded as Ad-dharmis in 1931 census. The significance of religion in the social and existential circumstances of men and castes remained at the centre of the Indian world-view. A typical example is of the most of the writings on caste in Punjab. These begin with the argument that caste has been weak in Punjab because of the influence of Islamic invasions and the Sikh religion. As a result of the end of domination of Hinduism due to the combined effect of Islam and Sikhism, the ideological basis of caste has been eroded. As a matter of fact nothing like that happened. Caste has remained the central feature followed by the religion, as is the case in the rest of the country. The only difference is that the corporate mobility of the peasant castes, which were basically Shudras, turned the caste hierarchy into a complex structure where different caste hierarchies began to compete with each other. The castes that emerged as the top most castes in the Sikh and Muslim religions did not practise untouchability the way it was practised by such castes in other parts of the country. The reason was simple. In Punjab, owing to religious differences, these castes became upper castes in the religious community, whereas the same level of castes in other parts of the country became 'dominant castes'. The caste hierarchy remained in existence within the framework of the Sikh religion, whereas the dominant castes in other parts of the country did not deviate from the prevailing caste practices.

Taking into consideration the present Punjab, it may be argued that the caste hierarchies among the Sikhs and the Hindus emerged as two distinct social formations that culminated into the construction of communalism among the Sikhs (Judge, 2002). The classic example of the significance of religion in creating two caste hierarchies is that of Singh (1977) who has studied caste in a Sikh village in which the existence of castes in the village is treated as synonymous with the prevalence of caste among the Sikhs. The moment we take into consideration the empirical fact that there are two caste hierarchies with different castes at the top, the understanding of Punjabi society undergoes a change. However, the most notable fact is that at the bottom of the society, the same castes with different nomenclature are located. Therefore, it could be stated that for the dalits the emergence of different caste hierarchies did not make much difference except for the change in names, besides an obvious absence of the practice of untouchability. The Hindu Balmiki—a Bhangi caste—became a Sikh Mazabi. In this context, the emergence of the Ad-dharm movement was an extension of what was happening in Punjab, but with one difference. In the recorded history of the dalits of Punjab, it was the first time that they organised into collective force as a result of their own initiatives and asserted a new religious identity. Obviously, the major gains were accrued to the Ad-dharmis from the movement. They became the most mobile dalit caste in the post-independent Punjab.

In the post-independence period, the dalits have been using different strategies, such as political participation and protest, to resist the upper-caste domination. There is, however, no empirical study that could map the dalit resistance at the local level in the first decade after independence. Nayar (1966) informs that in the early fifties the dalits largely recorded Hindi as their mother tongue, which was a kind of a protest against the domination of the Sikh landowners. Except for this the information is from the oral accounts of dalit protests at local levels, which were related with the sexual offences against dalit women. The sexual exploitation of dalit women emanated from the economic dependence of the dalits on the upper-caste landlords. Reaction to such cases of sexual abuse occasionally emerged and remained confined to the village level. Most of such cases were handled locally by the village panchayat.

The Green Revolution brought in economic prosperity as agricultural productivity went up in Punjab in which the landowners gained in the initial stages. The trickle-down effect of economic development to the working class took time and it was mediated by the struggles of the dalits for higher wages in the 1970s. Invariably, this struggle would take the form of refusal to work in the fields of the landowners unless the wages were not increased. Most of the times the landowners retaliated by banning their entry into their fields. The landlessness among the dalits worked against their ability to hold on to their strike for longer periods. Generally, the confrontation would end as a result of the intervention of the authorities (Judge, 1985).

The influx of migrant labour from UP and Bihar did not prevent the expected trickle-down effect on the working class as is evident from the actual rise in the wages of agricultural labourers (Gill, 2004). The Green Revolution gave boost to other sectors of Punjab economy. At this moment, the dalits began to move out of agriculture and started looking for new jobs. This process of moving out of agricultural labour however small in scale it was in the beginning contributed to the decline in the dependence of dalits on the landowners. More educated dalits joined white-collar occupations during this period. The changes that were taking place in the conditions of the dalits were not radical. These were slow and gradual and relatively small number among them could come out of the complete dependence on landowners. Even this dependence provided the context for certain kinds of assertion, which was essentially political. The conflict over formal power began to occur in the Green Revolution period, but it again remained confined to the village level. At the aggregate level, we may find such a conflict in many villages, but it never turned into societal conflict. There are many villages in the Doaba region that have dalit majority and such villages recurrently become the centres of conflict during the panchayat elections. In 1978, the manipulation of the Jats led to the protest among the dalits in village Ajram of Hoshiarpur district (Judge, 1985). Certain cases of the dalits and landowning castes confronting each other during or after panchayat elections in 2003 could be cited here. One of the clashes occurred in village Domeli in Kapurthala district between the dalits and a faction of the Jats after the dalit candidate defeated the Jat for the post of Sarpanch. The Jat landlord who lost election attacked the elected Sarpanch and his associates when they went for the thanksgiving to the religious place of the village. Timely intervention of the district authorities prevented the conflict from extending further.[2] The second case refers to the tension that erupted after a dalit woman defeated the Jat candidate for the post of the Sarpanch. This happened in village Pandori Khajoor in Hoshiarpur district. When the Jats stopped the dalit women including the Sarpanch elected from cutting grass from their fields the dalit families resorted to protest and road block.[3]

The third clash occurred in village Bhattian Bet in Ludhiana district. Kanchan Vasdev regarded it as another Talhan. She wrote, "The simmering tension between Jats and Dalits for the past one week over the election of a Dalit sarpanch finally came to the fore today when the Dalits tried to intervene when some Jats refused to let their women answer the call of nature in the latter's fields. This irritated the Jats and led to a clash. A dalit, Om Parkash, received an injury on his head as he was attacked with a sickle by a Jat.[4]

The major development in 1980s that culminated into the full-fledged dalit assertion in 1990s was the formation of the Bahujan Samaj Party (BSP) under the leadership of Kanshi Ram regarded as "the only successful player in the history of Dalit politics" by Dube (2001: 288). The BSP played power politics at the formal level, and it was and has remained the party of dalits with the objective of capturing formal power at the state and national levels. The BSP, in contrast to the Republican Party of India (RPI), brought a paradigmatic shift in the orientation of dalit assertion. Whereas the former approached the issue in terms of social equality for the dalits, the latter has been playing the game of power similar to that of other political parties. The ideological position of the BSP is a logical culmination of the dalit movements though the oppression and exploitation on the caste-class basis has not yet disappeared in India. The sustainability of dalit assertion has become a possibility largely due to the emergence of a sizeable middle class among the dalits, which find it difficult to be assimilated in the caste society as equals. The BSP has radically altered the nature of collective self-assertion of the dalits. The BSP-led activities began in Punjab in great earnest in late 1990s and culminated in its participation in elections. It seemed as if BSP was going to be a major political force in the electoral process of Punjab. Chandra (2000) studied the BSP in Hoshiarpur from the perspective of ethnic politics. In relation to caste and politics the usage of the term 'ethnicity' may not be new, but it is definitely misplaced. Chandra is not addressing to Indian audience and she is most irrelevant to the kind of debates on caste and dalits that are drawing the intellectual energies of Indian academia. Chandra's audience is the American and European scholars interested in Asia or South Asia. The consequence is that her views have become outdated in the specific context of Punjab. There is limited impact of the BSP in Punjab at the moment. The dalit politics has shifted to the Deras and saints who have established themselves as the sole and soul spokesmen (incidentally all such saints are men) of the dalits, particularly the Ad-dharmis and Chamars. A result of this participation of the men of god in public, social and political affairs of the dalits is the newly emerged context of the dalit assertion. According to the dalit informants, there are 176 Deras of Ad-dharmi saints that follow Guru Ravi Das as their deity. The notable among them is Dera Sachkhand located at village Ballan in Jalandhar district.[5]

A new form of dalit assertion and its contestation, which caught the social scientists unawares, has recently emerged. Mention may be made of the Ad-dharmi-Jat clash in village Talhan in Jalandhar district on June 5, 2003. The root cause of this clash was the struggle for the control over the Gurdwara Baba Nihal Singh in the village. The dalits wanted to be equal partners in the management of the Gurdwara (Judge, 2005). It may be pointed out that the conflict over religious places is a new form of conflict between the castes that has started emerging in Punjab. The entry of religion into social conflicts is not new even with regard to the dalit issue. We all know that Ambedkar began his movement from the issue of entry into Hindu temples meant for high castes. His subsequent conversion to Buddhism and rejection of Hinduism was a form of protest, which was based on the assumption that in Hinduism the caste is immutable. As mentioned earlier in Chapter 1, the dalits of Punjab did not follow Ambedkar as no mass conversions to Buddhism took place. A few cases of conversion to Buddhism in recent years indicate the changing orientation of the Punjabi dalits to Buddhism though it is largely confined to the intelligentsia. Some of the cases of conversion to Buddhism after the earlier attempts in late 1950s could be stated here. Virdi (2000) informs that in a function organised by Punjab Buddha Mahasabha, 3,500 converted to Buddhism on March 10, 1991. Buddh Vihars have been constructed in Hoshiarpur, Jalandhar and Kapurthala districts. Despite all such efforts by many prominent dalit leaders the response to Buddhism is confined as only 0.2 per cent of the population of Punjab is Buddhist. In other words, the dalit assertion seems closely linked with the Guru Ravi Das Deras.

The middle class among the dalits has changed its orientation from assimilation to participation. This class wants to be an equal partner in the conduct of the affairs of the village, city and state. Such an orientation may redirect the issue of castelessness in a somewhat different manner. The upper castes have been consistently coming out with social boycott as a weapon against the dalit assertion. Earlier, social boycott was regarded as the weapon of the strong, because the entire life conditions of the dalits depended on the landowners. In the changed socio-economic circumstances, when the dalits are no more dependent on the landowners the way they were before, social boycott cannot be used as way of suppression. It is now used as a weapon to deprive the dalits from being equal partners in the affairs of the society. It is the means to remind them that despite their improved conditions, they continue to be low caste. The Talhan clash followed after all negotiations to end the social boycott failed at the informal level. The dalits of Talhan were not dependent on the Jat landowners because of their better economic conditions (Judge, 2005). Why have the conflicts over religious places emerged in recent times? It is particularly important in the light of the fact that in many other villages, the possibility of such conflicts had existed in recent past. It may be reminded that in the past the religious places invariably depended on the patronage of the landed classes. The Jats of Punjab began to turn to Sikhism in a serious manner towards the end of the 19th century and then began the process of a shift to the religious places. The Talhan clash got a wide coverage and attention, but there are many such conflicts and contestations that have remained unnoticed.

Three recent illustrations among many, besides the explosive case of Talhan, may be succinctly stated here. The conflict between the Jats and the dalits in village Mahem in Nakodar tehsil of Jalandhar district has come to the fore.[6] The Jat Sikhs of the village forcibly occupied the Baba Khazan Singh Udasi Dera in 2003. It was looked after by the Ad-dharmis of the village. According to Kali (2003b), the major reason for this occupation should be located in the rising cost of land as well as the prosperity of the people of Doaba due to emigration to foreign countries. The donations and offerings have increased manifold. The Jat Sikhs removed all the symbols of Udasis and installed the Nishan Sahib[7] and Guru Granth Sahib in the Dera's building. With the help of the Pendu Mazdoor Union, the Ad-dharmis were able to file FIR and stall the further designs of the Jats. The village Mahem has total population of 1,967 out of which 893, that is more than half, belong to the scheduled castes. Most of the scheduled castes belong to the Balmiki caste, whereas the Ad-dharmis are about 20 per cent of the total population. The Jats are also about 20 per cent of the total population. In the present study, Mahem was one of the villages where the fieldwork was conducted. It will be worthwhile to provide a general outline of the characteristics of the sample. The number of total respondents was 54 out of which the Ad-dharmis and Balmikis were 27 each, that is, 50 per cent. Literacy rate of the village dalits was 81.48 per cent though only 14.81 per cent had got education above school level. All the respondents recorded their religion as Hindu.

There are two Gurdwaras that have been constructed and controlled by them. There is one each Balmiki temple and Ravi Das temple. The Udasi Dera is the fifth religious place in the village. Besides these religious places, there are two *mazaars* (graves) that are places of veneration. The dispute over the Udasi

Dera is now in the court and it will take some time to resolve it. The Ad-dharmis claim that for the last 60 years the Dera has been under their control. The Jats, on the contrary, claim that it is a Gurdwara. The counter-argument offered by the Ad-dharmis is that there are graves in the precincts of the Dera and it cannot be a Gurdwara.[8] Charan Das—a Balmiki by caste—is illiterate and is 47 years of age. He was the most vocal about the Dera though every dalit respondent talked about the conflict with the Jats. He said, "For the last 60 years we (Ad-dharmis and Balmikis) have been controlling the Dera. Two fairs were organised every year, one of which was on January 14, whereas the other in the memory of the founder saint of the Dera on 20th of *Asharh* (somewhere in the beginning of July). The flag of the Dera is distinct as it is decorated with the peacock's quails. The Jats forcibly installed the Guru Granth Sahib and began the construction and started claiming that it was a Gurdwara. We say that it is an Udasi Dera. There is lot of money involved. There are two localities of the Jats. All this had been done by one locality called the Sandhu Patti". Interestingly, he also informed that liquor is also offered at the Dera. The views of the respondents and the observers clearly shows that the moment the Dera became rich due to offerings from the people particularly those living abroad the vested interest led to the conflict. The dominant caste of Jats could venture into this act, because they thought that the dalits were vulnerable and would not resist.

One of the notable cases is related with Sant Bhaniarawala. Piara Singh Bhaniarawala is a phenomenon that should be understood from the perspective of how religion and dalit mobilisation are interlinked and in what manner it comes in conflict with the dominant castes. Meeta and Rajivlochan (2007: 1911) provide the necessary background to the emergence of Bhaniarawala phenomenon thus:

> Piara Singh, one of the seven children of a mason Tulsi Ram from the village Dhamiana in Ropar district had been working as a class IV employee with the state horticulture department at a sericulture farm in Asmanpur village. His father had been the caretaker of two mazaars on the outskirts of the village

Dhamiana. At the death of his father, Piara Singh became the caretaker of the mazaars. Soon he also came to be known as a healer, providing medicines for various ailments. His reputation grew since people believed that he did have healing powers. He soon came to be addressed as a 'baba', a local holy man. In course of time even the then union home minister, Buta Singh, who subsequently went on to become the governor of Bihar, solicited his advice in treating his wife's illness. As Baba Bhaniara's reputation grew, so did his number of followers. It was said by the newspapers at one time that he had 20,000 followers across the state. Most of them were mazhabis.

As the number of his followers and consequently his influence began to grow, the Baba alarmed the Sikh establishment. In 1998, the Jathedar of Akal Takhat excommunicated him on the pretext that he was disrespectful to the Sikh sacred text. Then began the state intervention in curbing his influence through various ways. He was arrested and has been put under trial. His Deras at different places have been appropriated by the Shiromani Gurdwara Parbandhak Committee (SGPC). Ram (2007) regards the clash between Dera followers, whether it is Bhaniarawala or Sacha Sauda, and the Sikh establishment as the symptom of the caste conflict in the Sikh community.

The case of Mahem is not an isolated phenomenon. It is spreading not as an aftermath of Talhan clash, but as a state-wide phenomenon, particularly in those areas where the dalits have been organising themselves and have become conscious of their rights. The third example is that of Nurmahal, where the dalits were trying to reclaim the Dargah of Hazarat Shah Fateh Ali. Kali (2003a) warned that this religious place might lead to the Talhan-like situation. In 1994 the Sikhs tried to convert this place into a Gurdwara and tried to demolish all graveyards. However, the people got organised and tried to prevent this demolition. Who these Sikhs were has not been clearly stated in Kali's report, but it was clear that the administration was hand in glove with these armed gangs. However, by this time, both the *samadhs* (graves) and the Gurdwara are in existence. The *Hindustan Times* (2005) provided the latest detail of this conflict thus: "The weekly prayers at the Fateh Ali Shah Samadh here were held under tight security today following tensions over the erasing of writings from the façade of the samadh." The Deputy Commissioner of Jalandhar district has announced that a partition wall would be constructed separating the two religious places. Since then, there has been a stalemate in the situation. Instead of using the 1989 Act of Prevention of Atrocities against the Scheduled Castes, the administration seems keen on working out an amicable solution through reconciliation.

It is clear from the above that dalit consciousness is rapidly changing along diverse trajectories that tend to suggest that the issue is not simply confined to the caste equality. It is a movement towards the construction of a society in which dalits can equally participate in social life and influence decisions. The mobilisation of dalits is also segmented along caste lines. Most of the discussion above remains confined to the collective actions of the Ad-dharmis/Chamars and all other castes are excluded from this dalit assertion. We may say that the Ad-dharmis/Chamars are showing the way to other castes. Unfortunately, other dalit castes are not as educated as the Ad-dharmis/Chamars are. Except for Balmikis and Mazabis all other dalit castes are numerically small. Their mobilisation cannot make an impact. From this perspective only the Ad-dharmis/Chamars have favourable objective and subjective conditions for political mobilisation. Objectively speaking, the Ad-dharmis/Chamars have been able to improve their economic conditions through education, emigration and entrepreneurship.[9] Their dependence on the landowning castes has considerably declined. At the subjective level, the level of political consciousness and preparedness to mobilising the caste members is quite high the example of which is the Jat-Ad-dharmi clash in Talhan in 2003 which had immediate repercussions on other areas. The only death that took place during the agitation was not in Talhan but in Boota Mandi—widely regarded as the capital of the Ad-dharmis, at a distance of about 20 km from the site of clash (Judge, 2005). The Ad-dharm movement has contributed significantly in raising the consciousness of this caste.

II
Empowerment from Above

As has been discussed earlier, the concept of empowerment from above is related with the political reservation for the scheduled castes. The reservation of seats in the Lok Sabha and Vidhan Sabhas had been introduced right from the beginning with the understanding that after sometime this provision would be discontinued. As a result, it is recurrently passed by the Lok Sabhas after every ten years, which implies that the need for continuation of reservation policy in Lok Sabha and Vidhan Sabha has been still felt. However, the popular usage of the word 'empowerment' began after the 73rd and 74th constitutional amendments that came into force on April 20, 1993. The 73rd Amendment Act enshrined in the new Part IV of the Constitution of India provides for the first time the national framework for the reservation of certain seats and positions for women and the scheduled castes in village panchayats. The 74th amendment is applicable to *nagar palikas* (urban local bodies). The reservation for the women and the scheduled castes in the local bodies is seen as empowerment at the grass-roots level. This section is largely about the actual scale of reservation at the level of local bodies—both rural and urban—and the perception of the respondents whether political reservation could be interpreted as a sign of empowerment.

More than a decade has passed since the 73rd and 74th amendments came into being. Studies have already been conducted to evaluate the effectiveness of the third tier of governance (e.g., Narayana, 2005; Kumar and Rai, 2006). Let us begin with the overall picture of Punjab. Table 3.1 provides the information about the number of the SC sarpanchas and members of the panchayats in the last elections held in 2003. The overall percentage of the SC sarpanchas is 28.07 in the state, whereas the total members of the panchayats in the state are 21.06 per cent. In Amritsar district the SC sarpanchas constitute 21.06 per cent and the percentage of the panchas is 17.95, whereas the corresponding figures for Jalandhar district are 43.34 per cent and 44.84 per cent. It is clear from the data presented in Table 3.1 that the distribution of reserved seats in different districts vary due to the fact that the population of the scheduled castes also varies across districts.

Table 3.1

Districtwise Distribution of Reserved Seats for Sarpanch's Post as well as members of the Panchayat in Punjab

District	*No. of panchayats*	*Election completed in 2003*	*SC sarpanchas elected*	*No. of members elected*	*No. of SC members*
Gurdaspur	1,591	1,591	275	9,060	1,560
Amritsar	1,287	1,287	271	9,030	1,627
Kapurthala	535	533	172	3,019	985
Jalandhar	886	884	384	5,372	2,409
Nawanshahar	445	443	168	2,675	456
Hoshiarpur	1,317	1,305	457	4,763	2,647
Rupnagar	852	851	245	4,698	1,148
Ludhiana	876	874	309	5,628	1,303
Firozpur	1,089	1,089	153	6,454	882
Faridkot	181	180	68	1,247	464
Muktsar	265	262	67	1,963	499
Moga	326	326	103	2,288	693
Bhatinda	306	306	92	2,164	683
Mansa	243	243	76	1,783	551
Sangrur	735	735	227	5,838	1,702
Patiala	1,080	1,080	285	6,332	1,742
Fatehgarh Sahib	430	430	134	2,358	706
Total	12,444	12,419	3,486	74,672	20,057

Source: Statistical Abstract of Punjab, 2005. Government of Punjab, Chandigarh. pp. 777.

Looking into the number of the SC sarpanchas and panchas may lead one to assume that a considerable change has taken place as a result of the 73rd amendment. It was difficult to imagine a few decades back that such a large number of the scheduled caste people would be elected to local bodies. In the panchayat elections the landowning castes dominated in Punjab till the end of 1970s. If we add the number of years during which no democratic elections were held in the state due to terrorism till 1992 (exception of course is of the 1985 elections), the change from the dalit perspective is phenomenal at the moment. To what extent the quantity has turned into quality is a matter of empirical research as well as opinion. Obviously, the former would give us the true picture of the reality to the extent possible. It may just be added that the empowerment of dalits is also linked with their objective and subjective conditions, which in certain areas of Punjab are quite favourable.

In view of the lack of availability of data on urban local bodies, we confine ourselves to the two cities that were studied, namely, Amritsar and Jalandhar. Table 3.2 shows the data on the reserved seats in the municipal corporations of the two cities. It is evident from the data that the proportion of the reserved seats for the dalits is higher in Jalandhar than in Amritsar. In comparison to the villages, the data in cities show a less number of representatives from the dalit castes. Obviously, it is largely due to the fact that the percentage of dalits in the cities is less than in the villages. The caste background of the mayors and sarpanchas is an important aspect to know the caste-politics dynamics in Punjab. Tables 3.3 and 3.4 provide the caste of the mayors and the sarpanchas respectively. In the case of mayors, it may be informed that the information is confined to previous three municipal elections, as the city corporations came to exist only in the recent past. It is interesting to note the predominance of the upper castes in the case of both the cities. Only Jalandhar has a dalit mayor because of 74th amendment. The case of villages is quite interesting. The Jats predominate among the sarpanchas in villages. Notably, the Ad-dharmis and the Mazabis follow the Jats in terms of numbers. Among the total sarpanchas at present in all the villages eight belong to the dalit castes. All of them became sarpanch under the 73rd amendment implementation. It is clear that before the 73rd amendment period there was hardly any dalit sarpanch and the landowning castes like Jats dominated the village politics. In an earlier study by Judge (1986), it was found that in the case of the five villages of Hoshiarpur district two had had dalit sarpanch. Otherwise, the picture was the same, that is, the Jat, Dogra or Mahaton landowners dominated in the village politics.

Table 3.2

Distribution of Seats in the Municipal Corporation in Amritsar and Jalandhar

Category	*Amritsar*	*Jalandhar*
General	47 (78.34)	34 (61.82)
Reserved for Backward Classes	02 (3.33)	02 (3.64)
Reserved for Scheduled Castes	11 (18.33)	19 (34.54)
Total	60 (100)	55 (100)

Table 3.3

Caste Background of the Present and the Previous Mayors

Caste Background	*Amritsar District*		*Jalandhar District*		*Total*
	Present	*Previous*	*Present*	*Previous*	
Brahmin	1	1	—	—	2
Khatri	—	2	—	2	4
Ad-dharmi	—	—	1	—	1

Table 3.4

Caste Background of the Present and Previous Sarpanchas

Caste Background	*Amritsar District*		*Jalandhar District*		*Total*
	Present	*Previous*	*Present*	*Previous*	
Brahmin	—	1	—	—	1
Arora Sikh	—	1	—	1	2
Jat	—	10	—	11	21
Kamboh	1	1	—	1	3
Ramgarhia	—	—	1	1	2
Ad-dharmi	—	—	3	6	9
Balmiki	—	—	1	—	1
Mazabi	3	5	—	—	8
Od	1	2	—	—	3
Total	5	20	5	20	50

Is a dalit mayor or a sarpanch a sign of empowerment? The issue is not easy to deal with. Apparently, gathering responses to the above question may not tell us about the fact of whether the dalits are empowered by it or not. But that is not the purpose of asking this question. The purpose is to see how the dalit respondents perceive the democratic process at the grass-roots level. Table 3.5 presents data on the responses of the dalit respondents in both villages and cities. It is clear from the data that having a dalit sarpanch/mayor is important for empowerment for more than half of the respondents. Interestingly, for the rural respondents it was more a sign of empowerment than dalit identity, whereas the urban dalits have begun to think of a dalit mayor in terms of dalit identity assertion. As a part of the general perception of politics as a game that involves power, some dalit respondents also understood the entire process in terms of power game. The significant aspect is related with the dalit perception.[10]

Table 3.5

Significance of Dalit Mayor/Sarpanch in the City/Village

Response	*Urban*	*Rural*	*Total*
Empowerment	389 (48.62)	415 (51.88)	804 (50.25)
Dalit identity	124 (15.50)	5 (0.63)	129 (8.06)
Caste is irrelevant	45 (5.63)	1 (0.12)	46 (2.87)
He/she should work for the city/village	44 (5.50)	317 (39.62)	361 (22.56)
Dalit sarpanch discriminates against other dalit castes	—	10 (1.25)	10 (0.63)
It is power game	134 (16.75)	42 (5.25)	176 (11.00)
Don't know	64 (8.00)	10 (1.25)	74 (4.63)
Total	800 (100)	800 (100)	1600 (100)

Still another question that was asked from the respondents was with regard to the conduct of elections. The respondents who told that there were malpractices in every election were above 90 per cent of the total. Their responses regarding the types of malpractices are shown in Table 3.6. These are interesting and are a gateway to the understanding of the conduct of elections in

India. Widespread corruption in the electioneering is a normal occurrence in Punjab and Haryana. There is a common saying in Punjab: *Hamari vote uski, Jo pillaye whiskey* (We shall vote for that candidate who will offer us whiskey).[11] The data substantiate the above saying as 78.62 per cent of the respondents informed that liquor has been served by the candidates during the panchayat and nagar palika elections.

Table 3.6

Malpractices during Elections

Malpractice	*Urban*	*Rural*	*Total*
Money/bribe	3 (0.38)	9 (1.12)	12 (0.75)
Liquor	467 (58.37)	791 (98.88)	1258 (78.62)
Bogus votes	5 (0.63)	—	5 (0.32)
All the above	235 (29.37)	—	235 (14.69)
Don't know	90 (11.25)	—	90 (5.62)
Total	800 (100)	800 (100)	1600 (100)

Figures in parentheses are columnwise percentages.

What is the desirability of political reservation for the scheduled castes? The query is essentially normative in the sense that it, at present, implicates the social position as well as the ideology of the person responding to it. It is now a well-established fact that there has been a widespread resentment against the proposed reservation for the Other Backward Classes (OBCs) in recent years. Passionate opposition to the implementation of the Mandal Commission's recommendations took place in 1990. It may be reminded that there have been protests and agitations against the reservation policy for the scheduled castes and scheduled tribes. Bains (1997) conducted an empirical study of the collective mobilisation of the non-scheduled castes against the reservation policy. It is thus clear that there is an opposition to the reservation policy for the scheduled castes. Owing to reservation policy, as we mentioned earlier, the upper-caste people call the dalits 'Government Brahmana' (Malagatti, 2007) and in Punjab 'government's sons-in-law'. If we come to the specific nature of this reservation policy, that is, political reservation, the nature of reaction may not be different. How important it is for the dalits is an altogether different dimension. Since the primary focus of discussion in this chapter is empowerment of the dalits through the constitutional amendments, it is important to first know how the dalits perceive it.

Table 3.7
Whether Political Reservations Should Continue

Response	*Urban*	*Rural*	*Total*
Good and should continue	440 (55.00)	402 (50.25)	842 (52.62)
Dalits need no help	—	7 (0.88)	7 (0.44)
Will continue but not sure whether useful	25 (3.12)	7 (0.88)	32 (2.00)
Helps only the rich dalits	31 (3.88)	100 (12.50)	131 (8.19)
No improvement	120 (15.00)	215 (26.87)	335 (20.94)
Casteism among dalit leaders	3 (0.38)	22 (2.75)	25 (0.12)
Undecided	181 (22.62)	47 (5.87)	228 (14.25)
Total	800 (100)	800	1600 (100)

Figures in parentheses are columnwise percentages.

The respondents were asked whether political reservation for the scheduled castes should continue. The responses have been presented in the Table 3.7. The responses are not in accordance with expectations. It was expected that the dalit respondents would wholeheartedly support political reservations. However, only slightly more than half of them regarded political reservations as good and thus desirable. Interestingly, one-fifth of the respondents stated it clearly that no improvement had occurred due to political reservations, whereas 14.25 per cent of them were undecided. Very few of them raised other issues that could be taken as important aspects of the reservation process. The fact that reservation for the dalits in the local bodies began in 1990s, the ambivalent response betrays many hidden realities. One of these is that there is a rich class among the dalits, which is gaining power through reservations. The second reality is that there is existence of castes and caste hierarchy among the dalits and the one who comes to power serves and protects the interests of his/her own caste people. The existence of caste and class inequalities among the dalits is not empowering the dalits as one creates differentiation and the other disjunction. The consequence is that the political reservation has failed to empower the dalits. It seems strange that social scientists are trying to give importance to a 'part' instead of the 'whole'. The 'whole' is empowered only when there is corporate mobility. One or few members occupying position of power does not make any difference except for symbolic relevance and significance, which serves its functions only when we understand it in terms of rupture in the historical tradition.

Has the empowerment taken place in practice? The question is related with the notion of power that was discussed in the beginning of the chapter. In other words, we may raise the issue whether the dalit sarpanch/mayor is able to carry out his will even against the resistance of the others It was found that whereas the dalit mayor was as effective in his functioning as anybody could be, the dalit sarpanchas were not. During the fieldwork a lot of situations were encountered where it became quite obvious that the landowning castes hardly bothered about the dalit sarpanchas. It was more pronounced in the villages of Amritsar district than those of Jalandhar district. It may be further added that in comparison to the three villages of Amritsar district where the sarpanchas belonged to the Mazabi caste, the three sarpanchas in Jalandhar district belonging to the Ad-dharmi caste still showed some degree of independence from the landowning castes. However, even the Ad-dharmi sarpanchas have not been effectively functioning. The example of Mahem village may be cited here. At present, the village has an Ad-dharmi sarpanch, whereas in the previous four panchayats the sarpanch always belonged to the Jat caste. As described earlier, in the conflict between the Jats and the Ad-dharmis over a religious site, the former are realising their will. Though the sarpanch belongs to the Ad-dharmi caste, they are unable to settle the dispute. Conversely, the dalit mayor of Jalandhar city is not facing any problems that could be related to intercaste relations. He is part of the Boota Mandi's Ad-dharmis and is a rawhide merchant. He is an entrepreneur and active politician. He is an illustrious case of empowerment. Let us discuss the case of the mayor of Jalandhar.[12]

Mr Surinder Kumar Mahey, an Ad-dharmi, has risen to become the first citizen of Jalandhar—the third largest city of Punjab, that is, he was elected to become the mayor of the city. Forty-nine-years-old, Mr Mahey had education not even up to matriculation though his father was a graduate. He has three brothers; one of them is settled in Denmark where he runs an Indian restaurant. His children are getting education but also keenly participate in the family business of rawhides, tanning and in the factory. He is a widely travelled man. He has travelled the whole world. His ancestral place is nearby village, Dhanal, from where his grandfather migrated to this place in 1932. His hereditary occupation is dealing with rawhides while his father also continued with the same business till his death. He started working with his elder brother, but, at that time, he was more interested in one or the other kind of a social work. He was busy more as philanthropist than as a businessman. To begin with, in 1978 he started helping the TB patients by getting them admitted to the hospital. Up to 1984 he had got almost one thousand TB patients admitted to the hospital. He used to follow the case at least for three years when he would procure medicines for them and would also help in fulfilling their other needs. His elder brother who was looking after the business would get angry with him for not taking interest in business. Mahey separated himself to start his own independent business for which he borrowed Rs 10,000 from his NRI friend and 3,500 from his sister-in-law. With that money he started his own business of rawhides in 1986. In his first sale at Ludhiana he lost lot of money. Then, he moved to Amritsar where he could earn profit worth Rs 5,000. Soon, there came traders from Madras who had sales worth Rs 40 lakh out of which Rs 17 lakh was his contribution. In this deal he could earn profit of Rs 4 lakh and thus he became a rawhides merchant. After his success in it he started diversification. He started manufacturing tool belts in 1999. This is an export-oriented product, as in India the workers do not wear it. The tool belt made of leather used to be soft and comfortable to wear to which a mechanic would attach various tools needed by him. Thus, he has emerged as a very successful entrepreneur. He has constructed a palatial house in the nearby posh colony.

Mahey elected as a councillor for the first time in 1991 when the democratic process was restored. He continued to win as councillor till June 2002 when he was elected to the post of the mayor of the city. There are total 55 councillors elected in the city, out of which 26 belong to scheduled castes and rest of them to the general category. In spite of opposition from upper castes, he was elected to the post of the mayor. After taking over as the mayor, he claimed to have carried out many projects particularly for the betterment of the scheduled castes. He thought that the earlier mayors ignored the development of all the four outer areas around the city that were mainly inhabited by the scheduled castes. He gave first priority to water supply and got installed 82 tubewells in the surrounding villages, which fall under the jurisdiction of the city corporation. Further, he took over the slum development project again with the emphasis on the drinking water supply and construction of residential quarters for the scheduled castes.

He is strongly of the view that society can develop on the basis of religion. He argues that the Sikhs have a distinct identity on the basis of religion. Similarly, the Hindus have their own distinct identity. All religious groups have their own religious holy book. The dalits are considered a part of Hinduism, but the Hindus do not regard them so in practice. He strongly believes that it is only when they have their own religious book—a collection of the ideas and philosophy of Guru Ravi Das is compiled and worshipped—the scheduled castes would be able to come up in the social hierarchy by having their own distinct identity. So long as they do not have their separate religion, they cannot improve their condition. The argument has simple economic explanation, that is, by placing the religious book at a place where devotees would come and the offering would be generated in the form of funds, which could be used for establishing schools/colleges and even universities besides the development of the people. So far they visit the Hindu or Sikh religious places and their offerings go to the common pool, which is used for the promotion of their own religion. He was also feeling disgusted at those dalits who after succeeding in life distinguished themselves by changing their religion and caste identity. They never helped their own community members. He was of the view that the scheduled castes have to come out of their prevailing conditions with their own efforts. For instance, if they stop doing dirty jobs, such as cleaning and sweeping, then, the people concerned would do such unclean jobs. It is the nature of one's work, which makes one low or high.

It is important to understand why a dalit mayor is effective, but the dalit sarpanchas are not. The answer lies in the qualitative and fundamental difference in the two settings, that is, between the city and the village. The municipal corporation is a large body, which has its own sources of revenue and, more importantly, a well-developed bureaucratic structure as well. The function of mayor is carried out with the help of both the resources that are based on instrumental rationality. The implementation of various development programmes is streamlined and the mayor does not have to seek the support of certain communities for functioning. On the contrary, the sarpanch has no source of income except the grants of the government. The sarpanch has to work within the framework of the village social structure in the absence of any bureaucratic structure. Since the functioning of the sarpanch depends upon the social structure instead of any bureau, the element of informal power structure enters strongly in anything that is done in the village by the panchayat. The result is the reinforcement of the dominant classes' position irrespective of whosoever is the sarpanch. Rajaraman and Sinha (2007: 2281) conducted a study of four states on the functional devolution to rural bodies in which they have argued, "The most astonishing feature of decentralisation of governance in India has been the complete absence of a uniform accounting system that would render transparent the transfer of functions mandated". It is important to understand that without the instrument of rational functioning and resource generation, the panchayat cannot function independent of the particulars of its social structure. The Indian village is not fit for local governance with autonomy that is being talked about. Caste and class inequalities intermingle, intertwine and overlap in such a way that it is not possible to work with consensus in villages. One is reminded of what Ambedkar said about villages in India thus: "In this republic there is no place for democracy. There is no room for equality. There is no room for liberty and there is no room for fraternity. The Indian village is very negation of the republic" (Moon, 1989: 26).

To conclude, it may be stated that despite all the limitations there have been certain changes that could be discerned in the case of political mobilisation of dalits of Punjab. With its history of the Ad-dharm movement in the colonial period, the dalits have significantly improved their political participation and have been engaged in continuous contestations with the landowning castes. There has been major shift in the dalit politics in Punjab, which is basically a reflection of what is happening in India. Sheth (2005) observes the prevalence of divergent discourses in the dalits politics, whereas Guru (2005) tries to make sense of atrophy in dalit politics. As a matter of fact, both of them are trying to capture the essence of changing paradigm of dalit politics, which is essentially losing its unilinear character. The heterogeneity among the dalits makes it sure that there is no single discourse in dalit politics. In contrast to the political mobilisation of the dalits, the efforts of the government have at least made it sure that particular percentages of the scheduled castes become sarpanchas and members of the panchayats in Punjab. However, actual empowerment is far from satisfactory. In nagar palikas the empowerment is becoming probable, but not in villages.

Notes

1. In Marxist tradition the notion of class consciousness has been well discussed by various scholars. Class consciousness is regarded as a distinct state of historical process from the consciousness that emerges from social existence. Lenin (1975) and, later on, Lukács (1971) pointed out that the class consciousness is imputed on the working class by the revolutionary vanguards. To put this obser-

vation in proper perspective, the role of leadership is of utmost importance in the emergence of social movements.

2. *The Tribune*, July 2, 2003, p.18.
3. *The Tribune*, July 5, 2003, p. 14.
4. Kanchan Vasdev, *The Tribune*, July 7, 2003, p. 1.
5. The founder of the Dera was Sant Sarwan Das. Virdi (2000) informs that at the time when Gandhi began his fast against separate electorate for the dalits, Mangoo Ram also sat on fast unto death. Sant Sarwan Das offered him the juice after the Poona Pact. What is known as Begampura, the Dera has become synonymous with the Ad-dharmi assertion in Punjab.
6. The village Mahem was part of the five villages covered for data collection for this study.
7. Nishan Sahib is the religious flag of the Sikhs generally found at the precincts of the Gurdwaras.
8. The issue of what is and what is not Gurdwara recently came up when the clash took place between the Jats and Ad-dharmis at Talhan. Whether the place of contention was a Gurdwara or not was raised by Jodhka and Louis (2003) who argue that in Talhan conflict the Ad-dharmis were justified in raising the issue, because there were graves in the Gurdwara, whereas the Sikhs do not worship graves. It is important to remind Gupta's (1991) use of binary categories of 'deemed' and 'actual'. There has always been the difference between what is called deemed Gurdwara and the actual Gurdwara. An example is one of the most visited Gurdwara in Amritsar is called Gurdwara Shahidan. This Gurdwara has grave.
9. The subsequent chapters deal with all these aspects and it clearly emerges from the findings that the Ad-dharmis/Chamars have fared better than other dalit castes.
10. During the panchayat elections held in June 2008 it emerged clearly that in many villages where the position of the sarpanch was reserved for the scheduled castes was in fact the competition between the attached labourers (*kamin/siri*) of the two dominant landowning families of the village.
11. The distribution of the local made liquor/whiskey during the elections has almost become a culture in Punjab and Haryana. In the 2008 elections the liquor was made available to everybody. The dalit women complained that ever since the election approached and the landowners began to serve liquor, the men stopped going for work.
12. At the time of data collection he was the mayor of Jalandhar city.

4

Emigration

The history of international migration of Punjabis dates back to the second half of the 19th century. It was inseparably linked with the emigration from other parts of the country, as both were a consequence of the colonial political economy. It is interesting to note that the dalits were always represented in the emigration that took place from India to the plantation economies under the indentured labour system. Various scholars have informed that the lower castes constituted substantial proportions of the indentured labourers recruited from India to various countries from time to time under the British imperial rule (Kumar, 2004; Lal, 2007). The possibility of the dalit migration could exist only in terms of indentured labour that took place in the early 19th century from India, as given their low socio-economic status they could not have emigrated voluntarily for which capital was required. Kumar (2004), citing various studies, informs that 26.2 per cent of the Indians who migrated to Fiji between 1879 and 1916 as indentured labourers belonged to the menial castes. Similarly, the Indian migration to Caribbean islands under the indentured labour system had considerable number of dalits and tribals. It may be noted that among the above-mentioned dalits, there was hardly any presence of the Punjabi dalits. Most of the migration under the indentured labour system took place from

Madras and Calcutta presidencies, including people specifically from Tamil Nadu and Chhotanagpur plateau areas. The Punjabi migration under indentured labour system has not been much noticeable. Singh (2008: 2) informs thus:

> Though there is a popular perception that Sikhs did not migrate as indentured workers since the main areas of recruitment for the indenture system were in Uttar Pradesh and Bihar, Fiji's immigration records show a number of registrations from Punjab. Migrants from Punjab went as indentured workers to Fiji and the Caribbean. It is, however, difficult to estimate the number of Sikh migrants who went to different countries in the early years of migration as religious identity was not used as a defining characteristic in those days. Most countries did not have a separate category for enumeration of Sikhs, and Sikh migrants were either placed in the category of Indians or referred to as Punjabis.

While referring to the Punjabis in Caribbean, Singh (ibid.) further writes, "Sikhs were not considered 'good indenture migrants' in the Caribbean because of their assertive nature. The plantation managers wanted docile, manageable workers to work in the cane fields". It is quite clear that though the Punjabis went to different parts of the world under the indentured labour system, yet their number was small. It was due to voluntary nature of the migration of the Punjabis in general and the Punjabi dalits in particular, which stands a class apart from their counterparts in other regions of the country in the 19th and early 20th centuries.

The British colonialism provided the impetus and reason to the Punjabis for the migration to places away from home. The major source that provided the information to the Punjabis regarding greener pastures elsewhere was the soldier who travelled to various places within the country and in certain cases beyond sea barriers. The Punjabis were not culturally very mobile and we do not find much history of their migration except, of course, for mendicants, saints, yogis, merchants and traders. The people were rooted to their village/native place where the community networks kept them safe. The scheduled castes were stifled by their socio-economic conditions characterised by bondage and misery in such a way that it was not possible for them to think of leaving their place of birth. Migration was not a feasible activity in a society that functioned and existed on the principle of community identity and belongingness. Cultivation was regarded as the best occupation (*uttam kheti*) the second to which was business (*madham vipar*) and the lowest in prestige was employment (*neech chakari*). Obviously, the cultivation attached the person to his land, whereas a search for employment could lead him to places away form his homeland.

The British colonialism was a major change in Punjab affecting all dimensions of the socio-economic milieu of the state. Two developments in the specific context of migration may be noted. The first was the British recruitment policy to the army that was premised on the notions of race. The identification of martial races in India was the exercise that was done under the growing influence of anthropology. However, there is also a reasonable basis to take into consideration the fact that after 1857—the first war of Indian independence—people of some regions of the country became suspect, whereas the Punjabis showed a loyalty to the British. Within the Punjabi society, the Jat Sikhs were included among the martial races that made them eligible for recruitment to the British army (Fox, 1987). They became the lions of Punjab. The second was the construction of irrigation canals and establishment of canal colonies in the western Punjab. The Punjabi farmers in the eastern part of the state where the size of landholdings had considerably declined began to move to the canal colonies. In a way the second half of the 19th century was full of changes introduced from above that positively and negatively affected the life of the people of Punjab. However, the Punjabis had begun to move to the far off places including other countries by the end of the 19th century. The history of Punjabi migration to foreign lands has been well recorded and given adequate attention and scholarly treatment. The contribution of Punjabi diaspora in the nationalist movement has been acknowledged among the intellectuals, historians and the state.

One of the most notable facts about the Punjabi pioneer emigrants is that most of them were Jat Sikhs. They were also farmers as well as the major source of recruitment to the British army. It is not possible to think of migration of the dalits from Punjab in terms of voluntary, adventurous exploration into the lands hitherto unknown to them, because all the social and economic factors were operative against them.When and how did the Punjabi dalits begin to migrate to foreign countries? There is no study that specifically focuses on the dalit migration. Three studies that inadvertently take stock of dalit migration are Kessinger (1974), McLeod (1986) and Juergensmeyer (1982). Kessinger (1974), in his study of the history of a village in the Doaba region, provides information about the international migration of the people and informs that some dalit families also migrated from the village in the 19th century. Similarly, Juergensmeyer (1982) has mentioned their migration to the USA from the Doaba region. However, McLeod (1986) provides a vivid detail of the caste background of the Punjabis that settled in New Zealand. He divides the period of immigration of the Indians into three phases, that is, up to 1912, between 1912 and 1921, and the 1922–39. Table 4.1 has been worked out of the information available in different tables in his book.

The data in Table 4.1 provide insights into the caste dimension of the international migration of Punjabis. Before interpreting data, it is important to make an observation with regard to McLeod's study. Owing to two reasons, it became possible to know the caste background of the immigrants to New Zealand. First, the number was smaller than that of other countries, particularly Canada. Second, the small size of New Zealand in terms of both area and population made it possible to know caste background of the Punjabis though in one of his tables, McLeod has put a column under heading 'Uncertain'. What does the Table 4.1 indicate with regard to the caste of the Punjabi immigrants in New Zealand? The foremost indication that may be discerned from the data is the overwhelming presence of the Jats. As is clear from the study, mostly these Jats are Sikhs. This fact is common in the case of international migration of Punjabis to all English-speaking western countries,

Table 4.1
Yearwise Immigration of Punjabis to New Zealand According to their Caste Status

Caste	*1890–1914*	*1912–1921*	*1922–1939*	*Total*
Jat	11	133	65	209
Chamar	—	24	15	39
Mahaton	—	10	7	17
Brahmin	1	10	3	14
Khatri	2	8	—	10
Saini	—	4	2	6
Chhimba	—	2	1	3
Sunar	—	2	—	2
Ahluwalia	—	1	1	2
Jhir	—	1	0	1
Labana	—	1	0	1
Nai	—	1	1	2
Rajput	—	1	0	1
Muslim	1	13	2	16
Total	15	211	97	323

Compiled from McLeod, 1986, pp. 56, 62, and 77 (Tables 1, 2 and 8).

Note: McLeod (ibid.: 137) informs that the 24 Chamars for the years 1912–21 also consisted of Julahas.

whereas in the case of migration to Africa, men belonging to the Ramgarhia caste might have outnumbered the Jats. The Jat Sikhs have continued to dominate in the post-independence period in terms of their proportion among the Punjabi emigrants. The most notable feature from the perspective of caste, keeping in mind the colonial political economy and powerful caste impositions in terms of hierarchy and purity and pollution, is that of the emigration of the Chamars/Julahas from Punjab. It is clear from the Table 4.1 that they are second only to the Jats in number. It poses a challenge to social scientists to explain how within the given stifling socio-economic conditions, some dalits could immigrate to foreign countries. There is another historical/empirical fact that should be mentioned before attempting any plausible explanation. Most of the migrants belonged to the Doaba region of Punjab. It is the fact that holds true of other migrations before independence. We know from diverse sources, but particularly from Juergensmeyer (1982), that migration of the dalits also took place to the USA. Mangoo Ram, who was to lead the Ad-dharam movement in the 1920s belonged to the Chamar[1] caste and hailed from the village Mughowal in the Hoshiarpur district.

The fact that colonial political economy enabled the dalits to migrate overseas, it is essential to indulge in an exercise of providing some plausible explanation of this occurrence. The effective way to examine the phenomenon of dalit migration is to look into the objective and the subjective conditions. The objective conditions that favoured the dalit migration have been elaborately analysed in the discussion that follows.

The colonial political economy contributed to the unleashing of certain forces that broke feudal relations on which caste and bondage were based. In this regard, Marx's (1975) view about Indian villages should help us in appreciating the role of British colonialism. The British administrators and other writers understood Indian villages as stable and unchanging and christened them as 'village republics'. Marx, assuming the unchanging character of Indian villages to be true, went on to understand why there was such a continuity of the society. He argued that the unchanging character of Indian villages is a consequence of failure of population growth to contribute to the emergence of more complex division of labour. The moment the village would grow in size, a new settlement emerged that was the exact replica of the original village. He was of the view that the British colonialism would be able to break this system. The colonial political economy made an impact on the occupational structure and it became possible for even the dalits to migrate out from their villages, even to the foreign countries.

Another aspect of the objective conditions is the flourishing of leather trade. The facts about the rise in the leather trade in Punjab during the First World War are well known. Briggs (1975) has pointed out that there was a rise in the volume of leather trade in India in the 19th century, which helped the Chamars in improving their economic conditions. Mangoo Ram, who migrated to the USA in the beginning of the 20th century was the son of a leather trader. Juergensmayer (1982: 42) informs, "His (Mangoo Ram's) father, like other ambitious Chamars at the time, had developed a flourishing trade in raw hides for the leather market". Without some improvement of economic conditions it was not possible for the Chamars to emigrate. Once we know that the Punjabis in general did not migrate as indentured labourers, it is to be kept in mind that their voluntary migration could occur only if they had financial resources. The fact that certain members of the Chamar caste had improved their economic conditions as a result of the rise in the demand for leather, there is a need to look at some of the dalit movements as a consequence of this improvement. It also partially explains why the Chamars dominated the Ad-dharam movement.

The third objective condition could be located in the nature of relationships characterising patronage and exploitation. Any village in Punjab could be identified in terms of a set number of people and castes. One was landowning castes, the second artisan castes and the third working classes belonging to different dalit castes. These three caste/class groups constituted the indispensable components of the village social structure. Between the landowners on the one hand and the artisan and some dalit castes there had developed *jajmani* relations that were durable across generations. When a relationship despite being characterised by asymmetry perpetuates across generations there develop certain degrees of patronage and proximity. Juergensmeyer (ibid.) writes, "Mangoo Ram's employer in the orchards of central California was the brother of a local landlord back home in the Punjab". Madhopuri (2004), in his autobiography, narrates the way these relations get constructed. Such friendly relations, particularly between the young boys belonging to different castes, create an environment of interpersonal trust where the fact of class/caste asymmetry is temporarily forgotten or overlooked. The story of Mangoo Ram, as narrated by Juergensmeyer above, clearly suggests that the boys belonging to the Jat caste in fact assisted his migration to the USA.

What were the subjective conditions that led to the emigration of dalits? Subjective conditions implicate consciousness, cognition and intentions of the actors in the situation. Juergensmeyer (ibid.: 284) writes, "In 1909 America was in the air. Scores of upper-caste farmers from Mangoo Ram's area of Hoshiarpur had gone to the United States, and those who had not gone were talking about it". The migration of the dalits to foreign countries had a lot to do with the climate of migration in certain regions of Punjab. The emigration that was initiated by the ex-soldiers snowballed into a movement. In the first two decades of 20th century, the returning migrants provided needed motivation to look for greener pastures overseas. The knowledge that the migrants while returning home for some time had earned lot of money could have become the major reason for other young people to think of emulating them.

It is clear from the above discussion that the usual push-pull factor analysis of migration does not work in the case of the dalits. Despite the fact that there were conditions that could have pushed them out of their socio-economic milieu, but such a rule is applicable under conditions in which the people could move out on their own will. In the case of the dalits, the identification of objective conditions implicates the examination of those forces that might have loosened the grip of the caste and community over individuals in the classical sense of the term. The role of Sikhism after it was constructed by the Singh Sabha movement in which it was claimed that all castes are equal in the Sikh community might have played some role. McLeod (1986: 172–181) has narrated the biography of one immigrant to New Zealand who was a dalit. His name was Baldev Singh Share. He was son of Giani Ditt Singh—the well-known ideologue of the Singh Sabha movement. Unlike all other Punjabis, Baldev Singh immigrated as a medical doctor. He met a tragic end as he was imprisoned on fallacious charges betraying blatant racism of the New Zealand society.

In the post-independence period, the emigration of the Punjabis grew in volume and dalits were part of it. It is alleged that out of the total Punjabi emigrants to England 10 per cent belonged to the dalit castes and among them

Chamars/Ad-dharmis constituted overwhelming majority. According to Juergensmeyer (1982: 246),

> One would not ordinarily expect Chamars to have access to international travel in such large numbers, and indeed in this case it was only that a fortunate selection of officials worked in their favor. Until 1952 it had been difficult for Chamars to thread the maze of upper caste bureaucracy and obtain the necessary emigration papers. In that year, however, the first Scheduled Caste gazetted officer in the Punjab, Ishwar Das Pawar, became the undersecretary for passports in the Punjab government and began handing out passports to Scheduled Caste applicants with an unaccustomed generosity. Pawar estimated that he helped five hundred Scheduled Caste applicants emigrate each year.

It is also important to mention that the scheduled castes constitute a substantial number among the Punjabi migrants to the Gulf countries. The process is still going on.

Notably, most of the dalit emigrants in the earlier stages and even at present belong to the Doaba region of Punjab. The Doaba region of Punjab is located between Satluj and Beas rivers and consists of four districts, namely, Hoshiarpur, Jalandhar, Kapurthala and Nawanshehar. McLeod (1986) informs that the Doaba region has four sub-regions, but for the purpose of the present study these sub-regions do not have much relevance. Over a period of time, emigration has become uniform from Doaba. One may raise an issue about the region-specific emigration of the Punjabis. In the colonial period, when the ex-soldiers initiated the international migration of the Punjabis, the people from Doaba were not in majority. The Punjabis' recruitment to the British Indian army predominantly took place from the areas other than Doaba. Obviously, the pioneer emigrants largely belonged to Amritsar, Ferozepur and Ludhiana districts. There were some from the Doaba region too. The region-specific emigration of Punjabis suggests that both the subjective conditions and objective conditions varied across the province. One may further point out that the conditions that led to the emigration of dalits were different from those that initiated the emigration of Punjabis in general. We may make an effort to identify certain conditions both objective and subjective to understand why Doaba became the major place from where emigrations took place.

Objectively, two important occurrences might have provided the conditions for emigration. First was the experience of migration within Punjab. The British, after annexing Punjab, began the construction of irrigation canals in the western part of the state. The establishment of canal colonies began towards the end of the19th century. A considerable proportion of the settlers hailed from the Hoshiarpur district where the size of landholdings was small and much of the land was uncultivable due to sand silting that was caused by the seasonal brooks, locally called *choes,* in the rainy season. The farmers who settled in the canal colonies experienced change in their conditions. The result of this experience of change could have motivated others who remained back in their native villages. It may be added that in most parts of the Jalandhar district the landholding pattern was different. The second occurrence could be the spread of epidemics of plague and influenza in the first two decades of the 20th century. During these decades the population of the state actually declined. Though it was common for Punjab but combined with the first occurrence it might have acted as a reason for migration.

The Doaba region of Punjab was predominantly characterised by the *ryotwari* system of revenue collection. Moreover, there was a thin presence of big *ryots*. The Malwa region of Punjab was largely comprised of princely states, like Patiala, Nabha, Jind and Faridkot, which covered its most of the area. The Majha region between Beas and Ravi rivers had a long experience of its proximity with the rulers, as the centre of power was located at Lahore. The emergence of landed aristocracy occurred in this region. Both the regions other than Doaba consisted of peasantry that was embedded in the land. Doaba region, particularly the Hoshiarpur district, had both yeomen with the land that were prepared to leave it for better opportunities and big *ryots* who were connected with land. Therefore, given the widespread impression that going abroad would lead to the better and prosperous life after return, the yeoman Jat lost no opportunity to move out of his home for adventure. This yeoman also encouraged the Chamar of his village who was better off than other dalit castes to emulate him. There was a durable relationship between the Jats and the village menials on family to family basis. These attached families with the landlords also called *kamin* used to do all kinds of work in the house as well as land of the landlord. Interestingly, the participation of the *kamin* even in the family feuds of the landlord provided it the basis of becoming a strong bond. Thus, it is no surprising fact if some Jat emigrants also took the dalit boys along with them.

In a way, at the subjective level emigration became a part of consciousness of the members of the society and an option to be successful in life. In view of the fact that there was a strong element of 'return' prevalent in the minds of the people, the idea was attractive and enchanting as if Sindbad the Sailor was moving out of his village for adventure and riches. There are considerable numbers of writers—a recent addition is those of Taylor, Singh and Booth (2007)—who are of the opinion that certain abstract concepts like esteem and honour have been very important in the Punjabi society. In fact, these are important for all societies in feudal age. It may not be lost in mind that all emigrations take place for better life conditions if the migrants know that they would not be coming back—as it is happening with the present transnational diasporas. All these emigrants who migrated in the beginning of the 20th century were aware that they would be coming back. Thus, their reasons were economic and what they wanted to do with the money earned provided them motivation, intention and reason to migrate. In an agriculturally dominant society the quest for buying more land and/or building a big house was natural and predictable.

In the backdrop of the above general historical and sociological understanding of dalit migration within the context of Punjabi diaspora, it was essential to assume that emigration was one of various sources of social mobility for the dalits. In the present times, the emigration of the Punjabi dalits is a unique feature in comparison to dalits of other states. Interestingly, the emigration of dalits under the indentured system from East India and Tamil Nadu in the 19th century was an event, whereas the emigration of the Punjabi dalits was a process. It is evident from the fact that the dalit emigration has been a continuous trend across time and is on the rise in recent years. The information was collected with regard to certain emigration related dimensions and the proceeding discussion is based on the data. It may be pointed out that the basic purpose of collecting information was to ascertain the level of emigration among the dalits. In view of the fact that the respondents living in their village or locality in the city could either be the return migrants or non-migrants, it is expected that their numbers were small. Keeping in mind this methodological limitation the information was gathered.

The discussion on the emigration-related issues with regard to dalits has been divided into five parts. Whereas the first part examines the extent and magnitude of dalit emigration, the second takes stock of their castewise emigration. In the third and fourth parts the issues of destination and their pattern of expenditure after returning home have been discussed respectively. The last part is an attempt at assessing the relationship between emigration and social mobility.

I
Magnitude of Dalit Emigration

It was pointed out earlier that one of the limitations of the data presented here is that it was only possible to know from the respondents regarding the emigration of their family members and relatives. In certain cases the respondents could be return migrants. However, a reasonable estimate could be worked out with regard to the magnitude of dalit emigration. Table 4.2 shows the distribution of respondents in terms of their relations with the emigrants. The question that was asked from each respondent was whether somebody among his or her relatives/families had gone abroad. The respondents identified their relatives/family members who had migrated to foreign countries.

Table 4.2
Relation with the Emigrants

Relation	*Urban*	*Rural*	*Total*
Self/spouse and/or children	16 (2.00)	40 (5.00)	56 (3.50)
Father/brothers and/or sisters	47 (5.88)	37 (4.62)	84 (5.25)
Sons and/or daughters	24 (3.00)	53 (6.63)	77 (4.81)
Father's relatives	9 (1.12)	7 (0.88)	16 (1.00)
Mother's brothers and their family	9 (1.12)	—	9 (0.56)
Sister's husband or his family	4 (0.50)	—	4 (0.25)
Wife's relatives	4 (0.50)	—	4 (0.25)
Don't want to reveal	15 (1.88)	—	—
Not applicable	672 (84.00)	663 (82.87)	1350 (84.38)
Total	800 (100)	800 (100)	1600 (100)

Figures in parentheses are columnwise percentages.

It is clear from the data in Table 4.2 that more people have gone from the villages (17.17%) in contrast to the cities (16%). Interestingly, in both the cases, the migration had occurred from the family of the respondents. Another fact that has not been revealed by the data, but is very important for proper understanding, is that in the case of rural respondents belonging to the Amritsar district none of them had any relative/family member who had emigrated. It implies that more than one-third of the respondents belonging to the Jalandhar district have relatives/family members who had migrated to foreign countries. Interestingly, even in the case of cities, there were only 12 respondents in Amritsar whose relatives/family members had gone abroad, whereas in Jalandhar the number of such respondents was 101 constituting 25.25 per cent. It is clear that Jalandhar district, which is a part of the Doaba region, is the major centre from where emigration has taken place, whereas in Amritsar district emigration is limited. The information coincides with all studies on emigration of the Punjabis. However, it may be added that there are certain areas in the Malwa region from where considerable emigration has occurred. The notable areas are Ludhiana, Moga and Faridkot districts.

The second dimension of the data given in Table 4.2 is regarding respondents' nature of relationship with the migrants. Obviously, in the majority of cases, the respondents' own family members had emigrated. It leads us to make a conjecture that the respondents might have informed about their own family members and avoided referring to distant relatives. Taking cue from this conjecture one may say that the actual number could be higher. To make an exact estimate of the magnitude of dalit emigration from Punjab is not possible within the methodological framework of the present study. It is so because of the simple fact that it is a study of the dalit respondents who are presently living in Punjab. Only an estimate of such dalits' family members or relatives is possible, whereas those families of dalits that have emigrated without leaving any family member behind could not be studied. However, such queries were made, but it all depended on the memory of the respondents which in the case of urban dalits was quite fickle. Even going by the information that has been gathered it may be stated that the dalit emigration is quite large if we keep in mind their economic conditions in general.

II
Caste and Emigration

In the earlier chapters castewise distinctions have emerged in relation to all variables that have been examined. As a corollary to these distinctions, it may be argued that some castes are likely to emigrate more than others. It has clearly emerged from the data that emigration is predominantly a process that characterises the Doaba region. It is thus important to know whether certain castes in the Doaba region have migrated in large numbers. Table 4.3 provides data on the caste of those respondents who informed that their relatives had emigrated. It may be mentioned that the data in the Table 4.3. pertains only to the Jalandhar district, the reason for which is that most of the respondents whose relatives/family members were emigrants belonged to the Jalandhar district. It is clear from the data that the Chamars/Ad-dharmis constitute an overwhelming majority among the emigrants. Interestingly, among the urban

Table 4.3
Caste of the Respondents having Emigrant Relatives (Jalandhar)

Caste	*Jalandhar City*	*Jalandhar Villages*	*Total*
Ad-dharmi/Chamar	88 (87.12)	92 (67.15)	180 (75.63)
Megh/Kabirpanthi	6 (5.94)	—	6 (2.52)
Balmikis	7 (6.94)	40 (29.20)	47 (19.75)
Bazigar	—	5 (3.65)	5 (2.10)
Total	101 (42.45) (100)	137 (57.55) (100)	238 (100) (100)

Figures in parentheses are columnwise percentages.

respondents, their proportion is higher than those of the rural respondents though in terms of actual numbers more rural respondents informed that their relatives had migrated to foreign countries. The Balmikis are second in number and their emigration has predominantly taken place from the villages. Emigration among the Meghs is limited though in the entire sample they are living in the cities. Conversely, the Chamars/Ad-dharmis are living in both the cities and villages and their emigration is equally high. In view of the fact that both rural and urban respondents' samples are equal, it may be argued that emigration is a predominant trend in the villages of the Doaba region of Punjab. At the same time, two major caste groups are emigrating from these villages and both are among the most numerous castes of Punjab. Moreover, the dalits living in villages are facing economic distress in face of limited opportunities. Many respondents informed that in most of the cases they take loan from informal sources. Most of their time, as we shall see little later, is spent on repaying the loan. The emigration from Amritsar's villages that were studied was nil in the sample though upon enquiry from the villages it came to our knowledge that some Mazabi men had gone to the Middle East countries. In the case of Amritsar city there were about 27 respondents who informed that their relatives had emigrated and they had gone to the Middle East and all such respondents belonged to Balmiki/Mazabi castes.

III
Destinations of Emigrants

It was pointed in the beginning that there have been certain phases in the pattern of migration of Punjabis to various countries. Equally important is the fact of the place of destination, which also reveals whether the emigrant is permanent or temporary resident in the foreign country. For example, it can be safely assumed that all emigrants to the English-speaking countries are permanently settled in there, whereas the emigrants to the Middle East countries are part of the transient diaspora and have all likelihood of returning to their native place. Table 4.4 provides data on the destination of the emigrants. This clearly brings out the rural-urban difference in the destination of the emigrants. There are more emigrants in the western countries from the cities than the villages. It implies that the permanent emigrants largely belong to the urban areas.

Table 4.4
Destination of Dalit Emigrants

Destination	*Urban*	*Rural*	*Total*
England	48 (37.50)	20 (14.60)	68 (25.66)
Germany	—	7 (5.11)	7 (2.64)
France	2 (1.56)	—	2 (0.76)
Austria	2 (1.56)	—	2 (0.76)
Italy	14 (10.94)	19 (13.87)	33 (12.45)
Greece	1 (0.78)	2 (1.46)	3 (1.13)
Denmark	1 (0.78)	—	1 (0.38)
USA	2 (1.56)	—	2 (0.76)
Canada	14 (10.94)	—	14 (5.28)
Australia	2 (1.56)	—	2 (0.76)
Dubai	35 (27.34)	70 (51.10)	105 (39.62)
Muscat	2 (1.56)	5 (3.65)	7 (2.64)
Kuwait	3 (2.35)	7 (5.11)	10 (3.77)
Bahrain	1 (0.78)	5 (3.65)	6 (2.26)
Japan	1 (0.78)	—	1(0.38)
Malaysia	—	2 (1.46)	2 (0.76)
Total	128 (100)	137 (100)	265 (100)

Figures in parentheses are columnwise percentages.

On the other hand, more than half of the rural emigrants have migrated to the Gulf countries the implication of which is that they are transient migrants and are not permanently settled at the place of their destination. Interestingly, for both rural and the urban emigrants, two major countries of destination are England and UAE (Dubai). Still another important finding is that Italy has emerged as an important place of destination. The data on emigration to England amply demonstrated the validity of the information provided by Juergensmeyer (1982) that in the beginning when migrations took place, an officer in passport office expedited the issuing of passports to the dalits applicants.

The destination of dalit emigrants clearly reveals that they are highly dynamic and are widely distributed in the world. Wherever they have gone they have constructed their religious places and have organised various societies for the welfare of their own people.[2] The dalits have not been able to organise themselves by understanding their specific interests but have considerably contributed to the welfare of their dalits brethren back in Punjab. At present, wherever there are dalits, they have one or the other organisation. For example, in the United States of America, there are seven major dalit organisations, of which Shri Guru Ravi Das Sabha of New York may be mentioned here. It was established in 1988 when the upper castes refused to allow the dalits to celebrate the birth anniversary of Guru Ravi Das in the local Gurdwara. Though most of these organisations have been established by the Ad-dharmis/Chamars, the one in Yuba City is worth mentioning simply because of the fact that it is called Maharshi Balmik Sabha. This Sabha also helps the young Balmiki boys in higher studies. In Canada, the dalits have organised themselves in almost every city. There is a reasonable basis to opine that the establishment of the Ravi Das temple began in reaction to their religious exclusion in subtle manner. Seven major organisations of the dalits exist in Canada. However, it is in England that the dalit organisations are numerous. There are more than two dozens of them. For example, Guru Ravi Das Sabha exists in almost every city. The Buddh Vihars (monasteries) exist in Birmingham and Wolverhampton. Similarly, dalit organisations exist in Germany,

Netherlands etc. Notably, there is one Shri Guru Ravi Das Parchar Sabha in Portugal. It all began with the plan to celebrate the birth anniversary of Dr B.R. Ambedkar on April 14.[3] First, the management of the Gurdwara and then that of Hindu temple refused to allow them. The Ravi Das temple was later on constructed by the Sabha.

There is a reasonable basis to inform that the Balmikis had also migrated before independence to various countries. In 1947 there were certain instances of killings of the Balmikis in Punjab the causes of which were economic. In Jalandhar district two Balmikis were killed by the Jat Sikhs (Virdi, 2000). In order to fight cases against the Jat Sikhs, the Africa Balmiki Sabha, Nairobi, sent the money.[4] It is clear from the information that the Balmikis had migrated to Africa during the British rule and they were large enough in Kenya to form the association. The existence of such a large number of dalit organisations in different countries makes it clear that their spread corresponds to that of the upper-caste Punjabis, particularly the Jat Sikhs.

IV
Pattern of Expenditure

In the light of the fact that the Punjabi diaspora shows a considerably strong tendency to invest/spend their earnings after returning temporarily or permanently, it is important to know the pattern of expenditure of the emigrant relatives of the respondents. It is evident from the data presented in Table 4.5 that there have been variations in the pattern of expenditure. However, two major areas of expenditure are renovation/construction of house and repayment of the loan. It is important to mention that the repayment of loan is something that has not been identified by various studies as the major component of expenditure. Earlier studies clearly identify construction of house and, more importantly, the purchase of land as the major areas of expenditure as these two were linked with the reasons for emigration (see Kessinger, 1974; Helweg, 1979; McLeod, 1986; Verma, 2002). However, these studies focus mainly on one particular caste community of Punjab, namely, the Jat Sikh, with the exception of Verma (ibid.), who has studied Mahaton caste of Punjab. It may be added that even the Mahatons are a part of landed peasantry of Punjab. It is therefore clear that since the dalits never became an exclusive focus of examination largely due to their small number in the earlier stages of Punjabi emigration, the caste-specific reasons were ignored in generalisations. It is evident from the data that the repayment of loan is an important part of the expenditure of the dalit emigrants after return. There are two implications of this predominant pattern of expenditure. First, the migration occurred to repay the loan and the second is that money was borrowed in order to emigrate. The second implication seems plausible, particularly in the light of the fact that emigration has become a culture in the Doaba region. It is seen as a solution to the economic difficulties as well as the way to earn handsome money.

Table 4.5

Pattern of Expenditure among the Returned Migrants

Pattern	*Urban*	*Rural*	*Total*
Started a business	—	2 (1.46)	2 (0.75)
Purchased land	10 (7.81)	10 (7.30)	20 (7.55)
Purchased house plot	4 (3.12)	4 (2.92)	8 (3.02)
Renovated the house	13 (10.16)	8 (5.84)	21 (7.92)
Constructed the house	30 (23.44)	53 (38.69)	83 (31.32)
Repaid the debt	18 (14.06)	59 (43.06)	77 (29.06)
Children's education	—	1 (0.73)	1 (0.38)
Don't know	53 (41.41)	—	53 (20.00)
Total	128 (100)	137 (100)	265 (100)

Figures in parentheses are percentages.

It may be noted that in the case of only two respondents' relatives the money earned abroad was invested in business. Business skills require cultural capital of a particular kind and the possibility of everybody starting a business seems remote. However, the proceeding case shows how emigration could improve upon the cultural capital.

Seventy years-old Ram Lal has seven brothers and all of them are settled in Boota Mandi and engaged in rawhides business. He is a middle level educated and staying with one of his brothers in Boota Mandi. He at the age of 20 in 1955 migrated to England when some of his friends from Jat caste who had earlier immigrated to England, sent sponsorship for him to come to England. He spent Rs 1,600 on airfare. He stayed for 22 years in England doing labour. During his stay he earned handsomely, but he was always feeling home sick and finally he returned to India in 1977 after that he did not go back. Now, as many as 10 members of his family are settled in England, Italy, America and Canada. His exposure to foreign land brought tremendous change in his outlook and standard of living. After returning back he renovated his house and fitted it with bathtub, septic tank, as there was no sewerage system till then, electric gas stove and also introduced western kitchen. He introduced the concept of separate kitchen and toilet in the house, which his other relatives also followed.

After coming back he resumed his hereditary business of rawhides and tanning and he employed some skilled workers who helped him to process the skins through wet blue tanning. Owing to his experience, he knew a lot on the quality of skins. It depends upon the type and age of the animal, its health and kind of care it got. For example, as he told this researcher, it is just like human skin, which with age gets hardened and wrinkled. The regular massage and patting of the animals leaves the skin soft which fetches more price than the usual. For instance, the skin of sheep is used for making jackets. Cow and ox's skin is used for making uppers of the footwears; similarly, it is also used for sofa covers and car seats. As buffalo's skin is hard, it is used for making horse saddles, suitcases and also for the soles and heels of the shoes. He has a sale of one crore rupees per annum. He feels that work available in this business has recently reduced. The number of animals has tremendously reduced with the tractorisation and the live animals are sold and even exported to Arabian countries. With the increased consumption of meat in our society the young and small animals are being slaughtered. The famous slaughterhouse of Punjab at Lalru near Chandigarh reveals the same story. Less proportion of fully-grown animals is available. In his view there are only ten to twelve shops of rawhides and nearly 25 vegetable tanning shops in Boota Mandi.

He believes that "the major drawback with our people is that they are very communal minded. With the efforts of government, through education and changing people's thinking and attitudes the change in the system is possible".

V
Emigration and Status Improvement

Respondents were also asked a question whether the process of emigration improves the status of the dalits. The reason for this question was the simple assumption that emigration implies improvement in the economic conditions. Therefore, it becomes pertinent to understand whether in the perception of the respondents, economic improvement also implies status enhancement. The responses to the question are presented in Table 4.6. It is evident from the data that the reaction to emigration in terms of its social consequences is ambivalent. However, much more number than those respondents whose relatives have emigrated (21.26%) were of the opinion that improvement in the status occurred after emigration. One of the reasons for ambivalence could be that most of the dalit emigrants migrate to Gulf countries and they have to come back. When they return, they become part of the socio-economic milieu of their native place. Over a period of time, they lose their economic prosperity if they do not invest their income in the productive ventures. The result is that they again emigrate by borrowing some money. The cycle goes on till they stop due to reasons of failure to get visa etc.

Table 4.6

Emigration Improves the Social Status of the Dalits

Response	*Urban*	*Rural*	*Total*
Positive improvement	137 (17.13)	33 (4.12)	170 (10.63)
Both social and economic status improves.	66 (8.50)	104 (13.00)	170 (10.63)
Caste does not change	1 (0.12)	—	1 (0.06)
Can't say	596 (74.25)	663 (82.88)	1259 (78.68)
Total	800 (100)	800 (100)	1600 (100)

Figures in parentheses are columnwise percentages.

The relationship between emigration and social mobility apparently seems simple, but it is complex due to various reasons. First of all, we have to make a distinction among the dalits in terms of the nature of emigration. The emigration to England, Canada and the USA could be technically regarded as immigration, as virtually all of them have permanently settled in these countries. Conversely, the emigration to the Gulf countries is transient in nature and all of them are bound to return to settle back in India. Whereas the former are settled as immigrants with their families, the latter migrate alone leaving behind their families who only receive remittances. In the case of the former the issue of social mobility has an altogether different context, as they cease to be a part of the Punjabi society, whereas the latter have to live in that society to which they originally belong.

The immigrant dalits in various countries constitute a part of the Punjabi diaspora and also the same community. Juergensmeyer (1982) rightly points out the caste differences among the Punjabis abroad. The Punjabi community, despite the same economic status, has constructed a replica of the Punjabi society. The result is the separate constructions of religious places despite common religion. Jats and Ramgarhias have separate Gurdwaras and the Ad-dharmis have their own. Judge (2002) has highlighted how the issue of intercaste marriages, when one of the parties is from the dalit caste, becomes volatile. The dalits have become active and they have started asserting their identities. An evidence of their assertion of identity could be found in the number of websites that are presently available for exploration among the dalit diaspora (Kumar, 2004).

In the case of transient diaspora, the issue of social mobility exists within the framework of the Punjabi society. The basic assumption entailed in the relationship between emigration and social mobility is that there is a link between the economic status and social prestige. It does not assume the end of caste, but foresees the possibility of rupture in the caste-based inequality. In other words, the sustained improved economic status would lead to the better quality of life that could be transformed into social prestige. Empirical observations suggest that at the microlevel there have been economic changes among the individual dalits and those migrants who start some business have been able to sustain their better economic conditions. Despite all these changes, social inclusion at the individual level is still far from what is required.

The lag between economic status and social prestige is shifting the dalit orientation to the public sphere, namely, politics. The dalit politics has begun to revolve around the identity issue. At the normative level, it is negative, because it implicates the perpetuation of caste system. Analytically, the assumption in the identity politics is that caste is immutable like certain other inequalities, such as race and gender. In a way, the issue of race was a logical culmination of identity politics. It seems that in the face of perpetuation of caste as both a social system and ideology, the only plausible way to social status is the assertion of identity. There is one danger involved in this way of moving up: the system that is responsible for all the wrong done to certain castes is upheld and legitimised. This is what is happening if we see the extent to which the dalit diaspora is getting involved in Punjab politics through remittances.

In the end, it may be commented as a conclusion that international migration of Punjabi dalits is their most distinctive feature in comparison to their counterparts in the rest of the country. The Punjabi dalits have settled everywhere in the world and form an inseparable component of Punjabi community abroad. It has contributed to the emergence of casteism (Judge, 2002) among the Punjabis, but the dalits have sought to construct a casteless social space in the modern world where the host populations emphasise merit rather than birth ascribed status. The dalit diaspora has also contributed to the changing social space in Punjab through various efforts the most important of which is their monetary contributions to help their brethren to build institutions that could enable them to sustain struggle for equality.

Notes

1. The Ad-dharm movement began in 1920s before which there was Chamar caste. However, a section among this caste had converted to Sikhism who had been given the name Ramdasia.
2. Most of the information has been taken from Virdi (2000).
3. Virdi (2000: 274) has not mentioned the year though it seems that the event occurred in mid-1990s.
4. Most of the information has been taken from Pandit Bakhshi Ram's (1983) account of the struggle of the Balmikis before independence. Pandit Bakhshi Ram was one of the most prominent leaders of the Balmikis during the last two decades of colonial period as well as after independence.

5

Entrepreneurship

The relevance and crucial importance of entrepreneurship among the dalits with regard to their status enhancement cannot be ignored. It tends to suggest that with the improvement in the economic conditions the social status automatically undergoes a change. To approach the issue by making a causal connection between economic conditions and status enhancement, the argument would reduce the understanding of the subjugation, exploitation, and misery of dalits to their poverty. We maintained that the issues confronting the dalits in India are not exclusively economic; rather, there is social deprivation and discrimination involved in it making it a complex ensemble of totality. After this caveat, it may be pointed out that better economic conditions could become a means to adopt other strategies more effectively than without any economic resource. Earlier chapters show that there is positive relationship between improvement in the economic conditions and struggle for higher status. It is in this context that the present chapter takes up the nature and extent of entrepreneurship among the Punjabi dalits and examines how effective it is to provide opportunities to the dalits to negotiate for the better social status. We begin by looking into the salient features of the history of entrepreneurship in India the purpose of which is to situate caste as an important and, to an extent, a defining variable.

The history of Indian entrepreneurship shows three important features that make it unique in comparison to the western experience. First, entrepreneurship has remained largely concentrated in the hands of few traditionally dominant trading castes, falling in the Vaishya varna, such as Baniyas, Khatris and Aroras. Second, it has been found among certain regional communities. In other words, irrespective of castes certain communities known as belonging to certain region/state/country excelled in trade and business. For example, the Marwaris belong to a region in Rajasthan, the Gujaratis, the Punjabis and the Sindhis are from states, whereas the Parsis are Zoroastrians who left their home country, Iran, after the Islamic invasion[1] (Bal, 1998; Das, 1999; Tripathi, 2004). Third, the family businesses are an integral part of the Indian entrepreneurship. We have family-owned businesses in which two or more members of family have financial control over the enterprise. The family members also organise and manage the enterprise.[2] All these categories overlap in most of the cases except the Parsis. The history also reveals certain exceptions. For example, the first person to start the industry in Ahmedabad was a Nagar Brahmin and even the second textile mill in Ahmedabad was started by a Kanbi Patel. We have a case of Kirloskar who was a Brahmin. Paradoxically, the Marwaris were the second to enter industry sometimes during the period of two world wars—the time when they were already well established in trade and business. Such kinds of paradoxes and intriguing issues are quite prevalent in the history of entrepreneurship. The exploration in the present context is confined to know what actually matters to become an entrepreneur. To explain the entrepreneurial activity of various social groups the debate in entrepreneurship research is going on between contextual and dispositional approaches. The contextual approach is primarily rooted in sociology, which holds that the features of social structure may encourage or retard entrepreneurial activity independent of the positions of the incumbents. Scholars have suggested a number of structural influences on entrepreneurial activity such as family of origin, work environment, social networks, and regional, cultural and material environment. By contrast, the dispositional accounts have been emphasised by the psychologists who argue that stable individual traits lead to entrepreneurial activity, independent of context. They link entrepreneurial activity to individual differences in entrepreneurial ability, need for achievement and other aspects of personality (Sorensen, 2007). To a large extent, the dispositional approach is weak or irrelevant in Indian entrepreneurial scenario, as we find that a majority of entrepreneurs are born in a few families rather than being randomly distributed in the society. In spite of aberrations due to high and dominant caste status[3] and economic influence, we find that certain communities and castes invariably take up commercial activities instead of any other occupation. Hence, we may say that the 'merchant ideology' is not uniformly distributed in the Indian society.

Ghurye (1969) and many other scholars have pointed out that there is a correspondence between caste and occupation in India. Historically, one caste never performed one occupation, the simple example of which is Brahmins who have been priests as well as landlords. However, even then, occupational choices were limited for each caste group. For example, a Brahmin could not take up defiling occupations. Even then, deviations could occur under certain conditions. One, due to industrialisation they may lose availability of work opportunities in their hereditary occupations forcing them to shift to other occupations. Two, with the diversification and modifications in the work some other caste groups, including the upper castes, might get interested in taking up some work which was hitherto restricted to a particular caste group. Third, with the increasing opportunities of work, the traditional caste group might shift exclusively to trade and business part of its work with the help of hired workers who actually would be performing the dangerous and difficult tasks of manufacturing. In the process, they may even move up in the caste hierarchy through the process of 'sanskritisation'. Under such conditions, the caste and occupation linkage breaks though this kind of linkage tends to break across space. The same caste group may be performing some other work at other places. For example, in Banaras, the Chamars are a weaving community who are engaged in its silk industry. They were working under the putting-out system for the Muslim masters (Ciotti, 2007).

The industrial development in India led to the emergence of new occupations, which acted as a catalyst in changing the rigid structure of the society. Linking occupation with the caste status definitely posed a problem in the case of new occupations. It also implies that such an occurrence could take place either through the intervention of some external forces or the society itself experienced cataclysmic changes. In the case of India, both the events took place. The British colonial intervention was the major factor that transformed the Indian society in a definite way. The political economy[4] of colonial development, though characterised by many limitations, created two interesting trends that broke the caste-occupation linkages combined with power and privileges. First, some of the hitherto stigmatised occupations became lucrative due to the rise in the demand of certain commodities, which led to upper-caste people joining the same. Secondly, new occupations emerged that were to be performed by the people who were traditionally linked with their caste occupations. Could they come out of their traditional occupations? Yes, they did. However, it involved both voluntary and involuntary compulsions. Economic development brought misery to the artisan production and the indigenous production system did not have the ability to compete with the industrial manufacturing. The destruction of artisan production turned the artisans into workers. The age-old correspondence with the caste and occupation was broken. Even then, the opportunities for the lower castes to go for any occupation were limited. It remained confined to the cities that were not growing at a fast rate.

As the colonial political economy linked India with the capitalist world system, any occurrence in the world did have ramifications for the economy of the country. It is in this context that the rural hinterland became a part of the capitalist mode of production, which was linked at the international level. For example, the indigo cultivation in India was essentially carried out for the international market and the invention of chemical dyes virtually ended its cultivation creating economic stress among the peasants. Though the Indian agrarian production got integrated with the world-wide economic system, yet the cities were the major platform where the caste-occupation correspondence could break easily. The pace of urbanisation was slow and the expected change could not have occurred. The beginning of World War I in 1914 contributed to the rise in demand for certain goods in India. One of such demands was for leather goods, particularly the shoes that directly affected the lower castes involved in leatherwork. Tripathi and Jumani (2007: 86) mention, "The most of the wartime promotions and acquisitions were consistent with the traditional work of Chamars such as trade in hides, leather manufacturing, footwear production". These 'war babies' initiated a chain reaction that began from the collection of raw hides from the villages to the process of making of leather goods.

How far the process of industrialisation and the state policies in India have remained successful in bringing transformation in the work and lives of the scheduled castes? A review of the existing literature reveals that historically there has been a multi-faceted attack to break the rigidity of the caste system. On the one hand, the intervention of the state as well as the reformers tried to change the caste system, while on the other hand, the scheduled castes used the political mechanism to uplift their status.[5]

The underprivileged sections also benefited from the overall economic development of the country though there could be certain doubts about the effective reach of the trickle-down effect. It may be argued that the issue of entrepreneurship among the marginal sections of the society, particularly the scheduled castes, is inevitably and inseparably linked with the development process as well as the nature of the state, which in the case of India may be characterised as liberal and welfare-oriented. However, entrepreneurship is linked with capitalism, as it believes in the individual's efforts to rise in the social and economic scale through business and enterprise. In this regard, the internal dynamism of the capitalist system and the policies of the liberal welfare state become more crucial as an explanatory variable for the present study

The chapter has been divided into four parts. In the first part, along with the general information about the number of entrepreneurs among the respondents, the discussion focuses on the prevalence of dalit entrepreneurship as available in the existing literature. The second part traces the general background of the dalit entrepreneurs, whereas the third explores the pattern and process of their entrepreneurial functions. Some case studies of dalit entrepreneurs given in the fourth part depict how entrepreneurship has acted as a means to their economic and social mobility.

I
Dalit Entrepreneurship

It may be stated at the outset that there is no distinctive feature of dalit entrepreneurship at the theoretical level. What is important to understand is the context of the problematic within the limitations of which the term has been used. Let us begin the discussion with the data on the extent of entrepreneurship among the dalits. Out of the total 800 respondents belonging to 10 different villages of Amritsar and Jalandhar districts, there were only 14 respondents who were involved in various trading activities. As compared to villages, quite a large number of them have become entrepreneurs in the urban areas. In the Jalandhar city 95 (23.75%) respondents and in Amritsar city relatively a few, i.e., 38 (9.5%), thus, in total 133 (16.63%) respondents from both the cities were involved in various entrepreneurial activities.

An attempt, therefore, has been made to map the nature and extent of entrepreneurship among the scheduled castes as well as to see whether it has brought about change in their social and political world. It may seem truism, but it may be pointed out that the moment we find entrepreneurship among the dalits a degree of change is subsumed under it. Entrepreneur is one who carries on any commercial activity, may it be trade, business or industry. Entrepreneurship, which is innovative, creative and risk-prone activity, requires capital, decision-making ability and leadership traits.[6] The meaning of 'entrepreneur' has undergone a change over the time, but it was always understood in terms of the dominant system and needs of the society. Meanings changed from soldier, adventurer, moneylender, agriculturist and merchant to trader and industrialist. An entrepreneur is essentially a modern man who has come out of the beaten track and explored the new vistas of opportunities. Therefore, taking to entrepreneurship is a sign of change in social and economic conditions of the dalits.

If a caste is involved in a particular enterprise or business, its implications are collective. Sociologists identify two kinds of social mobility, namely, individual and corporate. In the case of individual mobility only certain members are able to improve their condition through certain occupations. However, if an entire caste group gets involved in the new occupation that leads to the improvement of its conditions, then it becomes corporate in nature. However, the corporate character of social mobility is to be understood in the context of time and space. In other words, at what particular time does social mobility occur in a caste and whether it is local or universal? It is quite possible that a caste may have experienced corporate mobility in one region, whereas in another region no such change has taken place.

The understanding of dalit entrepreneurship in the case of Punjab in general and the present study in particular revolves mainly around two castes that have excelled in entrepreneurship. The first major group is that of the Chamars/Ad-dharmis located at Boota Mandi in Jalandhar city. The second largest group, which constitutes one-third of the total entrepreneurs, is that of the Meghs. There are also a few Balmikis, Mazabis and Dumnas among them. The most important among them are the Chamars/Ad-dharmis, who need special focus for examination. We begin by exploring their origin and background.

Most of the Chamars/Ad-dharmis of Boota Mandi actually belong to nearby villages situated at the outskirts of the Jalandhar city. The name 'Boota Mandi' was given to the market for the dead animals located near the village named Boota. These Chamars were frequently coming to this place for the sale and purchase of dead animals and many of them settled there. From then onwards it became Boota Mandi.[7] Still it is a commercial as well as a residential area. However, in the process of growth, the affluent among them moved to other residential localities and the old houses in many cases have turned into their offices.

The Chamars are scattered well over the Aryo-Dravidian tract as leather workers. The census figures of 1911 show that the Brahmins had preponderance over the Chamars and Rajputs in numerical strength. The Chamars may be traced back to early times as an occupational group. Tanners are mentioned in the Rig Veda, the late-Vedic literature and the Brahmanas (Briggs, 1975). The Chamars would take the hides of all dead cattle and the flesh of all cloven-footed animals. They made and mended shoes, thongs for the cart, whips and other leather items. They were the village artisans and were getting the customary dues as a share of the total agricultural produce in return for their duties. In the east and southeast regions of the combined Punjab, the village Chamars were also engaged in weaving for which they were paid separately (Ibbetson, 1974). Their traditional occupation was considered dirty and carried a low status. Kessinger (1974) discussed the change occurred in the traditional occupation of Chamars who after the decline of traditional *sepidari* system took to shoe manufacturing on a full-time basis, as they found it profitable enough to compensate for the low status it carried. In fact, the Chamars in Punjab were always placed at an ambivalent position. Among the artisans they were the lowest in the hierarchy and among all the dalit castes of Punjab they were the most progressive caste group and could be placed at the top of the 'dalit caste hierarchy'.

Saberwal (1990) has made a comparative study of the Ramgarhias, the Ad-dharmis and the Balmikis in an urban area of Punjab. According to him, the Ad-dharmis are more open to new experiences and exposures, learning new skills, venturing into the industry by restricting their consumption and ploughing the savings back for expansion. They have moved up in the social and political hierarchy through their entrepreneurial skills and could occupy many positions of political and social importance. Conversely, only a few of the Balmikis did learn leatherwork and started their workshops, the others fulfilled the increased demand for scavenging, particularly the municipal scavenging, in expanding towns. As stated in the previous chapter, many

Ad-dharmis migrated to foreign countries, such as England and Canada, in the second half of the last century where they took up various types of occupations and sent remunerations back home that further contributed to their economic well-being. Many of them improved their lifestyle and also ventured into the wholesale business of hides and skins and tanning industry.

A study on entrepreneurship by Dahiwale (1989) on five different scheduled castes—Mahars, Mang, Dhor, Chambhar and Bhangi—in Kolhapur city reveals that they moved up in the social hierarchy by taking up new and modern occupations. These castes attribute their social mobility to education, occupational mobility and the personal performance. The ruler of Kolhapur, Shahuji Chhatrapati, personally practised and monitored the policies and programmes to uplift the untouchables by giving them education and sending them to cities to learn new skills. They were also financed to start new ventures. At the social and interpersonal levels, he took exemplary lead by employing these people in his kitchen and palace. He encouraged interdining and intercaste marriages. Besides his efforts, the social reformers—Jotirao Phule, V.R. Shinde, B.R. Ambedkar and Christian missionaries—worked for their social and economic uplift. In their case, the entrepreneurial activities are the result of comprehensive action programme. On the other hand, in the case of the Chamars/Ad-dharmis, it is largely due to the process of development when they excelled in entrepreneurial activities with their initiative and hard work.

The leather shoemakers of Tamil Nadu have become international entrepreneurs by exporting their finished leather and shoes to European, Australian and North American markets. They belong to the Labbai community. Believed to be ex-untouchables they converted to Islam and were responsible for its industrialisation during 19th and 20th centuries (Flamant, 2003). For almost a century their tanneries were producing semi-finished leather with traditional tanning methods, but after 1960s the modern methods of tanning improved the quality and increased the production. In the 1970s, many of the Labbai Muslims set up the factories producing shoes for the international market. Lately, many high-caste Hindus such as Chettiars and Brahmins have also joined them and set up their factories. The leather goods entrepreneurs of Tamil Nadu have close business dealings with the entrepreneurs under study. The rawhides and semi-finished skins procured in Jalandhar mainly have one of their final destinations in Tamil Nadu's tanneries and factories. It is worthwhile to analyse data and examine various aspects of the entrepreneurial activity of the respondents.

II
Profile of Entrepreneur Respondents

In this section, the main endeavour is to precisely describe the socio-economic profile of the entrepreneurs. All the respondents are males. The data in Table 5.1 indicate that a large majority, i.e., 83.16 per cent in Jalandhar and 81.59 per cent in Amritsar, fall in the age group of 20 to 50 years. Therefore, taking to entrepreneurship is relatively a recent phenomenon, as they are predominantly young persons. In Jalandhar all of them are Hindus except for a Christian and a Buddhist. While in Amritsar 71.05 per cent are Hindus and 28.95 per cent are Sikhs. In Jalandhar majority (69.47%) of them are the Chamars/ Ad-dharmis by caste, followed by the Meghs/Kabirpanthis (27.37%) and the Balmikis 3.16 per cent, whereas in Amritsar, the highest (39.47%) proportion is that of the Meghs/Kabirpanthis. The Mazabis (26.31%) come next followed by Balmikis (18.42%) and both Chamars and Dumnas are equally represented, i.e., 7.89 per cent. In Jalandhar they (81.05%) are mainly the natives of this place as majority of them have moved to the present location from the nearby villages and most of the respondents are born here, though nearly 16 per cent of them have migrated from Pakistan in 1947 at the time of partition. In Amritsar only 45 per cent of the entrepreneurs are the natives of the place, whereas 48 per cent are from outside the state and largely they have settled here after the partition, as the Meghs constitute the majority among them and they have all migrated from Sialkot (now in Pakistan) where they were working with Muslim entrepreneurs in sports and surgical instruments industries. Only 5 per cent of them have migrated to this place from within the state. If we compare the educational level of the respondents in two cities it is clear that only one each in two cities is illiterate; all others are educated ranging from the primary level to post-graduation, but 32 per cent in Amritsar and 38 per cent in Jalandhar are matriculate. Nearly 18 per cent in Jalandhar are graduates while in Amritsar it is only 8 per cent. It is interesting to note that though the level of education is by and large same at both the places, yet we find Jalandhar as favourable towards the education of the scheduled castes. Even in the case of the fathers, 61 per cent are found illiterate in Amritsar and only 42 per cent in Jalandhar. Nevertheless, 32 per cent and 21 per cent in Jalandhar and Amritsar cities respectively have been found educated up to matriculation.

Table 5.1

Age of the Entrepreneurs

Age (years)	*Jalandhar*	*Amritsar*	*Total*
Up to 20	1 (1.05)	3 (7.89)	4 (3.00)
21–30	20 (21.05)	13 (34.21)	33 (24.82)
31–40	33 (34.74)	11 (28.95)	44 (33.08)
41–50	26 (27.37)	7 (18.42)	33 (24.82)
51–60	6 (6.32)	3 (7.89)	9 (6.77)
61–70	6 (6.32)	1 (2.63)	7 (5.26)
71–80	3 (3.15)	—	3 (2.25)
Total	95 (71.43) (100)	38 (28.57) (100)	133 (100) (100)

Figures in parentheses are percentages.

Among the entrepreneurs, the Chamars/Ad-dharmis in Jalandhar were traditionally engaged in business of rawhides, tanning of leather and snaring of skins, whereas in Amritsar they were mainly engaged in shoe-making. The traditional occupation of Meghs in Bhargo Camp area of Jalandhar as well as in Haripura and Tapaai of Amritsar is weaving, whereas the Balmikis at both the places were traditionally engaged in sweeping/scavenging. The Balmiki and the Mazabi respondents were engaged as casual labourers. A significant transformation has been found in the present occupational status of the respondents. As this chapter focuses on their entrepreneurial activities at small, medium and large levels, it is significant to note that the Chamars/Ad-dharmis and Meghs have become big entrepreneurs. They have performed exceedingly well as compared to other dalit castes. The Chamars/Ad-dharmis have become leather goods industrialists, rawhide merchants, commission agents of animals and wholesalers of hides and skins, and owners of tanneries. The Meghs have become manufacturers of sports goods and surgical instruments. However, the persons from other caste groups have also become large businessmen, medium and petty shopkeepers. We would focus on the nature, type and extent of entrepreneurship among the respondents in the next section.

III
Entrepreneurial Activities of the Respondents

Nature of Entrepreneurship

The data on the castewise activities of the respondents have been given in Table 5.2, which clearly depicts that 26 different activities have been taken over by them representing large, medium and small entrepreneurship. Only five castes among the respondents, namely, Chamar/Ad-dharmi (51.88%), Megh (30.83%), Balmiki (7.52%), Mazabi (7.52%) and Dumna (2.25%) have taken to various entrepreneurial activities. It is significant to note that most of them have ventured mainly into those activities that have some association with their hereditary/traditional caste occupations.

The Chamars/Ad-dharmis have modified and diversified their hereditary skills in processing the hides and skins. It is significant to note that nearly 4.5 per cent of them have become industrialists, out of which nearly 3 per cent are manufacturing a variety of leather goods, such as leather garments, purses, belts, and tool-belts—a hundred per cent export product, while rest of them own shoe factories. A large proportion, i.e., 21 per cent, has become rawhide merchants, and nearly 2 per cent of them have become commission agents of leather. The rawhides are procured from different parts of Punjab. It is relevant to note that

Table 5.2

Castewise Entrepreneurial Activities

Entrepreneurial activities/caste	*Ad-dharmi*	*Balmiki*	*Megh/Kabir-panthi*	*Mazabi*	*Dumna*	*Total*
Leather goods industry	4 (5.80)	—	—	—	—	4 (3.00)
Surgical instruments manufacturing	—	—	8 (19.51)	—	—	8 (6.00)
Shoe factory	2 (2.90)	—	—	—	—	2 (1.50)
Hosiery goods	—	—	1 (2.44)	—	—	1 (.75)
Confectionary workshop	—	—	1 (2.44)	—	—	1 (.75)
Sports goods industry	—	—	9 (21.95)	—	—	9 (6.77)
Rawhides merchant	28 (40.58)	—	—	—	—	28 (21.05)
Leather commission agent	3 (4.34)	—	—	—	—	3 (2.25)
Property dealer	1 (1.45)	1 (10)	—	—	—	2 (1.50)
Saw mill	2 (2.90)	—	—	—	—	2 (1.50)
Running a school	1 (1.45)	—	—	—	—	1 (.75)
Leather goods shop	5 (7.25)	—	—	—	—	5 (3.76)
Readymade garments	1 (1.45)	1 (10)	1 (2.44)	—	—	3 (2.25)
Flourmill	—	—	2 (4.88)	—	—	2 (1.50)
General store	3 (4.34)	—	6 (14.63)	1 (10)	2 (66.67)	12 (9.03)

Cont'd...

Cont'd...

Karyana shop	2 (2.90)	4 (40)	6 (14.63)	5 (50)	—	17 (12.78)
Music shop	1 (1.45)	—	—	—	—	1 (.75)
Shoe shop	11 (15.94)	—	—	—	—	11 (8.28)
Tailoring	2 (2.90)	—	—	1 (10)	—	3 (2.25)
Electric goods repair shop	1 (1.45)	1 (10)	2 (4.88)	2 (20)	—	6 (4.52)
Mechanical works	1 (1.45)	2 (20)	2 (4.88)	—	1 (33.33)	6 (4.52)
Meat shop	—	—	—	1 (10)	—	1 (.75)
Telephone booth	1 (1.45)	—	—	—		1 (.75)
Barber shop	—	—	1 (2.44)	—	—	1 (.75)
Sweet shop	—	1 (10)	1 (2.44)	—	—	2 (1.50)
Vegetable shop	—	—	1 (2.44)	—	—	1 (.75)
Total	69 (51.88)	10 (7.52)	41 (30.83)	10 (7.52)	3 (2.25)	133 (100)

Figures in parentheses are percentages.

one truck full of rawhides is worth Rs 5–7 lakh and they deal with a large number of trucks in a day. There are also small traders who purchase the hides by pieces ranging from Rs 700 to Rs 1,100 per piece and after the processing the same are sold for Rs 1,500 to Rs 2,000 per piece mainly to cobblers/*mochis*. Excessive heat and cold usually perishes many animals. As the data were collected during the months of December–January, the rawhide merchants and agents were visibly busy and contended having a good season. This trade usually takes place in the mornings, because the trucks are allowed in the city during night times only. Also trucks loaded with rawhides produce foul smell. It was therefore natural for many small rawhides' traders, who have ample free time during the day, to simultaneously run side business such as music shops, DJ owners, cassettes recordings and PCO/STDs, while others are running shops of various leather goods—coats, jackets, purses, bags, belts, etc. They have experienced a transformation in their work, as they manufacture the leather goods in their tiny workshops and are selling the same by opening their own shopping outlets. They usually get the material from the leather complex from where they get pieces of waste leather that can be used for many other purposes, such as making sports goods—bats, balls, footballs, etc. Similarly, another 8 per cent are running shoe shops. Besides diversifying their hereditary skills, they have taken to diverse type of trading activities both at medium and low levels.

The Meghs are manufacturing surgical instruments (19.51%) and various sports goods in Jalandhar city. As discussed by Singh (2002), after settling at Jalandhar in 1947, they ventured into manufacturing surgical instruments (they were engaged as workers in this industry in Sialkot) at the small level some of which have gradually grown to the medium level industries. In surgical instruments they manufacture scissors of all sizes, pair of tongs, tweezers, saw and all other instruments which we usually observe lying just on the table of the doctor, or used for the dressing of the wounds. These instruments are made of nickel.

Jalandhar is famous for manufacturing the sports goods, such as cricket balls, footballs, cricket bats and hockey sticks, besides the boxing and cricket gloves and cricket pads. The Meghs are predominantly engaged in the sports goods manufacturing at different levels ranging from skilled workers to the entrepreneur. It is relevant to mention here that except for one all of them have evolved a unique system of manufacturing. They procure the raw material for the sports goods from international market which is quite expensive. For the small level unit owners, it is difficult to procure the raw material on their own. Therefore, some of the Khatris and Aroras of Jalandhar have started the business of importing the sports goods material, which they pass on to the Meghs who have the hereditary skills in manufacturing the same. They in turn employ the skilled workers and under their supervision and control they manufacture the goods. The whole family of the entrepreneur is engaged in it. They own a few machines, such as sewing machines, cutting and pressing and lock-in machines. We have included this unique case in the category of entrepreneurs though they get the raw material from the businessmen and they manufacture the goods according to their specifications. The production relations are quite similar to the putting-out production system of the west prior to the arrival of the industrial system. In their view, there is lot of variety with high degree of specialisation in the making of sports goods and it also involves teamwork. For instance, in the making of shuttlecocks, somebody cuts the wings, another puts them into a thread, and the third one fixes it into the cork. They get returns according to the work performed. For making a dozen shuttlecocks, they would get Rs 60. While for a football it is up to Rs 25 per ball and Rs 20 for the gloves. By the evening, the family usually is able to earn reasonably well out of which it also pays the wages to the hired workers and spends on the upkeep of the machines. Though most of their products are exported to foreign countries, but all of them fear the fierce competition from the Chinese made goods.

The Meghs have also become business entrepreneurs. They have started general stores and grocery shops, mechanical and electrical goods, running of flourmill and repair stores. A few of them are found running shops of hosiery and readymade garments, which is close to their caste occupation—weaving the cloth. A small number of them have also started sweets and vegetable shops in addition to the one who, by hiring quite a few of the migrant workers, was running a workshop for preparing wafers, chips, toffees and other types of fries, which he has been selling to the retailers who in turn were selling the same in the rural market. The Balmikis, Mazabis and Dumnas are the least mobile, as they have started small shops of readymade garments, grocery, tailoring, electrical, mechanical works and meat though there was an instance of a Balmiki engaged as a property dealer.

It is quite clear in the case of the Chamars/Ad-dharmis that their traditional skills still have relevance in the changing economic scenario. This also explains why this artisan group could survive the onslaught of industrial development. However, many persons engaged in traditional vegetable tanning feel that they are losing their work, which has been taken over by the tanneries. A respondent who was carrying on leather tanning[8] for the last fifty years narrated his experiences thus: "Earlier, 100 persons were engaged in this traditional work and now only ten persons are left in the work to carry on the activities. It has ceased to be profitable as was in the past, because people prefer to buy machine made goods". He further lamented that "in 1950 there were 90 units of leather tanning in Boota Mandi, but now only five units of traditional tanning are left and this change has occurred drastically during the last five years". In the tanneries, many of the Ad-dharmis have become workers though more than half of the workers were migrants who were involved in cleaning, peeling, and stitching of the hides. It means that in order to meet the demand of the work, the migrants are also attracted. Some of the Ad-dharmis have also become workers in sports goods industry located in another locality, Basti Nau in Jalandhar. It is significant to mention that many younger generation Ad-dharmis were interested in immigrating to foreign countries[9] and many of their relatives had already settled abroad.

If we trace their genealogy in entrepreneurship, we find that a majority of them maintained that their grandfathers and fathers were carrying the same kind of business. In many cases fathers were doing business along with them or they started the business at a small level and gradually it grew. Their fathers (76.56%) and grandfathers (65.62%) were also running the businesses and were carrying on different trading activities. The rest of the respondents' fathers and grandfathers were engaged in other economic activities. It clearly shows that there has been a considerable continuity in the entrepreneurial activities of the respondents across generations. It implies that some of the dalit families began an upward mobility quite early in the 20th century. Table 5.3, showing reasons for taking the new occupation, reveals that at both Amritsar and Jalandhar, the respondents found trade and business more profitable and they were interested in it. Also quite a few of them left their earlier occupation as it was stigmatised and no more fulfilled their needs.

Table 5.3

Reasons for Taking up New Occupation

Reasons	*Jalandhar*	*Amritsar*	*Total*
Earlier occupation stigmatised	11	8	19 (14.29)
Not profitable	4	3	7 (5.26)
Got training	5	1	6 (4.51)
Lost/left the job	1	2	3 (2.26)
Education	1	2	3 (2.26)
Interest and profit	20	18	38 (28.57)
Non availability of work	3	4	7 (5.26)
Modification and diversification of the traditional occupation	50	—	50 (37.59)
Total	95 (100)	38 (100)	133 (100)

Figures in parentheses are percentages.

Most of them mentioned that their new business was linked with their caste occupation. Therefore, it was an extension of their traditional work though in some of the cases their education and acquired training and skills enabled them to become entrepreneurs. When did this process actually take place? The change started occurring after the independence of the country. A slow process of change in their occupations carried over up to the late 1970s (15%), another 11.28 per cent changed the occupation in the next decade. The pace accelerated in the 1990s when it reached 33 per cent. The first five years of this century have already witnessed transformation in 26 per cent cases. There are 15 per cent such cases that did not respond to this question. Looking into the process of their transformation it distinctly appears to be the phenomenon of the 1980s and then it rapidly picks up at both the places when its proportion triples and the process further accelerates in this century.

Looking into their motivating factors to become entrepreneurs, it is clear from the data contained in Table 5.4 that in nearly 72 per cent of the respondents, it largely happened because of their self-realisation/awakening on the one hand and was a matter of their economic survival, on the other. Thus, their threatened existence forced them to respond to the wake up call. They prepared themselves to take initiative in trade or business, which hitherto was the monopoly of the traditional Khatri/Banya castes. How did they acquire the business know-how/acumen? How did they prepare themselves to take to new occupation? What kind of preparation did they make for taking up the business activities? It is relevant to mention that 32 per cent of the respondents from Jalandhar mentioned that it was their hereditary occupation and other 45 per cent believed that they had prior experience. Only in the case of 8 per cent of the respondents in Jalandhar and 10 per cent in Amritsar, it was either through education or vocational training. Accordingly, the source of learning the skill was hereditary (61%) in Jalandhar, whereas in Amritsar for majority (68.42%) the source of learning the skills was on-the-job/through experience and private apprenticeship (16%).[10]

Table 5.4

Sources of Motivation to become Entrepreneurs

Sources	*Jalandhar*	*Amritsar*	*Total*
Self-realisation/awakening	24	7	31 (23.31)
Economic survival	36	28	64 (48.12)
Hereditary occupation	34	3	37 (27.82)
Impact of reformers	1	—	1 (.75)
Total	95 (100)	38 (100)	133 (100)

Figures in parentheses are percentages.

Having the right kind of motivation and job experience is an essential condition to set up a business, but it is not sufficient to start an enterprise in the absence of financial resources. Question arises as to how they started their enterprises. Sixty per cent of the respondents from both the places invested money in their enterprises which they earned through other occupations. While the relatives and friends helped 8 per cent of them financially, 7 per cent got financial assistance from the banks and only two got the finance from a moneylender. Three of them in Amritsar had started their enterprises under some government scheme.

As we know, to begin with, the small enterprises start from the residential area itself and as the growth takes place, either the entrepreneurs go and live at better places as has happened with the entrepreneurs of Boota Mandi who shifted to posh area of the city, while others would move their enterprises to the main market to fetch more customers. Our data reveal that 55 per cent of them in Amritsar were running their enterprises from the residential area and others had moved to the main market. On the other hand, in Jalandhar 59 per cent moved to the main market and rest of them were running from their residential places. So far as the conditions of work were concerned, it was found that these entrepreneurs were working for long hours. Nearly 71 per cent of them were working between 9 and 12 hours a day for six days in a week with the rest for one day.

Since it is a well-established view that in business the relatives, friends and primordial ties play a very significant role, an attempt was made to find out the participation of family members in various entrepreneurial activities. It was found that in the case of 40 per cent respondents, none of their relatives was working with them. In the rest of the cases, father/uncle (15%), brother (16%), son (24%) and wife (5%) participated in all business activities. Besides the family members, nearly half of them have up to five employees. In the case of big enterprises, more than twenty persons are hired to perform various jobs ranging from managerial services to accountancy, supervision and other jobs done by attendants/helpers and labourers. One may get interested to know the caste background of these employees.

Are there some persons who belong to upper castes? Interestingly, 44 per cent of the entrepreneurs have hired the persons from their own caste. Other 8 per cent have had some of their employees belonging to their caste, while some belong to upper castes, and 3 per cent mentioned that some of their employees belonged to the same caste, while others belong to lower castes. There are 30 per cent such cases in which the respondents were either not aware of the caste background of their employees or they did not want to disclose it.

In the market economy, commodities are bought and sold on the basis of their quality and performance and the personal profiles of the buyers/sellers become irrelevant. In this context it is worthwhile to examine the caste background of the customers. We may expect that the customers would be mainly from various dalit castes. The data do not corroborate with the expectation, because 95 per cent of the respondents mentioned that they had customers belonging to different caste groups of the society—including the upper and lower castes. This process reflects the transformation of the rigid social structure. So far as the extent of expansion of their market was concerned, the entrepreneurs of Amritsar (97%) had their market locally except for 3 per cent who had market all over the state. In Jalandhar, 63 per cent of the respondents catered to the needs of the local market, 5 per cent had it all over the state from wherever they got the orders, 2 per cent had it up to the whole of North India, and the other 3 per cent had spread their market throughout the country. There were 19 per cent of respondents who had the export business in addition to having business throughout the country. Their main export products were shoes, leather purses, jackets, gloves, tool belts, workman's gloves, industrial equipment pouches, sports goods like football, balls, bats, shuttle cocks and surgical instruments and many other leather items depending upon the orders.

Looking into the pattern of their investment, both initial and present, it has been found that the respondents were non-responsive. For instance, all visible indicators reveal that the Chamars/Ad-dharmis in Boota Mandi of Jalandhar were by and large doing well in trade and business, but the information we could gather from them on their investments was highly understated. The pattern of their investment remained traditional as usual. They started the small business initially with a few thousand rupees arranged through their meagre resources. Gradually, following the pattern of 'save and invest' they have investments up to a few lakh rupees and presently, some of them (6%) have increased their investments up to crores of rupees.

In the case of Chamars/Ad-dharmis, the entrepreneurship is a rapidly emerging economic phenomenon where more than a quarter of their family members have also become entrepreneurs. Some of them are running businesses at the same level while others are doing it at a larger scale. It is relevant to explore that with the globalisation where privatisation and liberalisation of the market have prevailed upon, whether they introduced any changes in the business to be competitive with world market forces. And, what kind of problems they were facing as a result of it. A significant number of persons have not yet awakened to the call. They were continuing with the already existing set up. Very few among them have introduced changes in the techniques and mode of work, besides the change in the organisational set up. Their major worry has been competition—both internal and external. A large number of respondents feared from the local competition. Besides the competition from other big companies and MNCs, another large section of them fear the rising cost of the production and non-availability of the raw material as major hurdles. The main competition they are facing was from China, which has been aggressively pumping its goods into the Indian market. Besides the infrastructural hurdles only an insignificant number of persons faced problems due to their caste status.

IV
Profiles of Successful Entrepreneurs

This section presents a few cases of the process of mobility and modernity experienced by the scheduled castes. The cases presented here somehow reveal that though the process of their mobility has accelerated for the last few decades, yet their fathers and grandfathers had already paved the way to success for them. In all the cases, their grandfathers, some 80 years ago, moved out of the villages to the place where ample opportunities were available in their traditional work. With their sheer hard work, perseverance, business acumen and innovativeness, they have become multi-millionaires, political representatives, and socially mobile persons. Since there are two castes, viz., the Chamars/Ad-dharmis and the Meghs, who are predominant in our sample, it is relevant to take the case studies of these two caste groups from both Jalandhar and Amritsar. The Chamars/Ad-dharmis belong exclusively to Jalandhar, whereas among the Meghs two each from Jalandhar and Amritsar are presented.

Becoming of a Seth: Rich, Famous and Honourable

Seth Sat Pal, son of Seth Milkhi Ram, 50 years-old multi-millionaire is a rawhides merchant. He is educated up to higher secondary while his father was educated at primary level. He has five brothers and two sisters, who all are educated up to matriculate/higher secondary level. His six daughters and a son are graduates and one of his daughters is doing her masters. Besides being rawhides merchant his grandfather had an agency in Calcutta of manufacturing of bone china. The same agency was carried over by his father till the partition of the country. Also hunters from far off places were coming with their hunts to him to process and stuff the skins. People were coming even with the skins of tigers and lions, dears, stags, and python snakes.

Sat Pal owns a big palatial house beautifully decorated in a nearby posh colony where people with money and status from different castes live. He very proudly comments, "they all invite us to their family functions, as we are rich, powerful and politically well-knit". He also narrated the history of concentration of the Chamars in Boota Mandi. He described that earlier the scheduled castes did not have the right to get the registration of their houses done. There used to be Rajatnama (a kind of agreement) only and it was to be stamped by the Namberdar (the local village revenue collector). His grandfather being the Namberdar would put stamps on the papers of the scheduled castes without any hitch.

He has visited most of the foreign countries including England, Canada, Germany, USA, and Arabian countries. One of his daughters resides in Dubai. Here again, he narrates an occurrence. Ishwar Das, a dalit, who did his graduation from Lahore, was appointed Passport Officer in Shimla and during his tenure he liberally gave passports to dalits as a result of which a large number of Ad-dharmis could go to foreign countries.

Despite being so rich, he himself actively participates in all the activities of rawhides. His office and godown are situated in Boota Mandi. He comes to work early in the morning as most of the sale and purchase of rawhides takes place in the morning. Sat Pal removes his jacket and trousers and dressed in Kurta-Pyjama sits on the heap of rawhides with a note pad. Meanwhile, the workers start unloading the truck and simultaneously he starts counting the pieces. Sometimes, it is mixed skins of buffalo, goat, sheep and calf, while it is separately loaded. The hides come to this place from whole of Punjab and are sold to local tanneries and Muslim merchants from Tamil Nadu. He has such a good rapport with outside merchants that he would himself participate in auspicious ceremonies like Id, Bakrid, Ramadan, etc. Some people of the locality even commented that he had converted to Islam, which of course is not the case.

In his view, Boota Mandi is the capital of the scheduled castes. If any dalit has a problem/trouble, he can come here and seek the assistance. Lakhs of rupees are collected for the birthday celebrations of Guru Ravi Das with lot of fervour and gaiety. The sources reveal that on one day the liquor sale from Boota Mandi's shop goes up to Rs 7–8 lakh. He says that there is a sharp decline in the rawhide market due to high cost of electricity, bank rate of interest, high labour cost and competition from China. Chinese synthetic leather has captured half of the market. He comments that all parts of animals are useful—bones, teeth and skin—and out of total 10–15 per cent are consumed in India while 85 per cent is exported.

A Case of Inter-Generational Occupational and Social Mobility

Steven Kaler, a successful industrialist, a post-graduate, 35 years of age, calls Boota Mandi as his native place though his grandfather migrated to this place in the first decade of 20th century from a nearby town, Nakodar. His grandfather was the first post-graduate from this area, while his father could not complete graduation. He has five brothers and sisters. All of them are educated and are well placed. His wife is a civil servant. His grandfather moved to Calcutta where he worked and learnt new skills in tanning. He learnt the bag tanning, which was better than the indigenous way of tanning, and was later on improved to wet blue tanning. His grandfather became Seth in those days and after learning the technique himself he taught many people in Boota Mandi that technique. His father started his factory in 1925–28 and did a lot of business in finishing the hides. His father also moved to Calcutta in 1960 where he stayed for 15 years and afterwards resumed his business of rawhides, and semi-finished processing of skins. They have an ancestral house in Boota Mandi and all are living in the joint family. One of his brothers fought elections for three times as the BSP candidate.

After completing his post-graduation in the first position, he was offered a job of lecturer by the local college, but his father decided to put him to business. As the family has three factories, he moved to Delhi in 1990 to join his factory. This is an export unit where leather garments are manufactured. He remained there for seven years and then he came back and joined the tannery where rawhides are finished and the leather is exported and sold to other companies. He has a turnover of Rs 10 crore. He has a big tannery with all the modern machines and techniques. He has employed engineers and other technical personnel besides the skilled workers who belong to different caste groups. They produce finished leather. His company specialises in calf leather, which is very fine and soft, usually used in manufacturing hush puppies. They supply the finished leather in the international market and their biggest consumer is the USA and other big shoe factories such as *Drish* shoes etc. in India. Many sports goods industries also located at Jalandhar procure leather particularly for making footballs. Even football shoes are exported from here to East Europe, Ukraine, Austria and Germany. They are facing competition from China, Singapore, Taiwan and Malaysia with regard to finished leather.

In the 1950s, a modern shoe company—Bawa—now collaborating with Lotus under the brand name *Lotus Bawa* started by a Khatri family near the Boota Mandi. They had latest technology and many of the Chamars, who had hereditary skill in hides, were employed in their factory and learnt new skills and techniques in the process. It is mentioned that these people who earlier were the employees with Bawa are now running nearly half of the units. He believes that education, exposures to foreign countries and money have remained very important variables in their success. For the uplift of the scheduled castes, he suggests that the only way is through education. But unfortunately they can afford to go to government schools where teachers are from upper castes that do not have any interest in their development. For him caste is not an important issue but after a certain level class position becomes more important. He narrates that his father in his times used to face the stigma of caste but during his time, particularly in college, he along with other boys of his caste used to fight back. His family is virtually a mixed one. The relatives—daughters-in-law of the family—are from Brahmin, Jain and Khatri castes. With regard to questions on interreligious and intercaste marriages many of the respondents including Kaler are of the view that a scheduled caste boy is acceptable, they may get girls but nobody is accepting the scheduled caste girls for upper caste boys. That is why, they themselves encourage marriages within their own caste.

The Making of Rich and Powerful

N.K. Mahey, 42 years-old, and a matriculate is the senior Vice President of local Congress Committee. He was born at this place while his grandfather migrated from a nearby village some eighty years ago. Both his parents are illiterate. His relatives from the maternal side are well placed in various high status government jobs, such as in the Reserve Bank of India and the Indian foreign services. His grandfather and father were merchants of rawhides and were also getting the same processed through vegetable tanning. He carried on his inherited occupation, but now with the improvement in techniques and demand, he, in addition to rawhide business, specialises in wet blue tanning. His annual sales have risen to 2 crore rupees and his profit runs into lakhs. Nowadays majority of skilled workers in tanning industry are from Uttar Pradesh and Bihar, but belong to the Chamar caste. Their own young people are interested in going abroad.

In 1998 he constructed his own big house in a posh locality and has given his hereditary house in Boota Mandi on rent. His fathers' brother and their sons are settled in England for the last five decades where they are running an Indian restaurant. It is interesting to note that all those who have good business and are well-off have shifted out of the traditional house to the posh and the costliest localities where different caste groups of people are residing and whose standard of living and level of earnings by and large are same. The sight of their big houses, lavishly and tastefully decorated, forces one to treat class as more important than caste. He believes that their interpersonal relationship is possible only at Boota Mandi where they have to come to attend family and other community functions.

Mahey believes that it is through his personal efforts and hard work that he has become rich and powerful. He is very clear that leather business has a future and he wants his children to pursue their career by getting specialised degrees, such as B.Tech or M.Tech in leather. He like many others is not in favour of intercaste marriages and the reason he gave was that "we accept *others'* daughters, but they do not take *our* daughters through matrimonial alliances". Therefore, we discourage marriage with others, primarily the upper caste groups.

Enjoying the Economic and Political Status

Sardari Lal, 75 years-old, has been a councillor in the Municipal Corporation of Jalandhar's Bhargo Camp locality since 1980. He has education up to middle standard while his father was an illiterate. Two of his brothers are graduates while one brother is a law graduate. He belongs to the Megh caste and follows Arya Samaj religion. He fondly remembers Lala Ganga Ram of Sialkot who helped them to convert to Arya Samaj and whose birthday is celebrated with great fervour. His hereditary occupation is weaving, but now he runs a factory of surgical instruments and most of his products are exported. He learnt the skills on-the-job in a factory at Sialkot. As he did not know any other work after migrating to this place, he decided to start this work over here in 1949 with just three thousand rupees. He is amongst the pioneers who started manufacturing surgical instruments and now the entire industry of Jalandhar fulfils the 90 per cent requirements of the country. His son is also assisting him in his factory. He largely deals with the marketing of the products. His main exports are to England and the raw material is locally available. This industry is still labour intensive, as most of the work requires manual handling. His younger brother is also manufacturing surgical instruments for the last 20 years in the city. Since this work is labour intensive, it requires a constant supply of skilled workers and learning of the skills takes a long time, which is not possible for the migrant workers. Moreover, this skill is largely confined to the Meghs and they would like to protect the secrets of the craft. Thus, the major problem this industry is facing is of labour. Most of them have not yet mechanised their whole production process, which is forcing them to cope up with the shortage individually.

Sardari Lal has four sons and all of them are educated while one of them has done graduation and immigrated to England in 1980 on marriage basis. He has a big house with all modern amenities. His neighbours are Brahmins and he is of the view that the Meghs are ex-Brahmins who by virtue of lifting a dead cow were relegated to a lower position in the caste hierarchy.[11] At present, owing to the lack of education, they occupy a lower position in the caste hierarchy. He also points towards existing hierarchy amongst the dalits. Dalits is not a homogeneous, uniform category; rather, it is composite, heterogeneous category. As we have seen, the Ad-dharmis are doing much better than others. He refers to the case of present dalit mayor of the city who is an Ad-dharmi and he is not in anyway helping the Meghs.[12] Though there is an emergence of class within the castes, yet caste affiliations are very strong. Caste system prevails strongly amongst the dalits.

Story of a Successful Entrepreneur

Raj Paul Mahant, 70 years-old of the Megh caste residing in the Bhargo Camp locality of Jalandhar, migrated to this place in 1947 due to the Indo-Pak partition from Sialkot district of Pakistan. He has studied up to matriculation. He is a Kabirpanthi. It is relevant to mention that the Meghs follow three religions—Kabir-panth, Arya Samaj and Sikhism. Though his traditional caste occupation is weaving, but he has always remained engaged in the manufacturing of sports goods. His wife is illiterate, but one of his sons has got MBA degree and a daughter is post-graduate. Seven years ago two of his sons immigrated to Australia.

He was employed in a factory manufacturing sports goods in Sialkot. After being displaced from Sialkot, for some years in Jalandhar he continued to work in different factories till he decided to start his own work in 1967. Since he had the experience in the manufacturing of sports goods, he started a factory of his own. In the beginning it was a small venture, but now he has a large business and specialises in manufacturing a variety of sports items. To begin with, he invested Rs 4 lakh in his factory, which now has investment worth crores of rupees. His son helps him in keeping the accounts and also marketing the products. Like many other entrepreneurs he fears the competition from MNCs, particularly, the Chinese goods. He in fact has suffered a major loss in his profit due to it. He also mentioned that they supplied footballs to European countries for World Soccer 2006. Though one may expect the rise in demand for cricket and soccer balls within the country, yet he feels that the margin of profit is more in case of exports of the goods.

Two Cases of Amritsar

Bachan Lal, aged 35 years, resides in Haripura locality of Amritsar. He is a native of this place and is educated up to the primary level. He is Hindu and belongs to the Megh caste. His hereditary occupation is weaving and working on powerlooms. His father was a powerloom worker throughout his life. The powerloom work has been facing a serious setback for the last many years in Amritsar and he could not get regular employment. Being more enterprising he ventured into a small-scale business of his own where he has set up a confectionary workshop making toffees, fries, chips and wafers and all other kinds of fries for the retail market. He gets good orders for his products. He set up this business five years back when he took loan from a bank and started his own workshop. He has employed five skilled workers of his own caste and three migrant workers who work as helpers/attendants. Machines are installed and a group of 10–12 persons are working at one time. In spite of a good business he wants to have government job as in his view the government jobs would certainly improve the condition of the scheduled castes.

Rattan Kumar Bhagat of Haripura locality in Amritsar city is of 48 years of age and belongs to the migrant family to this place from Sialkot district. He has done graduation while his father was matriculate and his mother is also educated. He has three brothers, one of them is post-graduate, and another has done B.Ed and is a teacher while the third brother is an employee in the Punjab State Electricity Board. He runs a flourmill on the main road, and earns up to 12,000 per month. He has two sons and a daughter who all are studying; one is doing B.Tech from Jalandhar, while the other is in college. His wife is a graduate and is a housewife as well. He has a good house with all luxury items. He is of the view that illiteracy is responsible for his caste's lower position in the caste hierarchy. "That is why I am very conscious about the education of my children", he told. He is also an active member of the SC/ST cell of Amritsar.

Before making concluding observations of general kind on the basis of both quantitative and qualitative data, a comment on Jalandhar is required. Besides the leather industry, Jalandhar is also famous for sports goods industry. As informed by the elderly people that the sports industry before partition was located in Sialkot (Pakistan) that later shifted to both Jalandhar and Meerut. In Jalandhar it is mainly concentrated in Basti Danishmanda. Most of the sports goods are exported to England, America and Germany. The goods are boxing and batting gloves, cricket bat and ball, carom and chessboards, hockey skeleton and its lower part. Most of these people are the scheduled castes from

Megh caste. Similarly, Jalandhar is known for manufacturing surgical instruments. These people have also migrated from Pakistan[13] due to partition and are now settled in Basti Nau. Many of the Chamars from Boota Mandi, who could not become entrepreneurs, have become skilled workers in sports goods industries.

By way of concluding the discussion on the scheduled caste entrepreneurs, we may discern certain features of their entrepreneurship. Boota Mandi, a native place of most of the entrepreneurs, has emerged as the most important economic and political centre of Chamars/Ad-dharmis in Punjab. Here, every day, trade of rawhides worth lakhs of rupees takes place. Now trading of rawhides has concentrated in the hands of big merchants who after its semi-finishing and processing send it to far-off places. The traditional vegetable tanning of the hides has been replaced by the use of modern chemicals and techniques to make it compatible in the national and international market. The enterprising Ad-dharmis finding the avenues modified their skills and ventured into leather and sports goods industries. They have started manufacturing leather garments, shoes, accessories, and other export-oriented products. As a result of their entrepreneurship, they have been able to earn enough profits, which raised their standard of living and they moved up in the social hierarchy. All those artisans who could not cope up with the brunt of industrialisation have become skilled workers in leather-based industries, tanneries and sports industries. As a commodity, leather still has relevance, usefulness and demand owing to which the Ad-dharmis find much demand for their work. Due to their affluence as a result of entrepreneurship and political representation, they have started asserting their caste status at a corporate level. Assuming their caste differences, they have been able to get equal economic status, political representation and social mobility in the society though the phenomenon is not uniform.

Notes

1. The review of top 50 business houses of India, 1997, shows that out of the top ten, four are Marwaris, three are Punjabi, one Gujarati and one is Parsi besides one Chettiar. The following table shows the caste and community background of top 50 entrepreneurs in 1997. All the major religious groups are represented, i.e., Hindu, Sikh, Jain, Muslim, Christian and Parsi:

Community/Caste/Religious group	*Number*
Marwari	19
Punjabi	8
Gujarati	7
Parsi	3
Sindhi	2
Brahmin	3
Chettiars	2
Malayali Nair	1
Syrian Christian	1
Unknown	4

Source: Dorin, (2004).

2. Indian business is overwhelmingly owned and managed by the families (nearly 99%). It is not surprising. As even in the US, the most professionalised nation, more than 80 per cent of all enterprises are family run. The family resources, networks and primordial ties have been found most conducive to run the businesses of all kinds.
3. Available information depicts the instances of non-traditional trading castes taking to entrepreneurial activities. But it is important to know who these persons are? They are from high castes—Brahmins and dominant agriculturalist castes—who could get technical and professional education, and had enough of resources and networks required to venture into business.
4. For instance, the development of railways was seen indispensable to handle dissent in a large country.
5. A detailed discussion of alternative strategies has been done in the introductory chapter.
6. An entrepreneur is an individual (could be a group or an organisation) who owns, organises and controls any business activity and the activity, which he performs, may be called entrepreneurship. An entrepreneur is an innovative, creative, decisive and moderate risk-taker. He provides leadership with a task-result orientation and a sharp vision for the future.
7. Boota Mandi is North India's major market of rawhides and skins.

8. The rawhides of animals—buffalo, bullock, sheep, goat—procured through the agents are then processed. The hides are soaked in limewater with little soda for fifteen days in summers and one month in winter. The skin exfoliates and hairs and flesh are removed with scraper. They are then again put in limewater to clean it further. After being taken out they are rubbed, scrapped, cleaned and washed with clean water. Now, it is ready for tanning. There are mainly two processes that are followed in Boota Mandi. One is traditional vegetable tanning, that is, it is soaked with tan barks (babul) and is coloured with the twigs of kiker/cheel. The second is wet blue tanning, which is largely carried on with the help of chemicals usually used in tanneries. Both these processes go on for a few days followed by various methods of drying the leather.
9. Immigration has been found a predominant trend amongst these people. In fact, it has been remarked by many respondents that "change in our people has occurred due to immigration particularly with the money sent by them they could improve upon their living conditions".
10. The people were really amused when we asked them the source of learning the skills. Their reply was that "in Boota Mandi nobody learns the skills in handling the leather". Perhaps, they meant to say that it is in their blood and veins.
11. One is reminded of Delie´ge (1999) who has collected a considerable number of myths of origin of the dalits in which they claim to be Brahmins and owing to their handling of dead cow, they became untouchables. Gupta (2000) mentions his personal field experience in a South Gujarat village of an old Dubla woman who narrated the similar kind of story of origin of her caste's low status.
12. At the time of data collection S.K. Mahey was the mayor of Jalandhar city.
13. Singh's (2002) study of surgical instruments industry at Jalandhar also traces its history that the city of Sialkot (Pakistan) emerged as the centre of two important industries, the sports and surgical instruments manufacturing and these industries flourished during the two world wars period. The religious composition of the workforce reveals that 85 per cent were Muslims, 10 per cent were Hindus, and remaining 5 per cent were Christians and others. The owners belonged to upper castes and workers were from lower castes. It may be that these workers having experience and training ventured into manufacturing at a small level.

6

Paradox of Changing Dalits

This chapter brings out the paradox involved in the changes that are taking place among the Punjabi dalits. Since independence of the country in 1947, the forces that have been unleashed to ameliorate the conditions of the dalits in the country include conscious efforts on the part of the Indian government through constitutional provisions, reservation policy and special development programmes. Besides, there have been numerous instances of the efforts of the dalits through political mobilisation towards the improvement in their conditions. All these efforts towards changing the socio-economic conditions of the dalits for the better were destined to have a bearing on the caste system as such. This chapter aims at examining whether at the empirical level all these forces have made an impact with regard to the conditions of the dalits in Punjab. Equally important is to see whether the caste system has been eroded at different levels of the life of the dalits. Ghurye (1969) identifies the following features of caste system: segmental division of society, hierarchy, restriction on feeding and social intercourse, civil and religious disabilities and privileges of the different sections, lack of unrestricted choice of occupation, and restrictions on marriage.

This chapter is the revised version of the article published in the *Economic and Political Weekly*, XLIII(41), October 11, 2008 under the title "Understanding the Paradox of Changing Dalits in Punjab".

In certain respects the present study is linked with the identification and examination of certain dimensions of the caste system that are expected to change.

In the specific context of Punjab, which consists of 28.85 per cent of dalits in the population of the state, attempts have been made to identify certain key dimensions of change in the socio-economic conditions of the dalits (Jodhka, 2002; Judge, 2004). Based on the empirical research are some of the dimensions that have been examined by these two studies, namely, social ecology, religious places and economic conditions.[1] Equal attention is needed for investigation into the issues that are linked with the way the dalits construct their orientation towards change with regard to caste endogamy and caste identity. It may be added that caste system and casteism are equally important in impeding and facilitating certain basic changes in the system. The caste system is marked by the political and economic asymmetry and cultural plurality, whereas casteism is the system of ideas and principles that justify the system. As a system of justificatory ideas, casteism is embedded in the minds and the world-view of the people and may persist longer than the changes in the caste system through education, occupation and social ecology. Keeping in view the central features of caste, following aspects have been examined here to map changing (and not so changing) contours of Punjabi dalits: social ecology, hereditary occupations, religious places, caste endogamy and caste identity.

Social Ecology

The social organisation of physical space is one of the most important dimensions of understanding change in a society. The notion of ghetto basically emerged in the Jewish context in which it was understood that the Jewish population was confined to overcrowded localities. There were historical reasons for the emergence of the phenomenon and in the post-holocaust period, the situation has somewhat undergone a change with regard to the Jews. The ghettos, however, have not disappeared. It has been found that ethnic communities and blacks live in ghettos. Two reasons are ascribed to the process, namely, low income level and socio-cultural/racial distinction from the dominant population of the community. The latter is so strong that it tends to become the only reason for ghettoisation. An informal network develops in which the dominant community creates a system of checks to ensure the denial of entry to the 'others' as residents in the locality. In other words, the social organisation of space occurs in such a manner that the economic dimension in the determination of physical space gets marginalised.[2]

It is important to mention that little attempts have been made to understand the social organisation of the urban physical space with regard to the dalits. One of the ways of understanding the social organisation of space is to know the caste background of the neighbours. It is important to begin our discussion on the neighbourhood patterns. Table 6.1 shows the caste background of the two neighbours of the respondents. It may be informed that the respondents were asked to reveal the caste background of the two neighbours residing on both sides of their houses.

Table 6.1
Caste Background of Two Neighbours

Caste Status	*Urban*	*Rural*	*Total*
Same caste	736 (92.00)	766 (95.75)	1,502 (93.88)
Both higher	7 (0.87)	15 (1.88)	22 (1.37)
One same, one higher	48 (6.00)	18 (2.25)	66 (4.12)
One high, one lower	9 (1.13)	1 (0.12)	10 (0.63)
Total	800 (100)	800 (100)	1600 (100)

Figures in parentheses are columnwise percentages.

It is evident from the data that the respondents have been predominantly living in the neighbourhood where the people of their own caste reside. The fact that draws an immediate attention is that even the cities are not free from caste-based neighbourhoods.[3] The social ecology of the urban areas acquires importance because of the general understanding that cities are the modern centres where caste distinctions do not operate in the market situation. Possession of capital and goods for exchange becomes the most crucial basis of interaction. So far as market is concerned, the similar principles may operate though the western experiences of immigrants reveal that even the market situation could create exclusionary practices on the basis of the birth-ascribed features. Influenced by the city life in the western countries and repulsed by the Indian village life, Dr B.R. Ambedkar did not only create a critique of the village republic the way it was constructed by the British administrators (Moon, 1989), but also asked the dalits to leave the villages and go to the cities (Virdi, 2004). However, as Judge and Bal (2005) have argued, the migration of the Punjabi dalits did not follow any such perception that their conditions would undergo change nor was there any increase in migration rate. Even now, the proportion of the dalits in the urban areas is less than that of villages in Punjab. As a matter of fact, the expanding cities enveloped the villages that made many of them city dwellers. The city represented to them as a place where market situation could be clearly separated from the residential space. In the case of residential spaces the concentration of dalits in certain localities was obvious. It is evident from Table 6.2 that in the case of 18 wards in Amritsar and 21 wards in Jalandhar the percentages of the scheduled castes were above their population percentage in the state ranging from 29 to 85 per cent.

Table 6.2

Number of Wards According to the Percentage of the Scheduled Castes in Amritsar and Jalandhar

Percentage of the Scheduled Castes	*Amritsar*		*Jalandhar*	
	Number of Wards	*Percentage of Wards*	*Number of Wards*	*Percentage of Wards*
0–5	16	25.81	6	10.91
6–10	11	17.74	4	7.27
11–20	13	20.97	18	32.73
21–30	4	6.45	6	10.91
31–50	16	25.81	13	23.64
51–85	2	3.22	8	14.55
Total	62	100	55	100

Source: Census of India, 2001.

There was another fact that came to the fore in the case of all the localities in both the cities. In Amritsar Balmikis in Gowal Mandi, Mazabis in Guru ki Wadali and Meghs in Haripura localities were in overwhelming majority. In Jalandhar Ad-dharmis/ Chamars in Boota Mandi and Mithapur, Balmikis in Ali Mohalla and Meghs in Bhargo Camp were living in their own caste localities. Such a situation in which social ecology corresponds with the caste background, the classical notion of the city is seriously challenged. The political economy perspective would lead us to the understanding that such a situation could have emerged due to the overlapping of class and caste positions. It may be partially true. But it was seen that even in the case of economic mobility, as is illustrated by the Ad-dharmis of Boota Mandi, social ecology is marginally altered. The prosperous Ad-dharmi respondents had then started living in the adjoining Guru Tegh Bahadur Nagar in palatial houses, but the locality was still mainly inhabited by the Ad-dharmis. Sharma (2003), in his study of small town in Rajasthan, has shown how the social organisation of space is closely associated with the caste. There is likelihood of small town showing the ecological segregation of castes. The interesting aspect is that all the big cities of Punjab like Amritsar, Ludhiana and Jalandhar have the same kind of pattern. Such a pattern organises the social space in such a way that the perpetuation of caste identities seems highly probable. At the same time, such aggregation of people of one caste at one place facilitates the mobilisation process.

The villages hardly provide any changed scenario with regard to the settlement pattern. As is evident from the Table 6.1, the dalits continue to have segregated houses. In the villages of Amritsar district the dalit locality is called *Thathi*, whereas in the Jalandhar district it is called *Chamarhli* (Judge, 2004). It is already informed by many scholars that location of the dalit colony is towards the south-western direction of the village.

Hereditary Occupations

Occupational mobility is an indicator of both economic and social mobility. Sociologists take occupation, education and income as the determining variables of the class position of the individuals and families. Occupations do not change in a makeshift manner, as there is a definite relationship between economic change and emergence of new occupations that require certain skills. Capitalism/industrialisation is accredited with creating occupational diversification that broke their traditional hereditary character. In the case of India, caste and occupation had close proximity to the extent that even the caste names could reveal the nature of hereditary occupation. For example, Chamar, Mochi, Bhangi, Lohar and Nai are some of the caste names that are the names of the occupations as well. In the existential world of village India, the caste name invariably invoked the occupation. For example, Jat meant peasant, Saini meant vegetable grower, Julaha meant weaver, and so on. Obviously, the arrival of capitalism with new occupations that required education was destined to break the correspondence between caste and occupation. There has been a lot of diversification of occupations in the case of the dalits, which was clear from the fact that the dalit respondents were involved in as many as 46 occupations in both the urban and rural areas. However, everything has not changed. As is evident from Table 6.3, still 28.75 per cent of the dalit respondents in the cities and 49.5 per cent respondents in villages are involved in the 'low' occupations. In the case of male respondents, sweeping and agricultural labour, and in the case of female respondents and male respondents' wives, to be a maidservant or domestic help was the predominant occupation. It was also noticed that many of them tried to conceal their occupation. Table 6.3 also shows that among the respondents 17.12 per cent in urban areas and 9.66 per cent in rural areas did not have any occupation. A probe into the matter revealed that they had actually concealed the fact that they were either sweepers or maidservants. Understanding the change and persistence in the occupations of the dalits depends upon how we look into the matter with regard to the occupational characteristics of the respondents. One way of understanding is that there has been a definite change in occupations as there is some percentage (about 6%) of the respondents occupying high prestige occupations as they are industrialists, big traders, big landowners etc., whereas the other would be that some of the respondents are still located at the lowest occupational ladder.

Table 6.3
Categorywise Occupational Levels of the Respondents

Occupational Prestige Category	*Urban*	*Rural*	*Total*
I	25 (3.12)	16 (2.00)	41 (2.56)
II	46 (5.75)	9 (1.12)	55 (3.44)
III	8 (1.00)	1 (0.12)	9 (0.56)
IV	58 (7.25)	20 (2.20)	78 (4.73)
V	171 (21.38)	147 (18.38)	318 (19.69)
VI	124 (15.50)	133 (16.62)	257 (16.06)
VII	231 (28.88)	396 (49.50)	627 (39.18)
VIII/NA	137 (17.12)	78 (9.66)	215 (13.43)
Total	800 (100)	800 (100)	1,600 (100)

Figures in parentheses are columnwise percentages.

It is also plausible to point out that there is class formation among the dalits. Another way of looking at the empirical reality is that change is taking place in a gradual manner. It may be reminded that dalit castes have also been at the bottom of class structure. They were involved in polluting occupations. There is a difference between caste and class mobility. One is related with status enhancement, whereas the other is economic. In the case of dalits the two were combined and it could be anticipated that if the dalits stopped doing the defiling occupations their status could undergo change. Such a change has limitedly occurred though the nexus between caste and occupation has been fractured.

Deliége (1999: 144) understands the occupational aspect of the dalits of India from the perspective of change and continuity thus: "The position of Untouchables within the economic life of India is a combination of change and continuity… . They are still poor, oppressed, and relegated to manual labour, menial tasks and agricultural work". The change that we can witness in the case of the dalit respondents in this study is confined to the individual families. Though the political mobilisation of the dalits, as we have seen in Chapter 4, creates horizontal solidarity within caste, but in economic terms there is an obvious absence of corporate mobility.

Religious Places

All the respondents, irrespective of their rural or urban backgrounds, were assertive with regard to one query, namely, whether they were allowed to enter the temple/Gurdwara belonging to upper dominant castes. What was that assertion? There was no restriction on their entering into any temple/Gurdwara. Rather, many Balmiki respondents in both Amritsar and Jalandhar cities laughed at the query and declared that "nobody could dare stop us from entering a temple". However, the dalits of Punjab are struggling against the upper dominant castes, particularly the Jat Sikhs, on issues concerning the religious places. The issue of religious places has historically evolved into two phases. First, it was related with the right to worship in the temple. Ambedkar led dalits to make forced entry in the temples in the initial stages of his struggle for equality of worship (Zelliot, 1970). The second stage began when the dalits either had their own religious places or they started 'reclaiming' the religious places. So far as the issue of entry in the religious places is concerned, it has almost been settled. Jodhka (2002) and Judge (2004) noted the practice of not allowing dalits to enter the temple in Patiala district. Otherwise, such instances in Punjab are rare.

The issue of religious place is an important dimension of intercaste interaction and caste system. One dimension of religious place is what Jodhka (2002) has pointed in his study wherein he noted that in 51 villages the dalits had their own Gurdwaras though the number of such villages could be much more. It has been informed that there are 10,000 dalit Gurdwaras in Punjab (Webster, 2007). The implication of this finding could be very interesting. One of the interpretations of this empirical fact is that the dalits are not allowed to enter the Gurdwara and in protest they have constructed their Gurdwaras (Jodhka, 2002; Bal, 2007). The practice of untouchability at religious places among the Sikhs is almost absent in the Doaba region comprised of Jalandhar, Hoshiarpur, Kapurthala and Nawan Shahar districts of Punjab.[4] There is a widely held belief that there is caste hierarchy among the Sikhs though the caste system lacks rigidity that is prevalent in other parts of the country. The existence of the practice of untouchability is invariably denied.

There is another way of understanding the issue of the separate Gurdwaras. Let us look into the historical and anthropological dimensions of the religious places and their caste-linked existence in Punjab, which, metaphorically, could be stated as "a religious place of one's own". Historically, the social structure of a Punjab village typically followed the all-India pattern in which the entire social organisation revolved around agriculture. In the present Punjab, prominent castes of landowners are Jat, Saini, Lobana, Kamboh, Mahaton, Khatri and Brahmin. The numerically preponderant and politically dominant caste among them in Punjab is that of the Jats. Since more information is available on the Jats, it is appropriate to select them for illustration of the entire issue. The Jat landowner traditionally had a large number of service castes that were related to him under the *jajmani* system. As the entire village community depended on the agrarian production for its existence and livelihood, the landowner occupied the central position so far as the economic life of the village was concerned (Judge, 2002). All other castes were limited in number except for the agricultural workers who invariably belonged to the dalit castes. This fact of the existence of the service castes and their proportion in the population of village has been noticed by Dirks (2002: 76) in India in general, "No village contained more than a few of these families ...". The construction of a religious place in such a situation could only be done under the patronage of the landowning caste.

Most of the villages in the Doaba region in particular are without any temple despite the presence of the Hindus, whereas all the Jat Sikh villages have Gurdwaras. Over a period of time, the number of Gurdwaras in the villages has begun to rise. There is a general impression that there is a caste basis of the Gurdwaras. Each caste tends to have its own Gurdwara. Such an observation is partially true, because the caste-based settlement of the people in the villages would show this as a fact like two plus two is four. To understand the reality underneath, one may raise a question as to why the Jats have more Gurdwaras if the logic of caste basis is taken into consideration. As a matter of fact, there is a Gurdwara for each locality called *patti* in Punjab. The dalits having their separate Gurdwara is a recent phenomenon. The Green Revolution process brought changes in the Punjab economy and society. The arrival of migrant labour pushed the dalits out of the agrarian relations, as they were displaced as agricultural labourers due to which they had to go to the cities to look for work in non-agriculture sector. The conditions of the dalits relatively improved and they diverted their attention to the affairs of God. The Balmikis constructed their temples, Ad-dharmis their Ravi Das temples and Ramdasias and Mazabis their Gurdwaras. It should be reminded that so long as a caste community is poverty-stricken and its members are finding it difficult to make both ends meet, it may not be able to construct its temple or Gurdwara in the village. In the case of the Sikhs it is quite probable that during the period of the Singh Sabha movement the construction of Gurdwaras according to the locality and caste was discouraged due to its claim of equality among all the Sikhs. The conversion of Jats to Sikhism in the Doaba region at the turn of the 20th century due to the proselytising activities of the Singh Sabha movement leads us to raise a pertinent question, that is, what did happen to their religious places of worship? Since the Jats as the landowning class had a Hindu past, it was expected that they might have constructed some temples. We know that so far as the ancestor worship is concerned those places are still intact. However, the question of temples relating the Jats to their Hindu past has not been settled. There are two possibilities. One, there were no temples of any sort in the villages of Punjab. Second, the Jats after their conversion to Sikhism appropriated the sacred place as well.

So far as the Doaba region of Punjab is concerned, the above argument holds well, but the Majha region in which the Amritsar district falls, presents a little different case. During data collection the Mazabi respondents of Amritsar district reported caste-based exclusion of religious practices. Many of them told that the upper caste Sikhs did not allow them to carry the sacred book to their residence for purpose of performing various rituals/ceremonies with the pretext that their houses were dirty. Similar information was given by the Mazabis of Guru ki

Wadali—an erstwhile village that has become a locality of Amritsar city. No such thing was reported in Jalandhar district. The respondents while asked about the religious places informed that their villages had common Gurdwara(s). It clearly shows that certain degree of religious exclusion is practised in certain parts of Punjab.

It may be reiterated that a separate Gurdwara does not imply that its existence is a consequence of exclusion. There are three kinds of Gurdwaras of the Sikhs. First, there are historical Gurdwaras. These Gurdwaras are linked with the Sikh Gurus or certain events in the Sikh history. The Golden Temple in Amritsar is one of the examples of historical Gurdwaras. The second type of Gurdwaras is what has now become very well known religious place, namely deras.[5] The deras are a part of both the Hindu and the Sikh religious traditions of Punjab; and if we take Sufi tradition into consideration, then it is possible to put even the places of Sufi fakirs as a part of the same tradition. In the early medieval period, there were deras of Nath yogis. Sufi saints had their own deras. After the emergence of Sikhism, the institution of deras could be found among them. The Nirmalas and the Udasis had their own deras. These deras have also come into conflict with the mainstream religious establishments. Recently, deras have also become the places of contestation among different castes. The third kind of Gurdwaras is called the social Gurdwaras. It is here that the issue of untouchability or exclusion has emerged. In the ten villages studied in Amritsar and Jalandhar districts there was no historical Gurdwara.

A question was asked about the number of religious places and their responses are given in Table 6.4. It is interesting to note that there was a clear-cut distinction between the Amritsar and Jalandhar villages. In the case of Amritsar villages, the predominant trend was to identify the Gurdwara with the caste, whereas the villages in Jalandhar district had the predominance of common Gurdwaras. Notably, the Mazabis and Balmikis abound in terms of religious places though the largest number of religious places in villages was that of Muslim Sufi saints. The Muslims of the eastern part of Punjab migrated to the western part of Punjab after partition accompanied by a large-scale

Table 6.4

Number of Religious Places According to Village

Village	*Jat/Kamboh Gurdwara*	*Common Gurdwara*	*Mazabi Gurdwara*	*Hindu Temple*	*Dera*	*Sufi Pir's Tomb*	*Church*	*Balmiki Temple*	*Ravi Das Mandir*
District Amritsar									
Gehri	1	—	1	2	1	1	—	—	—
Galowali	1	—	—	1	—	—	1	1	—
Bhoma	1	—	3	1	—	2	—	1	—
Kotli/Dhole / Shah	1	1	1	—	—	1	—	—	—
Nawan Pind	1	—	1	1	—	1	—	1	—
District Jalandhar									
Udhowal	—	2	—	—	—	8	—	1	—
Adharman	—	1	—	1	—	—	2	1	—
Mahem	—	2	—	—	1	2	—	1	1
Bath	—	1	—	—	1	16	—	—	—
Mehtpur	2	—	—	—	—	8	—	1	1
Total	7	7	6	6	3	39	3	7	2

communal riots in 1947. However, it may be noted that the signs of mosques in villages have disappeared, but the tombs of Sufi saints are well maintained. It implies that the composite religious tradition of Punjab has not been completely eliminated by the efforts at constructing singular religious tradition.

Finally, the existence of a distinct religious space is a different dimension from that of a separate Gurdwara if the issue implicates the religious practices of the dalits. Comparing to the ideal typical constructions of the deprivation of dalits from the religious observance within the great tradition of Hinduism, the existence of a place of worship is a major transformation in the conditions of the dalits. The issue of Gurdwara is complex because some of the respondents reported discrimination that comes close to untouchability. However, the construction of Gurdwara on the part of the Sikh dalits could be considered in terms of their ability to do so. Caste was always present and strong even earlier. It was not what Gupta (2007) thinks about rising tide of caste consciousness, rather the change is with regard to the rising awareness of the dalit castes and its manifestation in the public sphere. The political economy of the religious place indicates that there is some improvement in the economic conditions of the dalits. The existence of separate Gurdwaras for different castes presents an illustration of untouchability as well as of dalit mobility however limited it may be.[6]

The cremation of the dead is both a religious and caste-specific phenomenon. Recent occurrence provides an understanding that despite the egalitarian principles of Sikhism, the Jat Sikhs prevail upon others as a caste group to deny the right to the dalits to cremate their deceased in the cremation ground. The story, as appeared in the *Times of India,* is as follows:

> Many in the country face evil of caste-based discrimination in their lives. But in the case a Dalit woman in Bholuwala (Ferozepur district) village, it continued even after she died. The dominant Jat Sikhs of the village did not let Dalit families cremate the body of Gurdial Kaur, 75, at the cremation ground on Tuesday. She had died on Monday.

> Jat Sikhs of the village allegedly threw out the pyre wood from the cremation ground following which the situation got tense.
>
> District administration sent the local executive magistrate and SHO of Ghal Khurd police station to the spot to diffuse the tension and persuade Dalits to cremate the body at vacant land in the village late on Tuesday afternoon.
>
> According to sources, some Jat Sikh families had filed a case some time back to prevent Dalits from using the common cremation ground of the village, but the court had issued a stay order in favour of Dalits pending final decision (Sharma, 2008: 2).

Predictably, the Jat Sikhs denied having received such a stay order. Interestingly, this was not first time that such a thing had happened. The reason for taking up this case which has recently occurred is that both the dalits involved in the case and the Jats have common religion. Since they are Sikhs and Sikhism, as per the claims of the SGPC (Shiromani Gurdwara Parbandhak Committee) and other ideologues of Sikhism, does not recognise caste, the dalit Sikhs should be sharing the common cremation ground. Notably, the entire incident involves two more parties, namely, police and the judiciary and both the parties are not aiming at punishing the offenders but negotiating the intercaste interaction. One is reminded of the murder of a dalit constable in 1991 in Maharashtra who was killed because he entered the Hanuman temple. The way the police and judiciary negotiated the interaction between the dalits and the upper castes was not strictly in the light of the Prevention of Atrocities Against Scheduled Castes and Scheduled Tribes Act of 1989 (Rao, 2005).

Endogamy and Intercaste Marriages

Caste endogamy is regarded as one of the major citadels on which the caste system rests. The notions and practice of hypergamy and hypogamy existed in Indian tradition, but these are more a part of mythological stories than reporting of the actual cases. The combination of caste endogamy and the institution of arranged marriage have made the caste almost a permanent system. Caste endogamy is also a result of a principle that has transformed into a mentality. Vovelle (1990: 12) defines the examination of mentality "as the study of the mediations and of the dialectical relationship between the objective conditions of human life and the ways in which people narrate it, and even live it". In a way the notion of mentality implicates the combination of objective and subjective conditions with a difference from traditional understanding of this dichotomy. The subjective condition is understood in terms of how it is narrated/told. It seems natural to think, expect and anticipate that the people belonging to the lower castes whose stake is in the demolition and destruction of the system would support intercaste marriages. Caste identity presupposes endogamy in spite of the fact that in patriarchal system the identity of the male is more important than that of the female. The respondents were asked to give their views on the significance of caste endogamy if they thought that it was desirable. Table 6.5 indicates the views of the respondents with regard to caste endogamy.

Table 6.5
Significance of Caste Endogamy

Significance	*Urban*	*Rural*	*Total*
Tradition	518 (64.75)	775 (96.88)	1,293 (80.82)
Better understanding	20 (2.50)	1 (0.12)	21 (1.31)
Family support	24 (3.00)	1 (0.12)	25 (1.56)
Doesnot matter	233 (29.12)	23 (2.88)	256 (16.00)
Donot know	5 (0.63)	—	5 (0.31)
Total	800 (100)	800 (100)	1,600 (100)

Figures in parentheses are columnwise percentages.

It is obvious that the dalit respondents living in villages overwhelmingly considered caste endogamy significant in comparison to the urban dalits. Less than 3 per cent rural respondents stated that caste did not matter, whereas 29.12 per cent respondents in urban areas viewed endogamy as insignificant. In both the settings there was a comprehensive support for the caste endogamy. Tradition is a vague word and the caste system could be plausibly regarded as a part of Indian tradition. Since the rural respondents were supporting caste endogamy, it was clear that this view cut across caste lines. On the other hand, a considerable proportion of the urban respondents regarded caste endogamy as not significant. Interestingly, the preference for caste endogamy and disapproval of intercaste marriage are embedded in the caste system. It is evident from the fact that in a survey conducted by the Centre for the Study of Developing Societies for the IBN-CNN in January 2006, it was found that 74 per cent of the respondents disapproved intercaste marriages (c.f. Luce, 2006). From the overall perspective the urban respondents were slightly less than the respondents belonging to different castes mentioned above in not approving the intercaste marriages. Keeping in view this fact, it was thought proper to see the castewise responses of the urban respondents. The conjecture was that the Ad-dharmis and Meghs would be more tilted towards the insignificance of caste endogamy than those of Mazabis and Balmikis.

The data presented in Table 6.6 show clearly that among those who emphasised traditions as the reason for supporting caste endogamy the majority belonged to the Mazabi, Chamar/Ad-dharmi and Sansi castes. At the same time, among the Chamar/Ad-dharmi respondents one-fourth of them considered the issue unimportant. If we take a closer look at this table and see how each caste is distributed in terms of its emphasis on caste endogamy, then, only Meghs could be considered to be more amenable to marginalise caste endogamy. In that sense, our conjecture is partially substantiated. The second main caste that does not attach crucial significance to caste endogamy is that of the Balmikis. It may be concluded that the dalit castes consider caste endogamy significant as a part of the tradition.

Related with the issue of endogamy is the event of intercaste marriage. The respondents were asked whether intercaste marriages could end the caste system. The responses are given in Table 6.7. Again there were rural-urban differences in the sense that 96 per cent of the urban respondents were of the view that it was possible to end the caste system if intercaste marriages come into practice. Interestingly, most of the rural respondents showed

Table 6.6

Castewise Responses Why Caste Endogamy is Significant (Urban)

Responses/Caste	*Tradition*	*Better understanding between spouses*	*Family support*	*Doesn't matter*	*No response*	*Total*
Ad-dharmi/Chamar	150 (71.77)	2 (0.95)	4 (1.91)	53 (25.36)	—	209 (100)
Megh/Kabirpanthi	141 (57.08)	4 (1.62)	9 (3.64)	92 (37.25)	1 (0.40)	247(100)
Balmiki	109 (56.48)	7 (3.63)	5 (2.59)	71 (36.78)	1 (0.52)	193 (100)
Mazabi	108 (80.59)	7 (5.22)	5 (3.73)	13 (9.70)	1 (0.75)	134 (100)
Sansi	3 (100)	—	—	—	—	3 (100)
Dumna	7 (50.00)	—	1 (7.14)	4 (28.57)	2 (14.29)	14 (100)
Total	518 (64.75)	20 (2.50)	24 (3.00)	233 (29.12)	5 (0.62)	800 (100)

Figures in parentheses are rowwise percentages.

Table 6.7
Whether Intercaste Marriages can End Caste System

Response	*Urban*	*Rural*	*Total*
Possible	384 (96.00)	16 (4.00)	400 (100)
Desirable	107 (52.45)	97 (47.55)	204 (100)
Caste is deep-rooted	140 (92.72)	11 (7.28)	151 (100)
Such marriages do not succeed	36 (92.31)	3 (7.69)	39 (100)
Undecided	133 (16.50)	673 (83.50)	806 (100)
Total	800 (50.00)	800 (50.00)	1,600 (100)

Figures in parentheses are rowwise percentages.

uncertainty with regard to the intercaste marriages. They remained undecided about the issue. The urban respondents were more articulated with regard to the issue than the rural respondents. One of the reasons was that all the urban respondents had the personal knowledge of such marriages due to which many of them thought that such marriages never succeeded or caste was deep-rooted. An attempt was also made to further examine the urban respondents. Table 6.8 presents castewise data on whether intercaste marriages could end the caste system. Predictably, the Ad-dharmis, Meghs, Sansis and Dumnas constituted the major proportion of those respondents who were of the view that it was possible to end the caste system through intercaste marriages. The Balmikis and Mazabis were not sure of the proposition.

In terms of education, as shown in Table 6.9, the responses were predictable. It is widely understood that education creates awareness. Obviously, educated respondents in the urban areas considered the proposition as a possibility. It may be further reminded that even the educated respondents were not wholeheartedly supporting the view.

The issue of intercaste marriage has wider ramifications. In a society in which modern institutions provide space for interaction among people belonging to different castes, there is always a possibility of certain frequency of intercaste marriages. The issue is also related with how the other caste groups

Table 6.8

Castewise Responses to Whether Intercaste Marriages can End Caste System (Urban)

Responses/Caste	*Possible*	*Desirable*	*Caste is deep rooted*	*Such marriages don't succeed*	*No response*	*Total*
Ad-dharmi/Chamar	125 (59.81)	25 (11.96)	17 (8.13)	9 (4.31)	33 (15.79)	209 (100)
Megh/Kabirpanthi	138 (55.87)	38 (15.38)	35 (14.17)	2 (0.81)	34 (13.76)	247 (100)
Balmiki	71 (36.79)	28 (14.51)	52 (26.94)	9 (4.66)	33 (17.10)	193 (100)
Mazabi	40 (29.85)	16 (11.94)	32 (23.88)	15 (11.19)	31 (23.13)	134 (100)
Sansi	3 (100)	—	—	—	—	3 (100)
Dumna	7 (50.00)	—	4 (28.57)	1 (7.14)	2 (14.28)	14 (100)
Total	384 (48.00)	107 (13.38)	140 (17.50)	36(4.50)	133 (16.62)	800 (100)

Figures in parentheses are rowwise percentages

understand it. The following news may not represent the frequently occurring incident but such cases appear once in a while:

> This is what they feared the most. Despite filing a writ in Punjab and Haryana High Court for security, a couple—Ashwani Kumar and Baljeet Kaur—were murdered by the girl's relatives—a punishment for marrying against her family's wishes.
>
> Ashwani, a Valmiki, and Baljeet, a Jat, belonged to Rauli village falling under Mehtpur police station. (*The Sunday Tribune*, July 15, 2007, p. 1)

The case refers to the area in Jalandhar district from where the sample of villages was drawn for the present study. In contrast to the Amritsar district, the dalits of Jalandhar district, as we have seen, have done well in different walks of life. However, the upper caste dominant Jats do not think so. There is still another issue with regard to intercaste marriages. Can we look at the possibility of intercaste marriages among the dalits? The same rule applies here also. The caste hierarchy among the dalits prevents any possibility of breaking caste barriers through intercaste marriages (Judge, 2002).

However, it is equally important to know the actual cases of intercaste marriages in which at least one of the couple is from any dalit caste. Table 6.10 gives the data on the cases of intercaste marriages in which dalits were involved. The data could be interpreted in various ways of which three seem plausible. Let us first look into the dominant pattern. A majority of cases (56.35%) reported of intercaste marriages are that of between a dalit boy and non-dalit girl. One of the reasons of this fact could be that since the dalit boys are socially more mobile than dalit girls owing to the factor of patriarchy, the mobile and educated dalits could marry from the upper castes. An illustration of this could be given of the family of Steven Kaler in Boota Mandi, Jalandhar who is a factory owner. The castes of the wives of his three brothers are Brahmin, upper caste Jain and Khatri. Secondly, in some cases, the girls belong to the backward classes like Nai and Jheer where the differences in the positions in the caste hierarchy

Table 6.9

Intermarriages as a Means to End the Caste System according to the Education of the Respondents (Urban)

Response/Education	*Possible*	*Desirable*	*Caste is Deep rooted*	*Such marriages Don't succeed*	*No Response*	*Total*
Illiterate	28 (7.29)	11 (10.28)	33 (23.57)	11 (30.56)	30 (22.56)	113 (14.12)
Literate	11 (2.86)	2 (1.87)	8 (5.71)	3 (8.33)	4 (3.01)	28 (3.50)
Primary	55 (14.32)	21 (19.63)	24 (17.14)	5 (13.89)	25 (18.80)	130 (16.25)
Middle	59 (15.36)	16 (14.95)	36 (25.71)	4 (11.11)	21 (15.78)	136 (17.00)
Matriculation	99 (25.78)	35 (32.72)	28 (20.00)	7 (19.44)	37 (27.82)	206 (25.75)
+2	53 (13.81)	12 (11.21)	4 (2.86)	3 (8.33)	9 (6.77)	80 (10.00)
College/Graduate	53 (13.81)	7 (6.54)	5 (3.57)	–	5 (3.76)	71 (8.88)
Post-graduate	7 (1.82)	2 (1.87)	–	–	2 (1.50)	11 (1.38)
Diploma/Professional Degree	19 (4.95)	1 (0.93)	2 (1.43)	3 (8.33)	–	25 (3.12)
Total	384 (100)	107 (100)	140 (100)	36 (100)	133 (100)	800 (100)

Figures in parentheses are columnwise percentages.

could not have evoked hostile response. Thirdly, the cases of non-dalit girl marrying a dalit boy are invariably controversial and the family of the girl opposes it. The conflict tends to keep the case alive in memory. On the other hand, a dalit girl marrying a non-dalit boy makes the girl invisible as she leaves the locality and there is not much reaction to such cases. After sometime, the case is forgotten. However, it is clear that despite all preferences for cast endogamy and reactions against intercaste marriages, the change is also taking place. However, the general response of the dalit respondents regarding intercaste marriage had been negative.

Table 6.10

Incidences of Intercaste Marriages Involving Dalits

Caste status of the couple	*Amritsar*	*Amritsar District*	*Jalandhar*	*Jalandhar District*	*Total*
Boy dalit, girl dalit	13 (27.66)	3 (25.00)	8 (17.78)	3 (13.63)	27 (21.43)
Boy dalit, girl non-dalit	20 (42.55)	7 (58.33)	32 (71.11)	12 (54.55)	71 (56.35)
Boy non-dalit, girl dalit	14 (29.79)	2 (16.67)	5 (11.11)	7 (31.82)	28 (22.22)
Total	47 (37.30) (100)	12 (9.53)	45 (35.71) (100)	22 (17.46) (100)	126 (100) (100)

Figures in parentheses are columnwise percentages.

Dalit Identity

The project to end the caste system seems to have lost direction in the face of tradition and resilience of the caste. The defining features of caste clearly showed that the attack on caste has to take place from all fronts if it were to be wiped out. If the caste differences do not disappear or wither away with all round efforts, then, the next logical question is what is to be done? Is it possible to end a system that has been in existence for centuries with the stroke of a pen or micro-level efforts? Sociologists would argue against such a possibility with vehemence. The case of Punjabi dalits with regard to all these issues cannot be seen in isolation from the dalits in India as such. At present, there are three areas in which the dalit-centric issues are raised in such a manner that one is constantly reminded of the powerful prevalence of caste existence in India. The first is related to the question of dalit politics in the formal structure of the Indian polity in which dalit identity is articulated. The second is the emergence of dalit literature within which autobiography as the genre is also being used to articulate the life experience of the dalits. The third aspect is the entry of the dalit issues in the social sciences in such a way that questions are being raised whether social theory is egalitarian enough to handle the dalit experience. Let us discuss these issues in little more detail to understand how the same situate the question of the end of the caste system in a paradox.

Politics of Dalit Identity

One of the preconditions of the abolition of the caste system is the end of all caste-based identities. One of the numerous castes of Punjab is that of the Jats. They are also the dominant caste in the villages. They boast of their Jat identity—the fact that could be gauged from the number of Punjabi songs, which may be more than one hundred where the mention of Jat is made. Similarly, the graffiti written on four-wheelers like trucks in particular would show the arrogant Jat displaying himself. The most popular graffiti is *Putt Jattan De* (Sons of Jats). No other caste group has made such a proud and arrogant mention of itself in the public space in Punjab. Recently, the similar trend could be found among the Chamars of Punjab, as is evident from the following graffiti: *Putt Chamaran De* (Sons of Chamars), then 'Chamar Power'. However, the following graffiti behind a truck is notable for its identity assertion: *Awen Bharam ne Mutiaran de, Marhi neet rakhade munde Chamaran de* (Young women are mistaken in thinking that the Chamar boys have evil intentions). One important issue is that why the Chamars are asserting their caste identity. These assertions are absent among the Balmikis, Mazabis, Sansis or Bazigars. Two decades back 'Chamar' as a signifier could have evoked protest as it meant an offence. The reason seems simple. The Chamars are the most mobile in terms of economic and political aspects of their existence. At the same time, all the Chamars may not necessarily showing off their caste identity. Such examples may be rare, but present before us a different trend in caste issue. There has been a rise in the caste assertion and it is not from the upper caste Jats where it was always present. The dalits have begun to assert their caste identity. The contemporary political scenario is also favourable towards such assertion. Mayawati's coming to power in Uttar Pradesh is an important aspect of this assertion. Whatever might be her political strategy, she essentially represents dalits. The present is marked by the perpetuation of caste in which the politics of numbers has led to a situation where it is in the interest of the dalits to articulate, manifest and maintain their caste identities.

Dalit Literature

We may now turn to the most creative and dynamic dimension of the construction of dalit identity, that is, dalit literature. Nagaraj (1993: 61) identifies certain salient features of the dalit literature. According to him, "it explores the world of the untouchables and other humiliated castes, although the word 'Dalit' means the oppressed in general". More important is the fact that it is the creation of members of the dalit castes, which radically alters the structure of emotions. Moreover, the young generation who are involved in it are militant and they reject the Hindu society completely. As a result, one finds tremendous intensity of emotions in the dalit literature. Punalekar (2001: 214–15) holds the similar views, when he observes, "Dalit writers themselves are either victims of or witness to social inequities and violence. Some have direct or indirect links with social, political and cultural organisations of Dalits. A few among them are staunch social activists and often use literature as a vehicle to propagate their views on Dalit identity and prevailing social consciousness".

Owing to intense emotional expression of the experience of atrocities and other forms of discrimination, a considerable number of dalit writers have written their autobiographies. Gaikwad (1992), Valmiki (1998), Moon (2002), Das (2006) and Malagatti (2007) could be mentioned as some representative writings of the dalits belonging to the genre of autobiography. As a matter of fact, these writings are first-person narratives of the existential conditions of the dalits. Shah (2001), Punalekar (2001) and Nagaraj (1993), to mention few, have analysed dalit writings in Marathi and Kannada. Dalit literature is an emerging phenomenon in Punjabi. Lal (2004) and Bharti (2004) have tried to show that the Punjabi literature has shown sensitivity towards the dalit issues though both of them forget to mention "Jug Badal Gaya" (The Epoch Has Changed)—a novel written by Sohan Singh Sital in which a dalit becomes one of the main characters. Since we have already defined the features of dalit literature, it is important to mention that Lal and Bharti examine those works in which the dalits are objects of aesthetic concerns. The dalit literature has made its presence felt in poetry where some prominent poets have made the subjective experience as the central motif of the poetry. Sirsa (2008) has noted a large number of emerging dalit poets though he begins with some earlier poets who were dalits. Two of them were Naxalite poets, namely, Sant Ram Udasi and Lal Singh Dil. Only the latter began to write poetry towards the end of his life which could be put in the category of dalit literature. Novel and short stories are rarely written. Only recently Des Raj Kali and Bhagwant Rasoolpuri have begun to make their presence felt in short stories. In the field of autobiography, the only serious effort that has drawn the attention of everybody is "Chhangia Rukh" by Balbir Madhopuri. One may argue that as a part of the construction of dalit identity and bringing to the fore the subjective experience, the dalit literature is emerging as a powerful movement in Punjab. However, unlike rest of India, it has not definitely shifted to Buddhism by rejecting Hinduism. Rasoolpuri's (2008) short story "Jarhan" has unambiguously shown how the Hindu past mediated through Guru Ravi Das prevails upon the minds of the Punjabi Chamar.

Social Science and Dalit Experience

As a part of dalit identity construction, the literature is not the only medium through which dalitism is getting constructed. Guru (2002: 5003) argues that "Indian social science represents a pernicious divide between theoretical Brahmins and empirical

Shudras". He goes on to argue that privileged status of theory in relation to empirical research is not a simple process as it is also related to who is privileged to do theory and who is condemned to do empirical research. In a way this divide in which most of the intellectual elites are concentrated in Delhi also represents intellectual hierarchies. The conditions in which the dalits, tribals and OBCs have been living for centuries were devoid of freedom without which no social group can do theory. Most interestingly, Guru (ibid.: 5007) also regards that claim as ontological blindness according to which "non-dalits have an innate inability to comprehend dalit reality because of their different social location. Thus, although dalits do not generate any theory, their research can always contain some valuable theoretical insights, their experience alone can illuminate aspects of human relations". He strongly argues that the dalit intellectuals should go for theory instead of becoming objects in somebody else's formulations.

The dalits, according to Guru, need theory as social necessity and inner necessity as well. Therefore, the project of theory building must not only be based on universal principles of oppression and exclusion but on the combination of specific subjectivities of the dalits. The argument seems quite convincing. Interestingly, when a large number of dalit organisations and intellectuals were combining their voices for the acceptance of correspondence of caste with race in the UN conference mentioned earlier in the beginning of this work, they were essentially looking for an already established theory. Blacks have already done it. The notion of negritude, as articulated by Césaire and given attention by Fanon, makes it clear that collectivity at the bottom of society has been looking for abstract conceptualisations to articulate its own autonomy.[7] The most important condition of doing theory is that it should be understood and handled by every member of the collectivity. In the process of doing theory of such a kind there would be reinforcement of certain identities, which the logic of universal principle of equality may not find suitable. The divide between empirical research and theory is an artificial construction, because the relation between the two is dialectical and discursive in most of the cases. Social sciences (should) move from facts to theory and again to facts and the process is going on. Claimants of privilege simply because they are doing theory are basically parasites on the empirical research done by others. Sarukkai (2007: 4048), following Habermas, comments on Guru's basic premise of experience of suffering and exclusive right of the sufferer to theorise it, "In fact, the crucial point here is that experience cannot dictate authorship. Habermas' theory is for us—namely, those who have not participated in that experience. It is we, who are outside this experience in all sorts of ways, who can build upon this theorisation".[8] Guha (2003: 1122) has made the following interesting point on the question of the nature of debates in Indian society:

> Thus, in 2003, one can speak meaningfully of two distinct discourses: one conducted within India, one conducted outside but apparently on India. These discourses have different inflections, different theoretical orientations, different purposes. Also, for the most part, different and largely overlapping casts of characters. Thus Indians living and working in India write primarily in Indian journals and (increasingly) foreign scholars write primarily in journals published in north America.
>
> The separation of the two discourses comes home most powerfully when one reads dissertations produced in America, which often tend to be ignorant of relevant Indian literature in the field, while quoting to excess works of social theory which seem to have little bearing on the dissertation's themes.

Guha's remarks are important in many ways, but here, we may just point out that first of all Guru has failed to make a distinction between the nature of these two discourses and secondly, he could not identify the essential marginal position of Indian social sciences in theorisation at the global level.

It is clear from the discussion of dalit identity, the way it has manifested itself through politics, literature and social sciences that there is a need to have certain specific ingredients for the egalitarian discourse. Political and cultural reproduction of dalit identity would both be of pragmatic and transformative nature without ending the caste system. It would be pragmatic in the backdrop of how and to what extent it is useful to articulate dalit identity for demanding a share in the resources, whereas it would be transformative because it questions the legitimacy of privileging other collective identities. Essentially, the politics and culture of identity in the case of dalits should be aimed at confronting and contesting hegemonic discourse.

In the end of the chapter, let us conclude by starting from Marx (1973: 146), who wrote, "Men make their own history, but not of their own free will; not under circumstances they themselves have chosen but under the given and inherited circumstances with which they are directly confronted. The tradition of the dead generations weighs like a nightmare on the minds of the living". There is no revolution that can bring about a complete break from the past traditions, practices, customs, mores, etc. The ethnic upsurge in Europe after the collapse of Soviet Union has given boost to the idea of persistence of certain identities. That is why, it is said that "more things change, more they remain the same". It is not simply a matter of confronting the idea of change with a certain set of continuities, but an issue of understanding why certain elements of the structure persist after basic changes have taken place. The question is why we should expect the change to take place in every aspect of social life. It is quite possible and probable that certain changes and continuities may pass each other by. Or certain formations may remain functional in the changing social reality.

Despite all these complexities involved in expecting that certain changes would always be followed by the introduction of certain forces consciously or otherwise, it seems empirically convenient to argue that it is possible to predict change. It is equally difficult to ascertain and identify various aspects of society that would undergo change. Therefore, the safest bet is to argue that there is no predictable pattern of change of society rather than going for empirical projections. Change certainly is an integral part of the society. As the positivist understanding and expectation is a part of sociological tradition that has dominated over the years, there has been a tendency to understand change as an effect of certain causes. The reason why certain aspects of the society do not change quickly could be examined and understood. Owing to these reasons the issues of change have been examined with the help of empirical data that tend to suggest that there are strong reasons to argue that change does not take place uniformly in all aspects of social life. The basic premise of the contention is that change is in the nature of society, but the kind of change that is occurring in Indian society does not break away from the basic fabric that constitutes it.

Findings of the empirical study point towards the paradox of change in the case of dalits. At the level of caste system inequalities and exclusion continue to show their existence the evidence of which could be ascertained on the basis of data on social ecology, occupation and access to religious places. Secondly, at the level of casteism as a world-view, the dalits are unable to construct the plausibility of a society without caste. The relevance and indispensability of caste in marriage have been largely accepted by them though there are apprehensions that without ending caste endogamy the caste may not disappear. Articulation of dalit identity for political gains in the electoral process is again the important issue of concern. From the perspective of the dalits the end of caste system is the most radical change that could be thought of. The traditions, however, do not allow the dalits to emerge as a homogenous category. Casteism is powerfully embedded in the collective consciousness of the dalits as a result of which their orientation towards the caste system is ambivalent. For them, the caste system is oppressive due to discrimination, exclusion, exploitation and untouchability, but, at the same time, it situates them in the system as a collective identity. Their desire is to end all kinds of discrimination, oppression and exclusion, but not the caste system. It is an instance of deep-rooted internalisation of a world-view—a process of reification in which like the Marxian market and relations emerging from that caste becomes a natural, absolute and ahistorical fact for the members of the society. Whereas the need of the hour is to think of Indian society without caste, the possibility of caste differences without inequality seems real.

Notes

1. Jodhka (2002) has examined the issue of untouchability by further probing into the issues like access to village streets, sharing of

drinking water sources, unclean occupation, practice of untouchability in modern institutions, police behaviour, etc.

2. There could be exception to the general rule in the sense that in the class society some rich Blacks, such as Oprah Winfrey, may be living in the posh and white dominated neighbourhood.
3. Judge and Bal (2005) have shown how the organisation of the social space in Amritsar and Jalandhar cities in the case of the dalits exhibits strong association with caste.
4. The following empirical observation may be important in understanding how untouchability has declined in the Doaba region: In village Ajram in Hoshiarpur district there are three Gurdwaras out of which one belongs to the Jats and the other non-dalit castes, and two to the Ad-dharmis. When the authors attended a Bhog ceremony in the Gurdwara meant for the Jats and other non-dalits, it was interesting to find that the priest belonged to the Julaha caste. This priest was a stopgap arrangement, because the Gurdwara priest was unwell and he belonged to the Mazabi caste. The person who prepared the *langar* (community food) belonged to the Ad-dharmi caste. On top of that, the women who were cooking *chapattis* belonged to the Bazigar caste.
5. Recently, clashes between Sikhs and the followers of Sacha Sauda sect have made the word 'Dera' common.
6. The issue of religious places provides for varying interpretation largely due to the complexity involved in the situation. Having a separate Gurdwara thus could also be understood as "assertion for autonomy" as stated by Jodhka (2002) though religious communities tend to construct horizontal solidarity unless there are internal sectarian fissions.
7. Aime′ Césaire was Fanon's teacher and his influence could be seen in the writings of Fanon. There is some similarity between the concept of negritude and the present dalit assertion of identity. Zahar (1974: 64) argues that negritude may be "understood as a reaction to the racist colonialist ideology of white superiority. By emphasising black authenticity it turns against the cultural self-alienation of the colonised and instils in them an awareness of their own historical and cultural tradition which embraces an awareness of all deformation suffered at the hand of colonialism". If we look at the way the dalits are asserting their identity and through autobiographical accounts the dalit intellectuals are arguing for the autonomy of their experiences there seems to be certain common grounds between the two at the level of collective self-understanding.
8. The reference here is to the Nazi holocaust.

7

Conclusions

The present study was conducted from the perspective of alternative strategies of change among the scheduled castes. The scheduled castes in India, also called as dalits, constitute a significant minority of the society. They suffered from disabilities, oppressions and exploitation due to their birth-ascribed status. The colonial intervention brought renaissance in certain parts of the country that began to question the legitimacy of keeping them at the lowest rungs of the society. The post-colonial state undertook affirmative actions in order to ameliorate their conditions. They also made their efforts in this direction by organising and struggling to end various discriminations. Any study of the scheduled castes is an attempt to contribute towards ending the caste-based inequality. The significance of the present study is two-fold. First, it assesses the level of change that has occurred among them by taking into consideration key variables that are universally recognised as markers of change. Secondly, it examines and identifies the areas that have not undergone change at the expected level.

The sample size (1,600) was reasonably large and the major attempt was to map the rural and urban differences owing to which the data have been presented for rural and urban respondents separately. Still another issue that was operationalised for examination was the caste differentiation among the scheduled castes. Most of the data were lopsided, in the sense that properties exhibited in most tables were strongly in favour of one element of the whole. Therefore, it was possible to draw conclusions without applying statistical tests of association and correlation. It is thus important, in the end, to bring out issues that provide us an understanding about the present and probable immediate future of the conditions of the scheduled castes in Punjab. The subsequent discussion about the changing conditions of the scheduled castes in Punjab is based on the findings of the study.

As asserted in the first chapter, the sample drawn was highly representative of the number of the scheduled castes as all the major castes, namely, Chamar/Ad-dharmi, Megh, Balmiki, Mazabi and others were included in the sample. However, there was one limitation with regard to the representative character of the sample, that is, it covered only two of the three regions of Punjab. Therefore, it may be stated that whereas the sample was representative of the castes as it covers numerically the most preponderant castes, there was absence of complete regional representations. However, the issue is not that serious due to three factors. First, geographically, Punjab is a small state without any serious spatial variations. Second, the religious features of the three regions do not show much distinctiveness among the dalits and the dominant castes. Thirdly, the numerical preponderance of dalit castes does not show any distinctive pattern in the third region that has not been included for study. In the light of these facts, it may be argued that the sample could reasonably provide a general understanding of the dalits of Punjab.

The issue of social mobility among the dalits has remained central in any discourse on social inequality in India. The concept of social mobility in India has different context and paradigm from that of the West. In the West the concept of social mobility was understood in terms of the movement of people in the occupational and income hierarchy, whereas in India social mobility implicates the context in which it is studied. Caste mobility has not been simply a movement along the income and occupational lines. It has been inseparably linked with status improvement of the underprivileged castes as a result of various alternative strategies. The present study focused on four major areas that have been understood as the central dimensions of understanding dalit mobility in Punjab. One of the dimensions, namely, emigration, is specific to the Punjabi dalits, whereas other dimensions are general and could be applicable to the dalits all over India. The changes examined in the four dimensions were consequences of various strategies that have been discussed in detail in the introductory chapter. Important findings of the study with regard to the four dimensions have been presented in the subsequent discussion.

There are 37 scheduled castes in Punjab, out of which seven castes were represented in the sample. The socio-economic profile of the respondents clearly showed that there are caste divisions among the scheduled castes in relation to the level of various changes. All the castes did not show uniform pattern. The emergence of economic inequality within castes came out sharply. Interestingly, the dalits are also divided along caste lines. The support to the caste endogamy among them amply demonstrated that there are differences among the dalits on caste basis. In a certain sense, it may seem truism, as it is well known even to the layman that caste hierarchy and differences exist among the dalit castes. The relevance of this issue is with regard to the construction of dalit identity independent of caste heterogeneity among them.

The findings pertaining to the education and occupational changes provide a mixed scenario, because there is change in the educational levels of dalits across generations. The literacy rate has gone up manifold in three generations. At the same time, education as a vehicle of occupational mobility has not come out strongly due to the low proportion of highly educated dalits. Thus, it is interesting to note that the occupational diversity is not a direct result of educational mobility; rather, the changes in the Punjabi society have given rise to occupational diversification. The meeting point of education and occupation is limited in terms of the former being the factor. However, an increase in the overall literacy rate must have led to certain changes in consciousness and political process. Predictably, the urban dalits have fared much better than the rural dalits in terms of all criteria related to education and occupation. Dalits of Jalandhar city and villages of Jalandhar district are better placed in relation to all aspects of socio-economic levels and education. In terms of castewise distribution of the respondents, the Chamars/ Ad-dharmis and Meghs are more educated and occupationally better placed than the Balmikis, Mazabis and others. These two castes have also done well in terms of going for high-prestige occupations.

The issue of empowerment has been the most complex of all as the earlier studies have maintained that there is a positive relationship between political mobilisation and status improvement. It has already been pointed out that in the case of the dalits the concept of social mobility corresponds with the improvement of status in which economic and political dimensions are enabling variables. The organisational struggles are as important as the improvement in economic conditions, for both are not simply the ends in themselves, but rather means to an end, which in the class society may seem an abstract goal. The end is to improve social status. It was found that the intercaste contestations are taking place only in Jalandhar. The Chamars/Ad-dharmis of Boota Mandi have effectively used their resources and organisation to capture not only power at the local level, but they are also striving towards the pan-Indian dalit unity. All other dalit castes have not effectively exploited opportunities that have been offered to them by the constitutional amendments (73rd and 74th). Despite the fact that the Mazabis were sarpanchas of certain villages in Amritsar district, but there is no evidence of their experiencing the empowerment. In most of the cases they are confronting with the landowners, who largely belong to the Jat caste.

International migration is the unique feature of the dalits of Punjab. No other state has as many dalits in the Indian diaspora as Punjab has. A large number of the dalits immigrated to English-speaking western countries after independence, which was estimated to be 10 per cent of the total migration to England by some experts. Again, the magnitude of international migration is largely confined to the Jalandhar district. The Chamars/Ad-dharmis have gone to these countries. The emigration to the foreign countries has contributed towards the rise in the standard of living and quality of life, but more importantly, it has infused the dalits with a sense of equality among human beings. The western experience of social equality where no caste system prevails and also a sense of sharing the same level of class position with the non-dalit Punjabis have provided the dalit diaspora a context for contributing to the cause of their brethren in Punjab. The migration of dalits to the Gulf countries has also contributed to the inculcation of a belief among them that it is possible to improve one's conditions through emigration.

There is low percentage of dalits who are involved in entrepreneurial activities. There is hardly any presence of entrepreneurs among the rural respondents, whereas in the case of urban areas Jalandhar has done far better than Amritsar. Interestingly, two castes have shown entrepreneurial acumen, namely, the Chamars/Ad-dharmis and the Meghs. Both the caste groups have excelled in the ventures in which their forefathers were involved. The Chamars/Ad-dharmis have done very well in the rawhide trade at Boota Mandi. Some of them have improved upon their traditional activity by starting leather goods industry. The Meghs of Jalandhar are involved in the manufacturing of sports goods and surgical instruments. Interestingly, the Meghs of Amritsar have not shown the level of entrepreneurial skill comparable to their caste brethren of Jalandhar. It is quite clear that as a matter of fact, there is one caste that has remained the most mobile, namely, Chamars/Ad-dharmis. Secondly, it is the dalits of Jalandhar, both urban and rural, who have fared better than those of Amritsar. It may be added here that Jalandhar is part of the Doaba region. What applies to the dalits of Jalandhar is also applicable to the Doaba region.

The last chapter was aimed at untangling the issue of change and continuity with the help of data. In contrast to the previous chapters that mapped the changing dimensions of the dalit status, the focus in this chapter was to identify the areas of no change or slow change. Continuity was examined as a problematic with regard to the essential features of the caste system. The findings are quite in favour of continuity in certain areas of the lives of dalits. They are still living in single caste localities in the cities. In villages their locality is separated from the non-dalits. Still most of them are engaged in their traditional or low status occupations though these occupations are no more as polluting as these were earlier. There is an articulation of caste identity, which has contributed to the political and social construction of exclusion. Most of them think that caste endogamy is the best option and intercaste marriages create many problems. There is also an emergence of assertion of Chamar identity. The celebration of dalithood is preventing them to break their own caste barriers.

The present study also throws up theoretical challenge with regard to understanding change among the dalits of Punjab. What are the ingredients of this challenge? Let us begin by pointing out what makes the change among the dalits a unique phenomenon to necessitate certain theoretical issues to be raised. The major challenge is related with the uneven nature of transformation. It is quite clear that beginning is made through certain changes in the economy followed by political mobilisation. Though the Chamars/Ad-dharmis are at the forefront of the change for better, but it is equally important to notice that there are poor families among them. Has the improvement in a section of the Chamars/Ad-dharmis led to the improvement in the status of those who have been left behind in economic terms? Have the dalits challenged the existing set-up of the caste system? The answer seems to be negative. The dialectics of change among the dalits points towards contrary trends to the modernist discourse of equality. It defies all notions of change from tradition to modernity. In the Marxist sense, we do not have any indication that ultimately class inequality would remain the most important form of social inequality in face of homogenising forces of capitalism. Class inequality has taken roots in the Indian society and has begun to become visible in the form of consumption patterns. However, caste is showing no signs of disappearance. Contrary to largely held views that the upper castes perpetuate caste inequality through the exercise of power, it has been found that the dalits are asserting their caste identity in the public sphere. They are equally against intercaste marriages. Some of the dalit castes insist on their identity. If the lowest of the low tend to perpetuate caste, then, it is not plausible to argue that social mobility should be understood in terms of the shift from birth-ascribed status to the achieved status. The emphasis has shifted from the end of caste to the irrelevance of caste. At the aggregate level, the change and continuity may be understood in terms of the levels of change in the sense that certain aspects of the society take longer time to transform than others. However, it may be stated that whatever is happening is the consequence of various changes that ushered in after independence either due to the direct intervention of the state or through the development process. The caste-specific changes have occurred due to the level of preparedness and political mobilisation of certain castes to take advantage of these changes. However, the politics of identity, emergence of class inequality within the scheduled castes, and existence of caste hierarchy are stifling any struggle for the end of caste. Caste differences and social equality may not go together. If the dalits do not break caste barriers among themselves, their struggle for equality will remain futile. Still, there is a long way to go.

Bibliography

Alexander, Jeffrey C. 1980. "Core Solidarity,Ethnic Outgroup, and Social Differentiation: A Multidimensional Model of Inclusion in Modern Societies", in Jacques Dofny and Akinsola Akiwowo (eds.) *National and Ethnic Movements*. Beverly Hills: Sage pp. 5–28,

Anderson, Charles H. 1974. *The Political Economy of Social Class*. Englewood Cliffs, New Jersey: Prentice-Hall, Inc.

Aurora, G.S. 1967. *The New Frontiersmen: A Sociological Study of Indian Immigrants in United Kingdom*. Bombay: Popular Prakashan.

Bailey, F.G. 1957. *Caste and the Economic Frontier: A Village in Highland Orissa*. Manchester: Manchester University Press.

Bains, Ravinder Singh. 1997. "Reactionary Mobilization against Change from Above", in Paramjit S. Judge and Satish K. Sharma (eds.) *Dimensions of Social Change: Essays in Honour of Professor P.N. Pimpley*. Jaipur: Rawat. pp. 122–152.

Bal, Gian Singh. 2007. "Viaktigat Suntarata, Dera Sacha Sauda Vivad ate Dalit-Kisan Samasya", *Nawan Zamana*. July 22. (Punjabi).

Bal, Gurpreet. 1995. *Development and Change in Punjab*. New Delhi: National Book Organization.

—. 1998. "Communities and Culture in Entrepreneurship Development in India", *The Journal of Entrepreneurship*, Vol. 7. No. 2. pp. 171–182.

Benedix, R. 1962. *Max Weber: An Intellectual Portrait*. New York: Anchor Books.

Beteille, Andre. 1966. *Caste, Class and Power: Changing Patterns of Stratification in a Tanjore Village*. Delhi: Oxford University Press.

—. 1999. "Empowerment", *EPW*, XXXIV (10 and 11), March 6–13. pp. 589–597.

Bharti, Dwarka. 2004. "Projection of Dalit Sensibilities in Punjabi Dalit Literature", Harish K. Puri (ed.) *Dalits in Regional Context*. Jaipur: Rawat. pp. 307–316.

Bingley, A.H. 1985. *The Sikhs*. Delhi: National Book Shop.

Brar, Gurbir. 1985. "Socio-Religious Reform Movements and Untouchables in Northern India", in P.N. Pimpley and Satish K. Sharma (ed.) *Struggle for Status*. New Delhi: B.R. Publishing Corporation.

Briggs, Geo. W. 1975. *The Chamars*. Delhi: B.R. Publishing Corporation. (First published in 1920).

Bouglé, Celelstin. 1971. *Essays on the Caste System*. Cambridge: Cambridge University Press.

Camus, Albert. 1992. *The Rebel: An Essay on Man in Revolt*. New York: Vintage. (First published in French 1951).

Chandra, Kanchan. 2000. "The Transformation of Ethnic Politics in India: The Decline of Congress and the Rise of the Bahujan Samaj Party in Hoshiarpur", *The Journal of Asian Studies*, 59 (1), February. pp. 26–61.

Ciotti, Manuela. 2007. "Ethnohistories behind Local and Global Bazaars: Chronicle of a Chamar Weaving Community in the Banaras Region". *Contributions to Indian Sociology*, 41 (3), September–December. pp. 321–354.

Cooper, David. 1971. *The Death of the Family*. London: Allen Lane.

Dahiwale, S.M. 1989. *Emerging Entrepreneurship among Scheduled Castes of Contemporary India*. New Delhi: Concept.

Dalit Jan Kalyan Samiti. 2003. *Protection Available to SC and ST Employees Under the Scheduled Castes and the Scheduled Tribes (Prevention of Atrocities) Act, 1989*. Kalka: Seema Bhadur, President, Dalit Jan Kalayan Samiti

Das, Bhagwan. 2006. *Main Bhangi Han*. Nakodar: Bahujan Hitt Parkashan (Punjabi).

Das, Gurcharan. 1999. "The Problem", *Seminar*, 482, October. pp. 12–21.

Davis, Kingsley and Moore, W.E. 1967. "Some Principles of Stratification", in Reinhard Bendix and S.M. Lipset (eds.) *Class Status and Power: Social Stratification in Comparative Perspective*. (Revised Edition). London: Routledge & Kegan Paul Ltd. pp. 47–52.

Deliége, Robert. 1999. *The Untouchables of India*. New York: Berg.

Dhesi, Autar S. 1998. "Caste, Class Synergies and Discrimination in India", *International Journal of Social Economics*. 25 (6/7/8). pp. 1030–1048.

Dirks, Nicholas B. 2001. *Castes of Mind: Colonialism and the Making of Modern India*. New Delhi: Permanent Black.

Dorin, Bruno (ed.). 2003. *The Indian Entrepreneur: A Sociological Profile of Businessmen and their Practices*. New Delhi: Manohar and ICHS.

D'souza, Victor S. 1980. *Educational Inequalities among Scheduled Castes: A Case Study in Punjab*. Chandigarh: Department of Sociology, Panjab University.

—. 1985. *Economic Development, Social Structure and Population Growth*. New Delhi: Sage.

Dube, Saurabh. 2001. *Untouchable Pasts: Religion, Identity and Power Among a Central Indian Community, 1780–1950*. New Delhi: Vistaar.

Dubey, Abhay Kumar. 2001. "Anatomy of a Dalit Power Player: A Study of Kanshi Ram", in Ghanshyam Shah (ed.) *Dalit Identity and Politics*. New Delhi: Sage. pp. 288–310.

Duncan, Howard. 2003. "Social Inclusion, Social Capital, and Immigration", *Canadian Issues*, April. pp. 30–32.

Flamant, Nicolas. 2003. "The Employer and His Enterprise: International Leather Shoemakers in Tamil Nadu" in Bruno Dorin (ed.) *The Indian Entrepreneur: A Sociological Profile of Businessmen and their Practices*. New Delhi: Manohar. pp. 101–135.

Fox, Richard G. 1987. *Lions of the Punjab: Culture in the Making*. New Delhi: Archives Publishers.

Fuchs, Stephen. 1981. *At the Bottom of Indian Society: The Harijan and other Low Castes*. New Delhi: Munshiram Manoharlal Publishers.

Gaikwad, Laxaman. 1992. *Uchchaka*. Delhi: Radhakrishan. (Hindi)

Gill, Sucha Singh. 2002. "Dropout Rate Cause for Concern: Collapse in Management much to Blame", *The Tribune*, October 1, Tuesday. p. 13.

—. 2004. "Socio-economic Transformation and Scheduled Castes in Punjab", in Harish Puri (ed.) *Dalits in Regional Context*. Jaipur: Rawat. pp. 225–240.

Ghuman, Ranjit Singh, Singh, Sukhwinder and Brar, Jaswinder Singh. 2006. *Rural Students in Universities of Punjab*. Patiala: Publication Bureau, Punjabi University.

Ghurye, G.S. 1969. *Caste and Race in India*. Bombay: Popular Prakashan

Gorringe, Hugo. 2005. *Untouchable Citizens: Dalit Movements and Democratisation in Tamil Nadu*. New Delhi: Sage.

Government of Punjab. 2004. *Human Development Report 2004: Punjab*. Government of Punjab, Chandigarh.

Guha, Ramachandra. 2003. "The Ones Who Stayed Behind", *EPW*, XXXVIII (12) March 13. pp. 1121–1124.

Gupta, Dipankar. 1991. "Continuous Hierarchies and Discreet Castes", in Dipankar Gupta (ed.) *Social Stratification*. New Delhi: Oxford University Press. pp. 110–142.

——. 2000. *Interrogating Caste: Understanding Hierarchy and Difference in Indian Society*. New Delhi: Penguin.

——. 2007. "The Threat from Within", *Hindustan Times*, July 28 (Editorial Page).

Gurr, Ted Robert. 1971. *Why Men Rebel*. Princeton: Princeton University Press.

Guru, Gopal. 1993. "Dalit Movement in Mainstream Sociology", *Economic and Political Weekly*, XXVIII (14) April 3. pp. 570–573.

——. 1997. "Understanding Dalit Protest in Maharashtra", *EPW*, XXXII (30) July 26. pp. 1879–1880.

——. 2002. "How Egalitarian are the Social Sciences in India", *EPW*, XXXVII. (50), December 14. pp. 5003–5009.

——. 2005. "Introduction: Atrophy in Dalit Politics", in Gopal Guru (ed.) *Atrophy in Dalit Politics*. Mumbai: Vikas Adhyan Kendra. pp. 11–32.

Hardgrave Jr, Robert L. 1970. "Political Participation and Primordial Solidarity: The Nadars of Tamil Nadu", in Rajni Kothari (ed.) *Caste in Indian Politics*. New Delhi: Orient Longman. pp. 102–128.

Helweg, A.W. 1979. *Sikhs in England: The Development of a Migrant Community*. New Delhi: Oxford University Press.

Hindustan Times. 2005. "Gurdwara-Samadh Row Re-ignited", August 26, p. 2

Hobsbawm, Eric. 1994. *The Age of Extremes: A History of the World, 1914–1991*. New York: Vintage Books.

Hooda, Sagar Preet. 2001. *Contesting Reservations: The Indian Experiment on Affirmative Action*. Jaipur: Rawat.

Ibbetson, Denzil. 1974. *Punjab Castes*. New Delhi: B.R. Publishing Corporation. (First published in 1916).

——. 1981. *Punjab Castes. Races, Castes and Tribes of the People of Punjab*. New Delhi: Cosmo Publications.

Jaffrelot, Christopher. 2003. *India's Silent Revolution: The Rise of Low Castes in North Indian Politics*. New Delhi: Permanent Black.

Jodhka, Surinder S. 2002. "Caste and Untouchability in Rural Punjab", *EPW*, XXXVII (19), May 11. pp. 1813–1823.

— and Louis, Prakash. 2003. "Caste Tensions in Punjab: Talhan and Beyond", *EPW*, XXXVIII (28), July 12. pp. 2923–2926.

Judge, Paramjit S. 1997. "Emerging Trends in the Caste Structure of Punjab", *The Administrator*, Vol. XLII, January–March. pp. 55–65.

—. 1997a. "Green Revolution and the Bahujan Samaj Party in Punjab", in Paramjit S. Judge and Satish K. Sharma (eds.) *Dimensions of Social Change: Essays in Honour of Professor P.N. Pimpley*. Jaipur: Rawat. pp. 48–65.

—. 1986. *Scheduled Castes Women's Participation in the Workforce in Rural Areas of Punjab.* Punjab State Institute of Public Administration, Chandigarh. (Mimeograph).

—. 2002. "Punjabis in England: The Ad-Dharmi Experience", *Economic and Political Weekly*, XXXVII (31), August 3–9. pp. 3244–3250.

—. 2002a. "Parvasi Mazdooron se Darr Kaisa", *Dainik Bhaskar*, October, 29 (Hindi).

—. 2002b. "Religion, Caste and Communalism in Punjab', *Sociological Bulletin*, 51 (2). pp. 175–194.

—. 2003. "Hierarchical Differentiation among Dalits", *EPW*, XXXVIII (28), July 12. pp. 2990–2991.

—. 2004. "Interrogating Changing Status of the Dalits", in Harish K. Puri (ed.) *Dalits in Regional Context*. Jaipur: Rawat. pp. 100–131.

—. 2005. "Caste Conflicts in Punjab: An Examination of Recent Jat-Dalit Clash in a Village", *Man & Development*, XXVII (3). pp. 151–168.

— and Bal, Gurpreet. 2005. "Dalits and Urban Social Space", *Indian Social Science Review*, 7 (2), July–December. pp. 98–120

Juergensmeyer, Mark. 1982. *Religion as Social Vision: The Movement against Untouchability in 20th Century Punjab*. Berkeley: University of California Press.

Kaistha, K.C. 1985. 'Urbanization and Scheduled Castes: A Study of North Indian State", in P.N. Pimpley and Satish K. Sharma (eds.) *Struggle for Status*. New Delhi: B.R. Publications.

Kali, Des Raj. 2003a. "Nurmahal Vich Vi Talhan Banan di Udeek Kar Riha Parshashan?" *Nawan Zamana*, August 29, Friday. (Punjabi).

—. 2003b. "Mahem Vich Udasi Dere te Kabaze Nu Nathia Dalitan Ne", *Nawan Zamana*, September 2, Tuesday. (Punjabi).

—. 2005. "Anusuchit Up-jatian", *Lakeer*, 95, October–December. pp. 60–63. (Punjabi).

Kallarmajri. 2008. "Rakhwankaran: Ajoki Sathiti, Sankat ate Chanautian", *Hashia*, No. 1, January–March. pp. 71–88. (Punjabi).

Kasturi, Malvika. 2002. *Embattled Identities: Rajput Lineages and the Colonial State in Nineteenth Century North India*. New Delhi: Oxford University Press.

Kessinger, Tom G. 1974. *Vilyatpur 1848–1968: Social and Economic Change in a North Indian Village*. Berkeley: University of California Press.

Kirpal, Viney and Gupta, Meenakshi. 1999. *Equality Through Reservations*. Jaipur: Rawat.

Kumar, Narender and Rai, Manoj. 2006. *Dalit Leadership in Panchayats: A Comparative Study of Four States*. Jaipur: Rawat (in association with Institute of Dalit Studies, New Delhi).

Kumar, Sanjay, Heath, Anthony and Heath, Oliver. 2002. "Determinants of Social Mobility in India", *EPW*, XXXVII (29) July 20. pp. 2983–2987.

Kumar, Vivek. 2003. "Dalit Movement and Dalit International Conferences", *EPW*, XXXVIII (27), July 5. pp. 2799–2810.

—. 2004. "Understanding Dalit Diaspora", *EPW*, XXXIX (1), January 3. pp. 114–116.

Lal, Brij (ed.). 2007. *The Encyclopedia of the Indian Diaspora*. New Delhi: Oxford University Press.

Lal, Chaman. 2004. "Dalit Life in Punjabi Novel", in Harish K. Puri (ed.) *Dalits in Regional Context*. Jaipur: Rawat. pp. 297–306.

Lenin, V.I. 1975. *What is to Be Done*. Moscow: Progress Publishers.

Luce, Edward. 2006. *In Spite of the Gods: The Strange Rise of Modern India*. London: Little, Brown.

Lukács, Georg. 1971. *History and Class Consciousness*. Cambridge: MIT Press.

Lynch, Owen M. 1969. *The Politics of Untouchability*. New York: University of Columbia Press.

Madhopuri, Balbir. 2004. *Chhangia Rukh*. Chandigarh: Lokgeet Parkashan. (Punjabi).

Malagatti, Aravind. 2007. *Government Brahmana*. Hyderabad: Orient Longman.

Marx, Karl. 1973. *Surveys from Exile: Political Writings,* Vol. 2. Harmondsworth: Penguin Books.

—. 1975. *Capital,* Vol. I. Moscow: Progress Publishers.

— and Engels, Fredrick. 1975. *German Ideology*. Moscow: Progress Publishers.

McLeod, W.H. 1986. *Punjabis in New Zealand: A History of Punjabi Migration 1890–1940*. Amritsar: Guru Nanak Dev University.

Meeta and Rajivlochan. 2007. "Caste and Religion in Punjab: Case of the Bhaniarawala Phenomenon", *Economic and Political Weekly*, May 26. pp. 1909–1913.

Mendelsohn, Oliver and Marika Vicziany. 2000. *The Untouchables: Subordination, Poverty and the State in Modern India*. New Delhi: Cambridge University Press.

Miller, D.C. and W.H. Form. 1980. *Industrial Sociology: The Sociology of Work and Organizations,* New York: Harper and Row. (II edition).

Mohanty, Manoranjan. 2001. "On the Concept of Empowerment", in Debal K. Singha Roy (ed.) *Social Development and the Empowerment of the Marginalised Groups*. New Delhi: Sage. pp. 22–31.

Moon, Vasant. 1989. *Dr. Babasaheb Ambedkar: Writings and Speeches,* Vol. 5., Bombay. Government of Maharashtra.

—. 2001. *Growing Up Untouchable in India: A Dalit Autobiography*. New Delhi: Vistaar Publications.

Murdock, George Peter. 1965. *Social Structure*. New York: Free Press.

Nagaraj, D.R. 1993. *The Flaming Feet: A Study of Dalit Movement in India*. Bangalore: South Forum Press & ICRA.

Narayana, D. 2005. "Local Governance without Capacity Building: Ten Years of Panchayati Raj", *EPW,* XL (26), June 25. pp. 2822–2832.

Narayanan, Pradeep. "Empowerment Through Participation", *EPW,* XXXIII (25), June 21. pp. 2484–2486.

Nayar, Baldev Raj. 1966. *Minority Politics in the Punjab*. New Jersey: Princeton University Press.

Nigam, Aditya. 2002. "Dalit Politics enters a New Phase", *EPW,* XXXVII (13), March 30. pp. 1190–1192.

Pandey, Gyanendra. 2006. "The Time of Dalit Conversion", *EPW,* XLI (18), May 6. pp. 1779–1788.

Pai, Sudha. 1997. "Dalit Assertion in UP: Implications for Politics", *EPW,* XXXII (37). pp. 2313–2314.

— and Singh, Jagpal. 1997. "Politicisation of Dalits and Most Backward Castes: Study of Social Conflict and Political Preferences in Four Villages of Meerut District", *EPW,* XXXII (23), June 7. pp. 1356–1361.

Pathak, Suman Lata. 1985. "Self-Images of Scheduled Caste Girl Students of Chandigarh" in P.N. Pimpley and Satish Sharma (eds.) *Struggle for Status*. New Delhi: B.R. Publishers. pp. 153–168.

Pimpley, P.N. 1980. *Profile of Scheduled Castes Students: The Case of Punjab*. Chandigarh: Department of Sociology, (Panjab University).

Prasad, Chandra Bhan. 2006. *Dalit Phobia: Why Do They Hate Us?* New Delhi: Vitasta Publishing Pvt. Ltd.

Punalekar, S.P. 2001. "Dalit Literature and Dalit Identity", in Ghanshyam Shah (ed.) *Dalit Identity and Politics*. New Delhi: Sage. pp. 214–241.

Puri, Harish K. 2003. "Scheduled Castes in Sikh Community: A Historical Perspective", *EPW*, XXXVIII (26), June 28. pp. 2693–2712.

Pushpendra. 1999. "Dalit Assertion Through Electoral Politics", *EPW*, XXXIV (36), September 4. pp. 2609–2618.

Rajaraman, Indira and Sinha, Darsy. 2007. "Functional Devolution to Rural Local Bodies in Four States", *EPW*, XLII (24), June 16. pp. 2275–2283.

Ram, Pandit Bakhshi. 1983. *Mera Jeevan Sangharash*. Brahamnian, Jalandhar: Punjab Pradesh Balmiki Sabha. (Punjabi).

Ram, Ronki. 2004a. "Untouchability, Dalit Consciousness and the Ad-Dharam Movement in Punjab", *Contributions to Indian Sociology*. Vol. 38, No. 3. pp. 323–349.

—. 2004b. "Untouchability in India with a Difference: Ad-Dharm, Dalit Assertion and Caste Conflicts in Punjab", *Asian Survey*, XLIV (6). pp. 895–912.

—. 2007. "Social Exclusion, Resistance and Deras: Exploring the Myth of Casteless Sikh Society in Punjab", *Economic and Political Weekly*, October 6. pp. 4066–4074.

Rao, Anupama. 2005. "Death of a Kotwal: Injury and the Politics of Recognition", in Shail Mayaram et al. (ed.) *Muslims, Dalits, and the Fabrications of History. Subaltern Studies XII*. New Delhi: Permanent Black and Ravi Dayal. pp. 140–187.

Rao, S. Srinivasa. 1997. "Dalits in Education and Workforce", *EPW*, XXXVII (29) July 20. pp. 2998–3000.

Rasoolpuri, Bhagwant. 2008. 'Jarhan', *Parvachan*, 30, January–March. pp. 61–69. (Punjabi).

Ray, Rajat K. 1994. (ed.) *Entrepreneurship and Industry in India, 1800–1947*. Bombay: Oxford University Press.

Roderigues, Valerian (ed.). 2002. *The Essential Writings of B.R. Ambedkar*. New Delhi: Oxford University Press.

Roy, Ramashray. 2001. "Meaning of an Alternative Strategy", in Debal K. Singha Roy (ed.) *Social Development and the Empowerment of the Marginalised Groups*. New Delhi: Sage. pp. 67–82.

Rudolph, L.I. and Rudolph, Susan H. 1967. *The Modernity of Tradition: Political Development in India*. Chicago: The University of Chicago Press.

Russell, R.V. and Hiralal. 1975. *The Tribes and Castes of the Central Provinces of India*, Vol. 11. Delhi: Rajdhani Book Centre, (reprint).

Sabarwal, Satish. 1990. *Mobile Men: Limits to Social Change in Urban Punjab*. Shimla: Indian Institute of Advanced Study in association with Manohar Publications, New Delhi.

Sachchidananda. 1974. "Research on Scheduled Castes with Special Reference to Change", in ICSSR (ed.) *A Survey of Research in Sociology and Social Anthropology*, Vol. I. Bombay: Popular Prakashan.

Sarukkai, Sundar. 2007. "Dalit Experience and Theory", *EPW*, XLII (40), October 6. pp. 4043–4048.

Seth, V.N. 1981. *Sociological Study of Harijan Protest*. Ph.D. Thesis (Unpublished). Department of Sociology, Punjab University, Chandigarh.

Shah, Ghanshyam. 2001. "Dalit Movements and the Search for Identity", Ghanshyam Shah (ed.) *Dalit Identity and Politics*. New Delhi: Sage. pp. 195–213.

Sharma, Dinesh K. 2008. "Casteism Raises its Head, Cremation Stopped", *The Times of India*, June 12, Thursday. p. 2.

Sharma, K.L., 2003, "The Social Organisation of Urban Space: A Case Study of Chanderi, a Small Town in Central India", *Contributions to Indian Sociology*, Vol. 37, No. 3. September–December 2003.

Sharma, Satish K. 2000. "Arya Samaj Movement in Punjab", in Harish K. Puri and Paramjit S. Judge (eds.) *Social and Political Movements: Readings on Punjab*. Jaipur: Rawat. pp. 93–110.

Sharma, Shalini and B. K. Aggarwal. 2004. "Educating Dalit Women for Development: A Study in Hoshiarpur District of Punjab", in Harish Puri (ed.) *Dalits in Regional Context*. Jaipur: Rawat. pp. 258–273.

Sheth, D.L. 2005. "Divergent Discourses in Dalit Politics", in Gopal Guru (ed.) *Atrophy in Dalit Politics*. Mumbai: Vikas Adhyan Kendra. pp. 33–42.

Singh, Indera Paul. 1977. "Caste in a Sikh Village", in Harjinder Singh (ed.) *Caste Among Non-Hindus in India*. New Delhi: National Publishing House. pp. 66–83.

Singh, Jagpal. 1997. "Dalits in Haryana Politics", *EPW*, XXXII (43), October 25. pp. 2785–2786.

Singh, K.S. 1999. *The Scheduled Castes*. Calcutta: Oxford University Press.

Singh, Manjit. 2002. "Surgical Instruments Industry at Jalandhar: A Case Study", *Economic and Political Weekly*, Vol. XXXVII, No. 31, August 3–9. pp. 3298–3304.

Singh, Shubha. 2008. "Punjabi Diaspora in the Pacific Region", paper presented in the International Conference on "Indian Diaspora: Migration and Development with focus on the State of Punjab" organised by Centre for the Study in Rural and Industrial Development, Chandigarh on January 14–15, 2008.

Sirsa, Sukhdev Singh. 2008. "Dalit Punjabi Kavita: Itihasik Pripekh", *Hashia*, January–March. pp. 22–34.

Sorensen, Jesper, B., 2007. "Bureaucracy and Entrepreneurship: Effects on Entrepreneurial Entry" *Administrative Science Quarterly*, 52. pp. 387–412.

Srinivas, M.N. 1966. *Social Change in Modern India*. Bombay: Allied Publishers.

Taylor, Steve, Singh, Manjit and Booth, Deborah. 2007. "Migration, Development and Inequality: Eastern Punjabi Transnationalism", *Global Networks*, 7 (3). pp. 328–347.

Throat, Sukhadeo. 2006. "Paying the Social Debt", *EPW*, XLI (24), June 17. pp. 2432–2435.

—. 2002. "Oppression and Denial: Dalit Discrimination in the 1990s", *EPW*, XXXVII (6), February 9. pp. 572–578.

Throat, Sukhadeo and Umakant (eds.). 2004. *Caste, Race and Discrimination: Discourses in International Context*. Jaipur: Rawat (in association with Indian Institute of Dalit Studies, New Delhi).

Tripathi, Dwijendra. 2004. *The Oxford History of Indian Business*. New Delhi: Oxford University Press.

Tripathi, D. and Jyoti, Jumani. 2007. *The Concise Oxford History of Indian Business*. New Delhi: Oxford University Press.

Upadhyay, Videh. 1997. "Panchayats and Paper Laws: Simmering Discontent on 73rd Amendment", *EPW*, XXXVII (29) July 20. pp. 2987–2989.

Valmiki, Om Prakash. 1998. *Jooth*. Ludhiana: Chetna Parkashan. (Punjabi).

Vasdev, Kanchan. 2003. "After Talhan, Now it's Bhattian Bet: Dalits, Jats Clash, Traffic Blocked", *The Tribune*, July 7, Monday, p. 1.

Velaskar, Padma. 2005. "Educational Stratification, Dominant Ideology and the Reproduction of Disadvantage in India", in S.M. Dahiwale (ed.) *Understanding Indian Society: The Non-Brahminical Perspective*. Jaipur: Rawat. pp. 196–220.

Verma, Archana. 2002. *Making of Little Punjab in Canada: Patterns of Immigration*. New Delhi: Sage.

Virdi, S.L. 2000. *Punjab Da Dalit Itihas: 1901 to 2000*. Phagwara: Dalit Sahit Academy. (Punjabi).

—. 2004. *Bahujan Manifesto*. Calgary: Guru Ravi Dass Society of Calgary. (Punjabi).

Vovelle, M. 1990. *Ideologies and Mentalities*. Cambridge: Polity Press.

Wankhede, G.G. 1999. *Social Mobility and Scheduled Castes: Receding Horizons*. Jaipur: Rawat.

—. 2001. "Educational Inequalities among Scheduled Castes in Maharashtra", *EPW*, XXXVI (18), May 5. pp. 1553–1558.

Watson, C.W. 2002. *Multiculturalism*. New Delhi: Viva Books.

Weber, Max. 1970. *From Max Weber: Essays in Sociology* (Tr. and ed. by H.H. Gerth and C. Wright Mills). London: Routledge & Kegan Paul.

—. 1976. *The Protestant Ethic and the Spirit of Capitalism*. London: George Allen & Unwin Ltd.

Webster, John C.B. 2007. "The Dalit Sikhs: A History?", in Tony Ballantyne (ed.) *Textures of the Sikh Past: New Historical Perspectives*. New Delhi: Oxford University Press. pp. 132–154.

Yagati, Chinna Rao. 2003. *Dalits' Struggle for Identity: Andhra and Hyderabad 1900–1950*. New Delhi: Kanishka.

Zahar, Renate. 1974. *Franz Fanon: Colonialism and Alienation*. Tr. Willfried F. Feuser. New York: Monthly Review Press.

Zelliot, Eleanor. 1970. "Learning to Use Political Means: The Mahars of Maharashtra", in Rajini Kothari (ed.) *Caste in Indian Politics*. New Delhi: Orient Longman. pp. 29–69.

—. 1992. *From Untouchable to Dalit: Essays on the Ambedkar Movement*. New Delhi: Manohar.

Index